THEORY OF MIND DEVELOPMENT IN CONTEXT

Theory of Mind Development in Context is the first book of its kind to explore how children's environments shape their theory of mind and, in turn, their ability to interact effectively with others. Based on world-leading research, and inspired by the ground-breaking work of Candida Peterson, the original collected chapters demonstrate that children's understanding of other people is shaped by their everyday environment. Specifically, the chapters illustrate how theory of mind development varies with broad cultural context, socioeconomic status, institutional versus home rearing, family size, parental communication style, and aspects of schooling. The volume also features research showing that, by virtue of their condition, children who are deaf or who have an autism spectrum disorder function in environments that differ from those of typical children and this in turn influences their theory of mind.

Although much important research has emphasized the role of nature in theory of mind development, this book highlights that children's understanding of other people is nurtured through their everyday experiences and interactions. This perspective is essential for students, researchers, and practitioners to gain a complete understanding of how this fundamental skill develops in humans. The book is invaluable for academic researchers and advanced students in developmental psychology, education, social psychology, cognitive psychology, and the social sciences, as well as practising psychologists, counselors, and psychiatrists, particularly those who deal with disorders involving social and/or communicative deficits.

Virginia Slaughter is Professor and Head of the School of Psychology at the University of Queensland, Australia.

Marc de Rosnay is Professor and Academic Head of Early Start at the University of Wollongong, Australia.

THEORY OF MIND DEVELOPMENT IN CONTEXT

Edited by Virginia Slaughter and
Marc de Rosnay

Routledge
Taylor & Francis Group

LONDON AND NEW YORK

First published 2017
by Routledge
2 Park Square, Milton Park, Abingdon, Oxon OX14 4RN

and by Routledge
711 Third Avenue, New York, NY 10017

Routledge is an imprint of the Taylor & Francis Group, an informa business

British Library Cataloguing in Publication Data
A catalogue record for this book is available from the British Library

Library of Congress Cataloging in Publication Data
Names: Slaughter, Virginia, editor. | De Rosnay, Marc, editor.
Title: Theory of mind development in context / edited by Virginia
    Slaughter and Marc de Rosnay.
Description: Abingdon, Oxon ; New York, NY : Routledge, 2017.
Identifiers: LCCN 2016022795| ISBN 9781138811584 (hardback : alk. paper)
    | ISBN 9781315749181 (ebook)
Subjects: LCSH: Philosophy of mind in children. | Child psychology. |
    Developmental psychology.
Classification: LCC BF723.P48 T44 2017 | DDC 155.4/13—dc23
LC record available at https://lccn.loc.gov/2016022795

ISBN: 978-1-138-81158-4 (hbk)
ISBN: 978-1-138-81159-1 (pbk)
ISBN: 978-1-315-74918-1 (ebk)

Typeset in Bembo
by Swales & Willis Ltd, Exeter, Devon, UK

CONTENTS

List of contributors   *vii*

Preface   *ix*

*Introduction: how should we conceptualise contextual influences on
young children's theory of mind development?*   *x*
    Marc de Rosnay

1   Learning a theory of mind   1
    Henry M. Wellman

PART I
Social contexts for development   **23**

2   Culture and the sequence of developmental milestones
    toward theory of mind mastery   25
    Candida C. Peterson and Virginia Slaughter

3   Family influences on theory of mind: a review   41
    Claire Hughes and Rory T. Devine

4   Why Montessori is a facilitative environment for
    theory of mind: three speculations   57
    Angeline S. Lillard and Sierra Eisen

5   Behaviour to beliefs   71
    Ted Ruffman and Mele Taumoepeau

PART II
Atypical developmental contexts   **87**

6   The role of institutionalization in theory of mind   89
    Bilge Selcuk and N. Meltem Yucel

7   The empathic mind in children with communication
    impairments: the case of children who are deaf or hard of
    hearing (DHH); children with an autism spectrum disorder
    (ASD); and children with specific language impairments (SLI)   106
    *Carolien Rieffe, Evelien Dirks, Wendy van Vlerken
    and Guida Veiga*

8   Environment and language experience in deaf children's
    theory of mind development   121
    Gary Morgan, Marek Meristo and Erland Hjelmquist

9   Mindreading as a transactional process: insights from autism   135
    Peter Mitchell

    Appendix: standard theory of mind tasks   151

Index   *155*

CONTRIBUTORS

Rory T. Devine
Centre for Family Research
University of Cambridge, UK
rtd24@cam.ac.uk

Evelien Dirks
Dutch Foundation for the
    Deaf and Hard of Hearing
    Child, Amsterdam, the
    Netherlands

Sierra Eisen
Department of Psychology
University of Virginia, USA
sle3jt@virginia.edu

Erland Hjelmquist
Department of Psychology
University of Gothenburg,
    Sweden
erland.hjelmquist@psy.gu.se

Claire Hughes
Centre for Family Research
University of Cambridge, UK
ch288@cam.ac.uk

Angeline S. Lillard
Department of Psychology
University of Virginia, USA
lillard@virginia.edu

Marek Meristo
Department of Psychology
University of Gothenburg, Sweden
marek.meristo@psy.gu.se

Peter Mitchell
School of Psychology
University of Nottingham, UK
Peter.Mitchell@nottingham.ac.uk

Gary Morgan
City, University London, UK
Deafness, Cognition and Language
    Research Centre, UK
G.Morgan@city.ac.uk

Candida C. Peterson
School of Psychology
University of Queensland, Australia
candi@psy.uq.edu.au

Carolien Rieffe
Institute of Psychology
Leiden University, the Netherlands
Dutch Foundation for the Deaf and
    Hard of Hearing Child, Amsterdam,
    the Netherlands
crieffe@fsw.leidenuniv.nl

Marc de Rosnay
School of Education, Faculty
    of Social Sciences
University of Wollongong, Australia
marcd@uow.edu.au

Ted Ruffman
Department of Psychology
University of Otago, New Zealand
tedr@psy.otago.ac.nz

Bilge Selcuk
Department of Psychology
Koç University, Turkey
byagmurlu@ku.edu.tr

Virginia Slaughter
Early Cognitive Development Centre
School of Psychology
University of Queensland, Australia
vps@psy.uq.edu.au

Mele Taumoepeau
Department of Psychology
University of Otago, New Zealand
mele@psy.otago.ac.nz

Guida Veiga
Department of Sports and
    Health, School of Sciences and
    Technology
University of Évora, Portugal

Wendy van Vlerken
Institute of Psychology
Leiden University, the
    Netherlands

Henry M. Wellman
Department of Psychology
Center for Human Growth and
    Development
University of Michigan, USA
hmw@umich.edu

N. Meltem Yucel
Departments of Psychology
Özyeğin University,
    Turkey and University
    of Virginia, USA
nmy2bg@virginia.edu

PREFACE

This book arose out of a celebratory symposium for Professor Candida Peterson, whose tremendously influential work with children who are deaf demonstrated the crucial role of everyday context on theory of mind development. This research, much of which was carried out in collaboration with Michael Siegal in the late 1990s, revealed that theory of mind development depends not on a child's hearing status per se, but instead on whether that status limits access to everyday conversation. With this unique and definitive evidence, Candida Peterson convinced a field that was focused on biological, maturational accounts that environment matters to theory of mind. Building on this work, she went on to produce more influential work demonstrating links between children's theory of mind development and their cultural context, their family context, and specific features of their home and school environments. Her approach to theory of mind shaped modern ideas of this central aspect of human development and life. The chapters of this volume bring together those ideas and celebrate her intellectual legacy.

INTRODUCTION

How should we conceptualise contextual influences on young children's theory of mind development?

Marc de Rosnay

Whichever way you look at it, the *false belief* (FB) task radically influenced many aspects of developmental science, and associated disciplines. In its most basic forms, such as the *Sally–Anne* or *Maxi* tasks (see Appendix), children are merely asked to make a behavioural prediction about a story protagonist: for example, will Sally look for her shoes where she left them (where she mistakenly expects them to be), or will she look for them where the child observing her actions knows them to be (the actual location)? Sally's mistaken expectation can be shown to be more than ignorance about the location of her shoes; rather, we can say that she holds an *FB* based on her previous actions or experiences. Classic FB tasks such as Sally–Anne have been taken by many to indicate whether a child does or does not possess a *theory of mind* (ToM). To put it simply, passing a classic ToM task is often inter-preted to mean that a child is maintaining in his or her construal of a given situation a distinction between the world as understood by a protagonist (i.e. Sally) and the world as understood by another person, in this case him- or herself. To achieve this, some have argued that the child needs to be able to *represent* the mental contents of another person's mind, a so-called *meta-representational* capacity (Perner, 1991; Wellman, 1990). Debate continues as to the significance of this particular develop-mental achievement – passing a classic FB task – against a growing research literature suggesting that infants' anticipatory looking patterns appear to track actions based on mistaken expectations by as early as 12 months of age (see Baillargeon, Scott, & He, 2010).

Leaving aside theoretical issues about representation and meta-representation, it is instructive to revisit the conditions under which ToM came to assume such prominence in the 1990s. The seminal research in the previous decade, which established an approximate age for passing classical FB tasks, about 4½ years, arose in the context of increasing interest and focus on children's awareness of mental attitudes, including other people's desires, knowledge, emotions, and so on (Harris, 1989; Wellman, 1990). Similarly, at the time ToM became prominent in the developmental literature, a great deal was already understood about young children's and infants' responsiveness to other people's agency (Bretherton, McNew, & Beeghly-Smith, 1981; Light, 1979; Trevarthen, 1980; Zahn-Waxler & Radke-Yarrow, 1982), although a great deal more has been learned in the decades that followed (Tomasello, Carpenter, Call, Behne, & Moll, 2005). That is to say, ToM research emerged during a time of expanding interest in the broader domain of children's *social-cognitive understanding*. Against this backdrop, the significance of *ToM mastery*, defined as passing FB tasks, was taken to imply a watershed moment in the development of social-cognitive understanding, not the beginning of social-cognitive understanding *per se*.

The profound significance of this particular developmental moment was elegantly described in Bartsch and Wellman's (1995) careful analysis of children's spontaneous reference to mental states in their natural language. They showed that it is not until just prior to the age that children start to pass FB tasks reliably that their spontaneous utterances and conversations reveal a crucial feature of our shared folk psychological explanatory framework: that sometimes a person's actions or responses can only be properly understood if one first takes into account the construal of the world held by that person, even if that construal is at odds with the true (or known) state of the world, and implies a mistaken expectation or a FB. In recognition of the fact that a person's beliefs can qualify the actions or responses that can be expected to flow from normal motivations – desires, preferences, wishes, inclinations, and so on – Bartsch and Wellman described the mature developmental state as a *belief–desire* (folk) psychology (also see Wellman, Chapter 1).

That children become belief–desire psychologists is considered a watershed moment because the shape of their psychological understanding and explanation comes to resemble that of the community of adult interlocutors they will enter, and it will maintain such a shape throughout their lives even if the content and the sophistication of such understanding and explanation will shift dramatically (and continue to reveal profound individual differences). Prior to this mature state, children can exhibit great sensitivity to other people's points of view and experience even when they are at odds with their own, and they can demonstrate tremendous awareness of another person's emotional state arising as a function of his or her own experiences (Harris, 1989; Tomasello et al., 2005). In fact, Bartsch and Wellman (1995) also show that children's early utterances and conversations reveal that awareness of (false) belief emerges prior to fully grasping the mature relation between belief and desire or passing FB tasks, leading young children temporarily to become *desire–belief* (folk) psychologists while they are sorting out the relations between these important facets of psychological understanding.

It is perhaps to be expected that a debate has arisen as to the relation between children's experience and the conceptual understanding that is so obviously on display when they grasp FB scenarios, such as the Sally–Anne task, or when they start to accept and utilise psychological explanations that imply an underlying belief–desire psychology. One view, which is often assumed when children are given FB tasks, is that the emergence of FB understanding at about 4 years is indeed a watershed moment for conceptual development, allowing the child to reorganise his or her folk psychological understanding and thereby draw on a richer psychological framework: it is this conceptual shift, for example, that is assumed to drive changes in the way children interact with their peers or tailor their communications in new ways (de Rosnay, Fink, Begeer, Slaughter, & Peterson, 2014; Fink, Begeer, Hunt, & de Rosnay, 2014). While many aspects of this account – ToM comes *online* at about 4 years of age – remain compelling, we can now say with confidence that such an account is too simplistic to capture what is known about children's ToM development. The most obvious problem for this kind of account comes from the study of ToM development in different contexts, which is the focus of this volume. In particular, two such research traditions have dramatically altered the way we understand the growth of children's social-cognitive understanding, including their mastery of FB scenarios: (1) the study of development within *social contexts*, and (2) the study of development in *atypical populations*.

Perhaps the most remarkable research finding in our understanding of children's ToM development has been the realisation that the communicative environments experienced by deaf children are of the utmost importance for their FB development and mastery. In this respect, the work of Candi Peterson and her colleague Michael Siegal (see Peterson & Siegal, 2000, for an overview) was instrumental in showing that when children are born deaf, their ToM development is essentially at parity with typically developing hearing children *so long as their parents are native speakers of a sign language*, which usually implies that at least one parent is also deaf. For deaf children who have hearing parents – the vast majority – FB understanding is usually profoundly delayed and sometimes even absent in late adolescence.

This opportunistic natural experiment, capitalising on the coincidental contextual interaction between hearing status and the communicative environment, brought sharp focus to the significance of the communicative environment for ToM development, but it did not in and of itself provide a window on why the communicative environment plays such a profound role. Is it the implications for children's language development or is it the act of communication *per se* that enhances ToM development? Is it both? Irrespective of the precise mechanisms, which are taken up shortly, the research field now understood where to focus attention. Indeed, the focus on atypical development continues to be of profound value in understanding how children come to understand others, including ToM development. In the second part of this volume, we see how the sustained focus on deafness and autism (Chapters 7 through 9) continues to present conundrums concerning the underlying mechanisms and processes that constitute or support ToM. For example, the work of Rieffe and her colleagues (Chapter 7) points to a *décalage* between the developmental course of *implicit* ToM skills (e.g. intention reading) and explicit ToM skills (e.g. FB understanding) in the context of atypical development – an issue we return to below. Also, in pioneering work by Selcuk and Yucel (Chapter 6), we see how the focus on institutionalised children has to some extent converged with insights from deafness: it is not so much the age of institutionalisation or even the amount of time in an institutional context that seems to be of significance for ToM development; rather it is the consistent opportunity to interact with adult interlocutors that appears to be critical.

In parallel with research on atypical development, there has been a long research tradition that seeks to understand how children's social sensitivity or understanding emerges through the social contexts in which they find themselves and the commonplace interactions they engage in. Whilst this research shares much in common with the approaches adopted with atypically developing children described above, it has tended to exploit individual differences amongst typically developing children in their social experience and personal capacities, at crucial developmental junctures. Building on the work of Dunn, Brown, Slomkowski, Tesla, and Youngblade (1991), Bretherton et al. (1981) and others (Light, 1979), many researchers turned their attention to associations between commonplace variations in family structure (e.g. are there siblings in the home and how many?), parental attributes (e.g. level of maternal education or family socioeconomic status (SES)), patterns of family interaction (e.g. emotional expressiveness, responsiveness, conversational practices or proclivities) and children's ToM development. In Chapter 3, Hughes and Devine provide a current meta-analytic overview of this literature and the current state of play. Their analyses confirm that both *distal* factors – family size and SES – and *proximal* factors – parental mental-state talk and *mind-mindedness* – explain variation in typically developing children's ToM understanding: children with more child-aged siblings, from higher-SES families, with parents who engage in more mental-state talk and tend to think of their children as independent psychological entities (i.e., more *mind-minded*) are very likely to have more advanced ToM understanding!

As Hughes and Divine (Chapter 3) observe, however, the differing contributions of these factors are not necessarily easy to disentangle empirically on current evidence. Indeed, in Chapter 4, Lillard and Eisen show how the pedagogical philosophy of early schooling, in this case the Montessori approach, can also influence ToM development and other aspects of children's social behaviour in positive ways. While such findings should give us pause for thought when considering how best to provide early-learning environments for children, it is also important to note that distal factors such as family size, SES and schooling philosophy are likely to stand in for other processes that occur between family members or between children and educators that may ultimately be underpinned by the same cluster of likely causal mechanisms already identified as existing proximal influences on ToM development (e.g. mental-state discourse). That is to say, the number of child-aged siblings a child has, for example, is likely to be of significance for ToM development because of the kinds of interactions that entail, which might include conversational exchanges that direct the child's attention to contrasting mental attitudes and other people's perspectives, or other processes such as conflict resolution, which might force children to negotiate with one another and thereby accommodate differing perspectives or needs. For sibling effects on ToM, there is some evidence that this interpretation will turn out to be correct (Brown, Donelan-McCall, & Dunn, 1996; Hughes & Ensor, 2005; Jenkins, Turrell, Kogushi, Louis, & Ross, 2003). Nevertheless, whilst such explanations of the association between distal factors and ToM development are plausible, we are not yet able to establish precisely how child-aged siblings promote children's ToM development, or why higher SES and Montessori schooling approaches are associated with better ToM understanding. The possibility that some other as yet unidentified factors may play a role is of course possible.

If we consider the proximal factors that have consistently emerged through the study of social determinants and correlates of children's developing ToM, the spotlight again falls on the early communicative environment. Unlike research with atypical populations, however, this research domain has been fruitful in highlighting qualitative aspects of the communicative interactions that occur between children and their parents. In their analysis, Hughes and Divine (Chapter 3) identify that parental mental-state discourse repeatedly emerges as robust correlate of children's ToM understanding. Furthermore, it is noteworthy that while *mind-mindedness* is conceived as an attribute of the parents, reflecting the way they conceptualise the child, there seems to be fairly good alignment between a proclivity to think of one's child as an independent agent with his or her own mental states, on the one hand, and the activity of communicating with one's child using a relatively high proportion of mental-state terms, on the other hand.

With these findings and observations in mind, it is understandable that higher levels of parental mental-state discourse are now widely believed to be causally predictive of children's ToM development, and it is worth considering the limits of this conclusion as the empirical literature currently stands. Interestingly, fairly wide-ranging correlations and longitudinal associations between various aspects of parent–child discourse and young children's understanding of mind and emotion (i.e. social-cognitive understanding) have been documented in the literature (see de Rosnay & Hughes, 2006, for a review; Ruffman, Slade, & Crowe, 2002). As noted by Hughes and Devine (Chapter 3), there are other ways of characterising parent–child discourse that have also shown links with children's mentalistic or emotion understanding of others; these include *elaborativeness* (i.e. the extent to which parents explain content and draw out their discussions with children) and *connectedness* (i.e. the extent to which the utterances of one interlocutor are meaningfully associated with the utterances of the other interlocutor), amongst others. By and large, these different ways of quantifying qualitative aspects of communicative interactions have not been pitched against each other, but where they have it is not always straightforwardly clear whether one better explains how communication supports ToM development than the other (e.g. Ensor & Hughes, 2008). Similarly, training studies have consistently shown relations between verbally mediated interventions and improvements in children's understanding of mind and emotion, without necessarily settling on an account of which aspects of communicative interactions *best* promote such understanding (see Hughes, 2011, for a discussion). What certainly seems likely is that, generally speaking, conversational interactions in which interlocutors are attuned and responsive to each other's offerings and perspectives are conducive to promoting various aspects of children's understanding of mind and emotion, including their FB understanding.

In contrast to this quite general conclusion, analyses undertaken by Ruffman and Taumoepeau (discussed in Chapter 5) and others (e.g. Ensor, Devine, Marks, & Hughes, 2014; Slaughter, Peterson, & Mackintosh, 2007) suggest that it may be possible to isolate very specific relations between the ways in which mothers speak to their young children (including infants and toddlers) and their children's growing understanding of mind and emotion. Thus, for example, Ensor et al. have shown longitudinally that mothers' *cognitive* state talk (e.g. specific references to thoughts, beliefs, memory, attention, etc.) with their 2-year-olds robustly predicts mental-state understanding 8 years later, when children are 10 years old. Importantly, Ensor and her colleagues also looked at the longitudinal impact of mothers' *desire* and *emotion* state talk, but these aspects of verbal interaction did not have the same long-range influence. It seems that being verbally inculcated into a familial culture of cognitive state discourse has a very direct impact on the child's subsequent *proclivity* to analyse human affairs and interactions in psychological terms.

That specific kinds of psychological discourse – in particular, cognitive state talk – show selective concurrent or longitudinal relations with ToM is an intriguing finding that has emerged from the study of individual differences: that is, within the normal range, and all things being equal, when a family conversational environment is rich in cognitive state talk, children in such a family are likely to have more advanced ToM understanding relative to their peers raised in families with lower rates of such talk. But how this finding is ultimately played out in the growing child's *capacity* to understand others in psychological terms is not a straightforward question. If we consider FB understanding specifically, one dramatic possibility is that, if a child is raised with no access to cognitive state talk, then he or she will never understand FB properly. Although this thought experiment may seem far-fetched, the analogy from the study of deaf children pushes in this direction: deaf children raised with hearing parents have profound difficulties with psychological understanding in general and FB in particular and, furthermore, their progress in this domain is inexorably connected to their burgeoning, albeit delayed, linguistic and communicative development.

This strong *experience-driven* account of ToM mastery is explored more deeply by Ruffman and Taumoepeau in Chapter 5, who draw on a small but important research tradition which examines how the balance of mothers' perspectival and mental-state discourse changes as children develop through the early years and reach specific milestones, such as participation in shared visual attention (e.g. Slaughter, Peterson, & Carpenter, 2008). Thus, in Western samples, when talking to their infants, mothers tend to focus initially on ostensive features of perception and desire, but increasingly refer to opaque mental states – such as belief, knowledge – as children get older. So not only are children exposed through communicative practices to mental-state words, which might direct their attention to unobservable psychological processes, it also seems that caregivers scaffold children's burgeoning mental state understanding verbally by both speaking to the child's current interests and sensitivities, and also by adjusting their input in ways that extend children's understanding and direct attention to other psychological processes. This account is broadly in keeping with Vygotsky's ideas on the influence of language and social interaction on the child's thinking (1978).

Naturally, caregivers' changing communicative patterns with their children will to some extent reflect maturational changes in the growing child but, as research with deaf children has shown, Ruffman and Taumeepeau (Chapter 5) are right to push the limits of verbally mediated accounts of ToM development and explore the extent to which our folk psychological understanding is achieved through specific features of the communicative tutelage that occurs between children and their caregivers. As the literature currently stands, both the general and specific accounts of how communicative interactions support children's ToM development have merit, and it is not as yet clear how they fit together or complement each other. Of course, it is important to remember that children's developing social-cognitive understanding is rich and diverse, taking in many aspects of psychological life and interpretation of action. While research may ultimately be able to show that specific patterns of communicative interactions or content influence the development of FB understanding – as defined by passing a Sally–Anne task – the richness of our person understanding and folk psychological explanatory frameworks may resist such a precise explanation.

Recognising that ToM understanding is far more than classical FB mastery is not any longer controversial (see Wellman, Chapter 1), even if it should turn out that FB mastery at about 4 years of age does indeed represent a watershed moment in psychological understanding (Bartsch & Wellman, 1995; Wellman, 1990). As noted earlier, there has been a sustained effort to examine whether infants can be said to understand, in so far as their rapid patterns of looking behaviour can indicate, a person's mistaken expectations, and there has been steady growth in our appreciation of the social attunement of toddlers to others' intentions and perspectives (Baillargeon et al., 2010; Liszkowski, Carpenter, & Tomasello, 2007; Tomasello et al., 2005). However, there has also been an important expansion of interest in the conceptual insights that constitute a child's ToM development. So, whereas ToM research once focused almost exclusively on FB, it is now clear that there are a series of ToM milestones that seem to follow a predictable time course in development, at least for typically developing children, and also a predictable sequence of development. Thus children understand that two individuals may have different desires, even about the same object (*diverse desires*: DD), prior to understanding that two individuals may have different beliefs about the same object (*diverse beliefs*: DB) or realising that something can be true but a person may not have access to that knowledge (*knowledge access*: KA). Interestingly, DB and KA vary in the sequence of acquisition by culture, but all three insights – DD, DB and KA – are mastered by children prior to FB mastery in every culture that has been examined, and yet FB mastery precedes children's capacity to understand that you might feel one thing but show another (*hidden emotion*: HE). In the chapters by Wellman (Chapter 1) and Peterson and Slaughter (Chapter 2), the implications of this developmental sequence are examined in detail. Here I draw out three themes that help to conceptualise contextual influences on ToM development.

First, it should be noted that, like the classical FB tasks, the ToM milestones outlined above are defined in terms of performance on very simple, story-like scenarios in which children have the opportunity to show that they are employing a concept in a minimal way. That is to say, just like previous research with FB tasks, the ToM milestone tasks could be viewed as a gross simplification of the richness of children's ToM understanding. However, we think that it is precisely this simplicity, along with the stability and replicability of FB tasks in multiple contexts and with different groups of children (see Wellman, Cross, & Watson, 2001), that has been their greatest strength. Amongst other things, the classical FB tasks have functioned as a bridge between the complexity of social processes underpinning mental state understanding, on the one hand, and the consequences of such understanding for children's social integration and behaviour, on the other hand. That researchers have been able to show how specific distal and proximal social and interactive processes relate to FB understanding (see above), while at the same time being able to show how FB understanding is related to children's peer acceptance and behaviour (see Slaughter, Imuta, Peterson, & Henry, 2015), has allowed the field to cut through some of the inherent complexities of conducting real-world research and move toward a better understanding of potential causal mechanisms.

The reliable measurement of FB has also allowed a distinction to emerge in the literature between the differential contributions to ToM development of (a) language development measured as a property of the child (e.g. the child's mastery of syntax or lexical semantics), and (b) the qualitative aspects of the communicative environment that have been discussed above. Indeed, the rapid acquisition of language clearly makes a contribution to children's ToM understanding that needs to be better understood (Hughes, 2011) but, in so far as current evidence extends, a distinction should be maintained between this aspect of child development and the social context in which children encounter different communicative practices (de Rosnay & Hughes, 2006; Hughes, 2011).

Second, as already noted, the ToM milestones articulated by Wellman (Chapter 1) have been shown to be scalable. That is to say, the order of acquisition in an individual child tends to be very predictable. Importantly, Wellman (Chapter 1) suggests that this makes sense from the point of view of conceptual learning, whereby earlier conceptions lead to later conceptions. With such a tool for understanding ToM development, the possibilities for hypothesis-driven cross-cultural research have greatly expanded. Indeed, there is already a growing body of research, to which Peterson and Slaughter contribute in Chapter 2, that suggests that ToM concepts unfold in a largely predictable manner over a large range of cultures and language groups, but that some differences also emerge and provide a window on *how* culture might mediate the contexts of children's learning. In particular, variation in the sequence of DB and KA performance between Western and Eastern cultures points to different child-rearing practices and cultural expectations about the respective importance of individual and collective concerns. Thus, the scaling ToM approach promises to broaden the questions we can ask about the different ways in which cultural contexts, and the interactions that occur therein, are exerting an influence on how children learn about the mind.

Finally, the scaling ToM tasks, like the FB tasks before them, present us with something of a paradox: while at one level it is clear that there are profound contextual influences on the growth of ToM understanding, it is also true that ToM unfolds in a remarkably consistent fashion across a broad range of contexts and children. Thus, while the time course of ToM development is very sensitive to contextual factors, both the way in which children appear to master the key constructs distilled in the scaling ToM procedure and the predictability with which they master such constructs are impressive. Even deaf children of hearing parents, who can show very profound delays on ToM acquisition, appear to follow an essentially predictable sequence in keeping with hearing children from their same culture. The only exception to this pattern appears to be children with autism, although they too are not radically different from their typically developing counterparts in the order in which they master ToM constructs, and in many respects they are the same (Peterson, Wellman, & Liu,, 2005; Scheeren, de Rosnay, Koot, & Begeer, 2013).

Furthermore, there is as yet relatively little evidence as to meaningful variations in the nature of the mature ToM state. So, for example, whilst we can say of young children that one may have mastered a specific construct whereas another may not have, it is not clear that such a distinction extends into adulthood. Are, for example, some adults actually better at understanding mental states than others? And if so, are they better because they have a more developed underlying ToM *competence*? Or do they vary in their *performance* such that they simply have a proclivity to approach human affairs in mentalistic terms (a proclivity that could potentially be reduced or enhanced)? There are not easy answers to these questions at present.

Faced with such consistency in ToM development, accounts such as those put forward by Wellman (Chapter 1) and Ruffman and Taumoepeau (Chapter 5) will tend to focus on the "common and robust set of developmental experiences" (Wellman, Chapter 1, p. 9) that the vast majority of people encounter. From such experiences – together presumably with language acquisition and other facets of intellectual development – the ToM-relevant information is extracted so that each person learns to participate in an essentially universal set of core assumptions about the psychological, internal or mental lives of persons. Of course, a culture could emerge in which this does not entail, but in this hypothetical case careful analysis of experience along the same lines discussed here should in principle yield a suitable explanation of any deviance from the kind of developmental sequence captured in the scaling ToM tasks. Others, however, will continue to view such consistency more directly as an overt manifestation of deep automatic, perhaps species-specific, capacities for understanding other people as autonomous agents acting in the service of their goals (see Chapter 5 for a discussion). To some extent this is a tension captured in the distinction between *implicit* and *explicit* ToM. The focus of this introduction and much of this volume is explicit ToM; that is, the child's capacity to *work out* or maintain as an object of thinking, in a way that is somewhat self-reflective (i.e., *conceptualise*), the psychological reasons and motives for people's actions and states.

As we have previously alluded, however, there is now good evidence that infants are highly attuned to other people's intentions, and may even be able show the rudiments of FB comprehension through their looking behaviour in enactments where a protagonist can be inferred to hold a mistaken expectation (see Baillargeon et al., 2010, for a discussion). Currently, there is not a compelling account of how implicit and explicit ToM are to be integrated in the course of development and, confusingly, it has also been shown that older high-functioning individuals with autism can actually pass a classic FB task while at the same time failing an implicit task (Senju, Southgate, White, & Frith, 2009). But, as before, it is noteworthy that the study of contextual influences on ToM continues to push forward the ways in which we think about ToM development. In their chapter, Morgan and colleagues (Chapter 8) provide a overview of current thinking on how young deaf children's implicit ToM is influenced by the communicative environment. They note the different ways in which hearing and deaf parents of deaf children communicate with their infants and toddlers: whereas the interactions between deaf parents and their deaf children are in many respects similar to hearing parents and their hearing children (e.g. good sensitivity to gaze and attention, accurate intention reading), the interactions of hearing parents and their deaf children are relatively impoverished in terms of the responsive face-to-face signals that characterise early parent–infant communication. Morgan and colleagues conclude that current evidence is pushing toward a very experience-driven hypothesis about implicit as well as explicit FB understanding because deaf toddlers raised by hearing parents also do not show the same expectancies in their looking behaviour as hearing infants in FB enactment tasks. It seems that even implicit ToM is to some extent experience-driven and, if Morgan and colleagues are right, the experience that is critical is participation in pre-linguistic communicative exchanges. Should these findings prove to be robust, they may not necessarily present an obvious solution as the nature of the relation between implicit and explicit ToM, but they will certainly add credence to the idea that communicative process goes to the very heart of the development of social-cognitive understanding.

Finally, in asking how the contextual influences on ToM should be conceptualised, it is helpful to consider some of the reflections in Mitchell's final chapter (Chapter 9) on mindreading as a transactional process. At the very centre of his argument is the assumption that interactive and communicative experiences are key to understanding the phenomenon that we describe as social-cognitive understanding. If we consider for a moment the implications of a transactional model, it specifies that it is not enough to recognise others' gestures or intentions, we must also be able to actually respond to such intentionality in ways that are comprehensible to our interaction partners or interlocutors so that more elaborate systems of communication can become established. This closely resembles the kind of process described in Trevarthen's pioneering work on *intersubjectivity*, wherein each partner must be able to accommodate him- or herself to the actions of the other (Trevarthen, 1980).

By drawing on his long-standing work with social cognition in autism, Mitchell presents us with an intriguing possibility that has hitherto escaped empirical investigation: that the social attention deficits or idiosyncrasies of autistic individuals, which are often quite subtle, may nonetheless be catastrophic for establishing early social, communicative interactions. On this view, the social and linguistic deficits that we associate with autism, to some extent, can be hypothesised to cascade as the cycles of interactive behaviour so characteristic of typically developing children fail to find traction. Sadly, if this speculation is correct, it is precisely because we are so sensitively attuned to others' social and communicative initiations that we fail to detect or cultivate them in children with autism. But there is an encouraging flip side to this possibility: if we can identify aberrant or idiosyncratic patterns of social attention and communication early in development, then we should in principle be able to accommodate ourselves to them and alter, if not fully change, the interactive experience of children with autism. It is a possibility that would seem to deserve close attention.

References

Baillargeon, R., Scott, R. M., & He, Z. (2010). False-belief understanding in infants. *Trends in Cognitive Sciences, 14*, 110–118.

Bartsch, K., & Wellman, H. (1995). *Children talk about the mind.* Oxford: Oxford University Press.

Bretherton, I., McNew, S., & Beeghly-Smith, M. (1981). Early person knowledge as expressed in gestural and verbal communication: when do infants acquire a theory of mind? In M. E. Lamb & L. R. Sherrod (Eds.), *Infant social cognition.* Hillsdale, NJ: Lawrence Erlbaum.

Brown, J. R., Donelan-McCall, N., & Dunn, J. (1996). Why talk about mental states? The significance of children's conversations with friends, siblings, and mothers. *Child Development, 67*(3), 836–849.

de Rosnay, M., Fink, E., Begeer, S., Slaughter, V., & Peterson, C. (2014). Talking theory of mind talk: young school-aged children's everyday conversation and understanding of mind and emotion. *Journal of Child Language, 41*(5), 1179–1193.

de Rosnay, M., & Hughes, C. (2006). Conversation and theory of mind: do children talk their way to socio-cognitive understanding? *British Journal of Developmental Psychology, 24*(1), 7–37.

Dunn, J., Brown, J., Slomkowski, C., Tesla, C., & Youngblade, L. (1991). Young children's understanding of other people's feelings and beliefs: individual differences and their antecedents. *Child Development, 62*, 1352–1366.

Ensor, R., Devine, R. T., Marks, A., & Hughes, C. (2014). Mothers' cognitive references to 2-year-olds predict theory of mind at ages 6 and 10. *Child Development, 85*, 1222–1235.

Ensor, R., & Hughes, C. (2008). Content or connectedness? Mother–child talk and early social understanding. *Child Development, 79*, 201–216.

Fink, E., Begeer, S., Hunt, C., & de Rosnay, M. (2014). False-belief understanding and social preference over the first 2 years of school: a longitudinal study. *Child Development, 85*(6), 2389–2403.

Harris, P. L. (1989). *Children and emotion.* Oxford: Blackwell.

Hughes, C. (2011). *Social understanding and social lives: From toddlerhood through to the transition to school.* London: Psychology Press.

Hughes, C., & Ensor, R. (2005). Executive function and theory of mind in 2 year olds: a family affair? *Developmental Neuropsychology, 28*, 645–668.

Jenkins, J. M., Turrell, S. L., Kogushi, Y., Louis, S., & Ross, H. S. (2003) A longitudinal investigation of the dynamics of mental state talk in families. *Child Development, 74*, 905–920.

Light, P. (1979). *The development of social sensitivity*. Cambridge: Cambridge University Press.

Liszkowski, U., Carpenter, M., & Tomasello, M. (2007). Pointing out new news, old news, and absent referents at 12 months of age. *Developmental Science, 10*(2), 1–7.

Perner, J. (1991). *Understanding the representational mind*. Cambridge, MA: MIT Press.

Peterson, C. C., & Siegal, M. (2000). Insights into theory of mind from deafness and autism. *Mind and Language, 15*, 123–145.

Peterson, C. C., Wellman, H., & Liu, D. (2005). Steps in theory of mind development for children with deafness, autism or typical development. *Child Development, 76*, 502–517.

Ruffman, T., Slade, L., & Crowe, E. (2002). The relation between children's and mother's mental state language and theory-of-mind understanding. *Child Development, 73*(3), 734–751.

Scheeren, A., de Rosnay, M., Koot, H., & Begeer, S. (2013). Rethinking theory of mind in high-functioning autism spectrum disorder. *Journal of Child Psychology and Psychiatry, 54*(6), 628–635.

Senju, A., Southgate, V., White, S. & Frith, U. (2009). Mindblind eyes: an absence of spontaneous theory of mind in Asperger syndrome. *Science 325* (5942), 883–885.

Slaughter, V., Imuta, K., Peterson, C. C. & Henry, J. D. (2015). Meta-analysis of theory of mind and peer popularity in the preschool and early school years. *Child Development, 86*(4), 1159–1174.

Slaughter, V., Peterson, C. C., & Carpenter, M. (2008). Maternal talk about mental states and the emergence of joint visual attention. *Infancy, 13*, 640–659.

Slaughter, V., Peterson, C. C., & Mackintosh, E. (2007). Mind what mother says: narrative input and theory of mind in typical children and those on the autism spectrum. *Child Development, 78*, 839–858.

Tomasello, M., Carpenter, M., Call, J., Behne, T., & Moll, H. (2005). Understanding and sharing intentions: the origins of cultural cognition. *Behavioral and Brain Sciences, 28*, 675–735.

Trevarthen, C. (1980). The foundations of intersubjectivity: development of interpersonal and cooperative understanding in infants. In D. R. Olson (Ed.), *The social foundation of language and thought: Essays in honour of Jerome Bruner*. New York: Norton.

Vygotsky, L. (1978). *Mind in society*. Cambridge, MA: Harvard University Press.

Wellman, H. M. (1990). *The child's theory of mind*. London: MIT Press.

Wellman, H. M., Cross, D., & Watson, J. (2001). Meta-analysis of theory-of-mind development: the truth about false belief. *Child Development, 72*, 655–684.

Zahn-Waxler, C., & Radke-Yarrow, M. (1982). The development of altruism: alternative research strategies. In N. Eisenberg-Berg (Ed.), *The development of prosocial behaviour* (pp. 109–137). New York: Academic Press.

1

LEARNING A THEORY OF MIND

Henry M. Wellman

In 1990 I was invited to talk on the then-new topic of "theory of mind" at a gathering of developmental scientists from Australia and New Zealand (the forerunner of today's meetings of the Australasian Human Development Association). Unknown to me, my invitation was masterminded by Candi Peterson, whom I met there for the first time.

Our next conversations were sparked by Candi's groundbreaking study, "Deafness, conversation and theory of mind" (Peterson & Siegal, 1995). Until then, discussion about serious delays in theory-of-mind understandings had focused on autism and had served to provide support for nativist, modular accounts of theory-of-mind development more generally. From such a perspective, the rapid development of person understandings apparent in normal children worldwide, revealed in an understanding of false belief, reflected a specialized theory-of-mind mental module (ToMM) "coming online" in early development. From this neurological-maturational perspective (Leslie, 1994; Baron-Cohen, 1995), ToMM could be intact or it could be impaired, as apparently occurred in individuals with autism. An additional implication of positing this sort of theory-of-mind module, however, is that individuals who are *not* impaired in the relevant module or modules should achieve mental-state understandings on a roughly standard maturational timetable.

This is where the studies of deaf preschool children raised by hearing parents have been so revealing. As charted first by Candi and then by others, deaf children of hearing parents show delays and deficiencies on theory-of-mind tasks comparable to children with autism. Yet these deaf children have not suffered the same sort of neurological damage that autistics have. Their damage is peripheral – in the ears, not the mind. This is clear in the fact that deaf children raised by deaf parents do not show theory-of-mind delays. Findings such as these challenge accounts of theory-of-mind development relying heavily on neurological-maturational mechanisms and instead underwrite learning accounts of that development. Theory of mind develops dependent on the social-interactive experiences of the child, and it is this perspective that informs the current volume. A hallmark of these social-interactive experiences is that they can differ according to the child's circumstances – his/her social context.

After that 1995 article, communication between Candi and me accelerated because we both favored an experiential-learning account of theory-of-mind development over a nativist, maturational one. Then in 2005 I was able to visit with Candi in Australia for three months. That visit sparked collaborations that produced much of the research I will emphasize in this chapter. Since my focus here is experience-dependent learning, it is fitting to emphasize at the start how much my own learning has benefitted from the experience of knowing and collaborating with Candi Peterson.

As a final piece of background, my first visit to Australia coincided with the release of *The Child's Theory of Mind* (Wellman, 1990) and the current chapter follows on from the publication of its sequel, *Making Minds: How Theory of Mind Develops* (Wellman, 2014). A fuller treatment of the ideas sketched here is available in that book.

Theory of mind, in brief

Philosophers (Churchland, 1984; Fodor, 1987) and social scientists (D'Andrade, 1987; Wellman, 1990) have long agreed that theory-of-mind reasoning is organized around three large categories of mind and behavior: beliefs–desires–actions. Because people have beliefs and desires they engage in intentional actions. Or, in everyday thinking, we construe people as engaging in acts they *think* will get them what they *want*. Because Romeo and Juliet want to be together, but believe their families will violently disapprove, they proceed to see each other in secret.

Beyond beliefs, desires and actions, theory-of-mind reasoning includes other important constructs and connections, such as those depicted in Figure 1.1. Romeo *loves* Juliet so wants to be with her. But Juliet is a Capulet and Romeo has *seen* his family's hatred of the Capulets so he thinks they will violently disapprove. That's why he tries to meet Juliet in secret. And when successful, Romeo *reacts* with happiness, indeed, he's ecstatic and lovestruck; when unsuccessful he's sad, dejected and forlorn.

Figure 1.1, then, sketches a framework for thinking of multiple sorts of theory-of-mind reasoning. Note that this is a very general framework. What, exactly, are Romeo's beliefs and desires? This framework does not tell us. Shakespeare tells us, but a framework like that in Figure 1.1 only says Romeo has some beliefs and desires (and emotions and perceptions), and they're important.

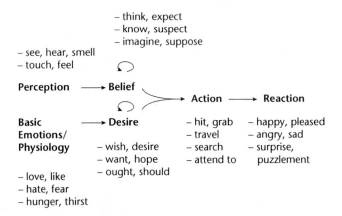

FIGURE 1.1   Simplified framework for depicting belief–desire reasoning. Centrally, beliefs and desires shape one's actions. But also, basic emotions and physiological states fuel one's desires; perceptual experiences ground one's beliefs and knowledge; actions result in outcomes to which the agent has reactions. Reprinted with permission from Wellman, H. M. (2014). *Making Minds: How Theory of Mind Develops*. New York: Oxford University Press.

False belief

Beliefs play a special role in the framework shown in Figure 1.1. We construe agents as engaging in acts they *think* will get them what they want. Of course, they can be mistaken. And when mistaken, agents not only think wrongly, they act wrongly. At the end of Shakespeare's play, there is Romeo down in the crypt with Juliet right beside him alive and well. Romeo kills himself. Why? Because he thinks Juliet is dead. This slippage between mind and world is an essential feature of theory of mind, and is one reason there has been so much research on children's understanding of false beliefs.

Box 1.1 sketches a common, "standard" false-belief task – one that deals with unexpected contents (also see Appendix). As outlined in Box 1.1, in several meta-analyses of hundreds of studies (Wellman et al., 2001; Milligan et al., 2007; Liu et al., 2008), 4-year-olds, 5-year-olds and 6-year-olds consistently answer correctly, like adults. These meta-analytic data clearly show early achievement coupled with developmental change. By 4 and 5 years many children are largely correct; on a vast array of false-belief situations they judge and explain correctly. But there is also clear change. By going backward to 2 and 3 years there is consistent below-chance performance, that is, classic false-belief errors.

Box 1.1

False belief tasks have children reason about an agent whose actions should be controlled by a false belief. Such tasks have many forms, but a common task employs unexpected contents, as depicted above. The child (not shown below) sees the two boxes and explores them to find the Band-Aids are in the plain, nondescript box, not in the Band-Aid box. Then she is asked about her friend Max, who has never seen these boxes before: "Max wants a Band-Aid, where will Max go for a Band-Aid?" Or, "Which box will Max think has Band-Aids?" Older preschool children answer correctly, like adults. Younger children answer incorrectly; they are not just random, they consistently say Max will search in the plain box (where the Band-Aids really are). Note that the task taps more than just attribution of ignorance (Max doesn't know); rather it assesses attribution of false belief (Max thinks – falsely – Band-Aids are in the Band-Aid box).

A frequently used alternative task uses change of locations (rather than unexpected contents). See Appendix for details.

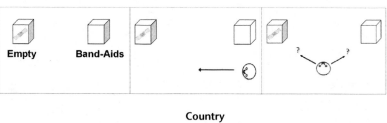

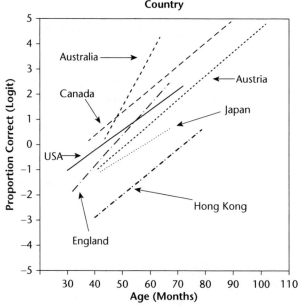

> Several task factors make such tasks harder or easier, but nonetheless children go from below-chance to above-chance performance, typically in the preschool years. Moreover, as shown in the graph above (combining results from Wellman et al., 2001 and Liu et al., 2008), children in different cultural-linguistic communities can achieve false belief understanding more quickly or more slowly, yet in all locales they evidence the same trajectory – from below-chance (below zero in this graph) to above-chance performance in early to later childhood. This is true even for children growing up in non-Western cultural communities speaking non-Indo-European language. And it is true even for children in traditional, nonliterate societies.

Perhaps more interesting, the graph in Box 1.1 organizes the data by the country where the children lived and were tested. Across countries, cultures, and their related languages there are some differences in timetables – some children in some locales come to understand false belief a bit faster, some slower – but granting that, there is very similar conceptual development in all countries. To be clear, these sorts of childhood data do not mean that adult folk psychologies worldwide are equally similar, or that cultural construals of mind all look exactly like the Euro-American one which inspires Figure 1.1 (see Luhrmann, 2011; Wellman, 2013). Nonetheless, it is also true that in some culturally appropriate form or another, just as shown in Box 1.1, young children everywhere come to understand that a person's actions are importantly controlled by what he or she thinks and intends, not just reality itself.

Infant "false belief"

A picture like that in Box 1.1, of false belief development as concentrated in the preschool years, represented the consensus view until about 7 or 8 years ago. But since then, as is well known, multiple findings have emerged claiming that even 12-, 15-, and 18-month-olds understand false belief. These data come from infant looking-time studies (Onishi & Baillargeon, 2005; Surian et al., 2007; Scott & Baillargeon, 2009), but also from anticipatory-looking, eye-tracking methods (Southgate et al., 2007; Neumann et al., 2008), and from studies using active–interactive paradigms where infants hand objects to others or otherwise actively interact with them (Buttelmann et al., 2009; Southgate et al., 2010).

For several reasons, I will not tackle the infant false-belief data in this chapter. First, I do so at length in Wellman (2014), where I make clear that we are far from a clear understanding of infant theory-of-mind development (see Morgan, Meristo & Hjelmquist, this volume). And second, importantly, it is the preschool conceptual developments (as in Box 1.1) that are directly related to children's everyday life, actions, and interactions.

As is clear in Box 1.1, there is significant variation in timetables across countries in preschool achievement of theory of mind. Not directly obvious in that graph is that there is considerable variation across individuals as well. Although almost all normally developing children eventually master false belief, some children come to this understanding earlier and some later. This variation has helped researchers confirm the impact of achieving preschool theory-of-mind understandings. Children's performance on false-belief tasks is just one marker of these understandings, but differences in false-belief understanding alone predict how and how much preschool children talk about people in everyday conversation (e.g., Ruffman et al., 2002), their engagement in pretense (e.g., Astington & Jenkins, 1995), their social interactional skills, including secret keeping (e.g., Peskin & Ardino, 2003) and lying (e.g., Lee, 2013), and consequently their interactions with and popularity with peers (e.g., Watson et al., 1999; Diesendruck & Ben-Eliyahu, 2006; Fink et al., 2014; see Slaughter et al., 2015, for a meta-analysis). False-belief understandings predict such social competences concurrently *and* longitudinally and do so even after IQ and executive function skills are controlled for.

These findings importantly confirm theory of mind's real-life relevance and moreover they demonstrate that something definite and important is happening in children's theory-of-mind understandings in the preschool years. Clearly, theory of mind has a foundation in infancy, but open questions remain as to how and why these understandings originate and change over time. For now, preschool data provide the best look at these developmental questions.

Theory theory

My approach to the preschool data, to theory of mind, and to much of cognitive development goes by the name *theory theory*. Theory theory has this name, because it is a theory proposing that children are constructing theories of the world from their evidential experiences. In this way, theory theory is an heir to Piaget's constructivist account.

According to theory theory, human cognizers not only have coherent, framework representations of the world – like the framework outlined in Figure 1.1 – in the course of development we acquire these representations, they are learned. Theories and theory development, then, depend on a crucial interplay between hypotheses and data – between theory and evidence – that propels development. We use theory and data, together, to learn and revise more specific theories and framework ones as well.

I advocate theory theory, but the central claim – that cognitive development proceeds like theory development – raises a crucial question: how could this sort of learning be possible? Lack of a satisfying, clear answer undermined Piaget's constructivism; it has been a weakness of theory theory as well. However, over the last 10 years things have changed due to theoretical and computational advances in learning. Of particular relevance to theory theory are advances in computational models that explore and exploit probabilistic Bayesian learning and especially hierarchical theory-based learning (e.g., Tenenbaum et al., 2006; Griffiths et al., 2010; Goodman et al., 2011). As Alison Gopnik and I argued (2012), these advances promise to reconstruct constructivism, and reinvigorate theory theory.

These computational approaches are Bayesian because they take off from Bayes' law:

$$P(H/E) \propto P(E/H)\, P(H)/P(E)$$

Bayes' law is a simple formula to relate together two things: the probability of a hypothesized structure (H) and the pattern of the data or evidence (E) that you see. Together these generate the probability of H given E, or P(H/E). Conventionally, P(H) is called the "prior," your initial belief in the hypothesis; P(E/H) is the "likelihood" (the likelihood of the evidence you did see given the hypothesis under consideration); and P(H/E) is the "posterior" and captures learning (your revised belief in the hypothesis after you've considered the evidence). So, Bayes' law says that the posterior probability of the hypothesis is a function of the likelihood of the evidence, and the prior probability of the hypothesis.

Here is a common illustrative example. You go to the doctor's and get a positive diagnostic blood test, the E; a test that when positive indicates having cancer. Possibly having cancer, then, is the focal H. If the blood test is diagnostically appropriate, then the likelihood [P(E/H)] might be quite high; if you have cancer you are very likely to have a positive test. But at the same time the prior [P(H)] might be quite low – in general you or anyone might be very unlikely to actually have cancer and other factors can also lead to a positive test. So the posterior [P(H/E)], the probability that you have cancer now that you've received evidence from a positive test, might still be relatively low; it only changes a little. Eventually though, enough evidence (other tests, a biopsy, newly discovered family histories) could lead you to accept even an initially very improbable idea; many positive tests and other evidence might indeed lead to the initially unlikely conclusion that indeed you do have cancer.

With this example it's clear that Bayesian learning depends on the learner's "diet" of evidence, coupled with sensible hypotheses. Different diets of evidence (or different prior hypotheses) can result in different learnings, or different trajectories of learning.

Bayes' law has been around a long time, but its integration of hypothesis and evidence to yield learning can be very difficult to implement. For example, often, in fact usually, there are many hypotheses that could produce a particular pattern of evidence. Any single structure is underdetermined by the evidence. This is one reason that led Chomsky (1975) and others in the nativist tradition to argue that the structure must be innately given. However, the new advances in machine learning and computational modeling have successfully overcome many of the difficulties. These approaches are not just Bayesian; they rely on probabilistic procedures for Bayesian inferences. Bayes' law itself deals with probabilities, of course, but these learning models are probabilistic in still further ways. *Probabilistic* Bayesian methods tell you whether some hypotheses are more likely than others given the evidence – the positive test increases the probability of cancer. You can learn, even if any one hypothesis is always underdetermined by the evidence, by adjusting posteriors among the many hypotheses as evidence accumulates.

These rational probabilistic models have both attractions and limitations as theories of the actual learning mechanisms of cognitive development. But here are some features that are attractions to me:

- They focus on probabilities and exploit probabilistic evidence. One of the most consequential advances in our understanding of cognitive development over the last 20 years is increased understanding that and how young children engage in statistical, probabilistic learning (Saffran et al., 1996; Siegler, 2007).
- They emphasize that prior hypotheses influence how you treat the evidence but at the same time that evidence updates and changes one's hypotheses. In fact, under the right circumstances this interplay between evidence and hypotheses can lead to new hypotheses (Gopnik et al., 2004), including hypotheses about unobservable constructs and forces, variables not observable in the evidence itself (e.g., Walker & Gopnik, 2014).
- Hierarchical Bayesian learning goes still further (e.g., Tenenbaum et al., 2006) and assumes that hypotheses – theories – come at several different levels. Some are more specific and in direct contact with the evidence, others more abstract – frameworks that contact the evidence only through the specific theories they help generate. Computational demonstrations with hierarchical Bayesian models demonstrate how, in principle, evidence at the bottom can revise and generate not just specific hypotheses but also framework ideas (e.g., Goodman et al., 2011).
- Finally, as the dynamics of learning unfold in these systems, learning proceeds in sequences through intermediate series of steps (Ullman et al., 2012).

To my mind, the overall integration of prior knowledge and new evidence – including more framework ideas and not just specific ones – is exactly the kind of thing Piaget had in mind when he talked about assimilation and accommodation. It is also the sort of thing I've had in mind, in imprecise form, when talking about theory change on the basis of experience and evidence (Wellman, 1990; Gopnik & Wellman, 1994). Probabilistic Bayesian learning processes, as demonstrated in current computational models, reveal characteristics of learning that, I believe, also characterize children's learning in basic domains, including early theory-of-mind development. Indeed, when these learning algorithms play out in real time they show three signature characteristics of constructivist learning: (a) learning proceeds in progressive conceptual sequences; (b) sequences and timetables are experience-dependent (and hence context-dependent); and (c) prior conceptual knowledge influences the presence and amount of learning. In the next sections, I describe research that demonstrates these three features in theory-of-mind development.

Conceptual sequences

To begin to think about sequences, consider these related things a child could know (or not know) about persons and minds: (a) people can have different desires, even different desires for the same thing (diverse desires: or DD); (b) people can have different beliefs, even different beliefs about the exact same situation (diverse beliefs: DB); (c) something can be true, but someone might not be privy to that knowledge (knowledge access: KA); (d) something can be true, but someone might falsely believe something different (false belief: FB); and (e) someone can feel one way but display a different emotion (hidden emotion: HE). These notions capture aspects of mental subjectivity, albeit different aspects (including mind–mind, mind–world, and mind–action distinctions). Listing them in this manner suggests that one could devise a set of tasks, all with similar formats and procedures, similar to false-belief tasks, for example, and see how children do.

Studies using such a battery of tasks (see Appendix), encompassing hundreds of preschoolers in the USA, Canada, Australia, and Germany, evidence a clear and consistent order of difficulty. It's the order listed above, with diverse desires easiest and hidden emotions hardest. For shorthand, call this sequence, DD > DB > KA > FB > HE. This sequence is highly replicable and significant when assessed via Guttman or Rasch statistical modeling (e.g., Wellman & Liu, 2004; Peterson et al., 2005; Kristen et al., 2006). More simply, about 80 percent of the children in these various studies showed this pattern. Thus this theory-of-mind scale establishes a progression of conceptual achievements that pace theory-of-mind understanding in normally developing Western children, as well as a method for measuring that development.

Scaling and variations

But how invariant is this sequence and what accounts for this consistency of sequence? Clearly, a consistent sequence could result from innately programmed maturations. Or similarly, it could result from maturationally unfolding gains in basic cognitive processes; for example, increases in executive function or in cognitive capacity. But alternatively, a consistent sequence might result from processes of conceptual learning in which initial conceptions lead to later conceptions, shaped by relevant information and experiences. Consistency, in this case, would arise to the extent that most children encounter a common and robust set of developmental experiences. If theory-of-mind conceptions are more shaped by relevant information and experiences, however, then, in principle, sequences could be very different.

Cross-cultural research can help address these possibilities. Consider research with Chinese children, and assume that theory-of-mind understandings are the products of social and conversational contexts that vary from one community to another. If so, then Western and Chinese childhood experiences could be crucially different. Various authors describe a common Asian focus on persons as sharing group commonalities and interdependence and a contrasting common Western focus on persons as distinctively individual and independent (e.g., Nisbett, 2003). These differences include differing emphases on common knowledge and perspectives versus diversity of individual beliefs and perspectives. Moreover, others distinguish an everyday Western epistemology focused on truth, subjectivity, and belief versus a Confucian-Chinese epistemology focused more on pragmatic knowledge acquisition and the consensual knowledge that all right-minded persons should learn (Li, 2001; Nisbett, 2003). Indeed, in conversations with young children, Chinese parents comment predominantly on "knowing" (Tardif & Wellman, 2000), whereas in comparison US parents comment more on "thinking" (Bartsch & Wellman, 1995).

In accord with such conversational-cultural preferences for emphasizing knowledge acquisition versus belief differences, Chinese preschoolers evidence a consistent but different theory-of-mind sequence where KA and DB are reversed: DD > KA > DB > FB > HE (Wellman et al., 2006, 2011). Both Western and Chinese children first understand basic aspects of desire (DD), but after that Western children first appreciate belief differences (DB), whereas Chinese children instead first appreciate KA. This is not some singular peculiarity of Chinese mind and development; the same alternative sequence appears in Iranian preschool children (Shahaeian et al., 2011). Despite profound differences in Iran's Muslim traditions and beliefs in contrast to Chinese Confucian/Communist ones, both China and Iran share collectivist family values emphasizing consensual learnings, knowledge acquisition, and low tolerance for childhood assertions of disagreement and independent belief. Similarly, children in both China and Iran share a conceptual theory-of-mind sequence where KA precedes DB.

Hypothesis-driven cultural comparisons like these approximate a natural experiment – naturally occurring differences in some key socio-environmental factors are exploited as akin to an experimental variation. Exploiting natural experiments is a crucial tool in examining developmental learning. Moreover, such experiments can address not only issues of developmental sequences but developmental timetables as well.

The false-belief data in Box 1.1 already show that timetables can vary; some children are quicker, some slower to achieve false-belief understanding. But, at the same time, pretty much everywhere children achieve a similar understanding of false belief in the preschool years. Indeed, reconsider the sequence data as well: although sequences differ between the USA and China, nonetheless children apparently proceed through more or less the same steps and at more or less the same time – in the preschool years. Tightly restricted – not identical, but restricted – timetables (or sequences) might well reflect development of theory of mind as largely under maturational control (see Callaghan et al., 2005). But if early progressive theory-of-mind understandings are built one upon the next, shaped by relevant information and experience, that process should be able to produce very different timetables.

It is well known that false belief has a very different timetable for children with autism. Most adolescents and adults with autism perform poorly on false-belief tasks (e.g., Baron-Cohen 1995). But, autism provides a noisy natural experiment for considering learning and/or maturation because autism is replete with neurological impairments and general across-the-board cognitive impairment and delays. Autism could certainly have its own delayed maturational timetable. A more telling test case concerns deaf children. Moreover, because there are two main groups of deaf children to consider, they provide a still more precise natural experiment.

Deaf children of deaf parents – often called *native signers* – grow up with ordinary conversational, language experiences. Although this occurs in sign language, native signers grow up with others who communicate and interact with them profusely. But most deaf children – about 95 percent – are born to hearing parents (Lederberg et al., 2013). They grow up with very different early experiences. For example, despite valiant efforts to learn sign, hearing parents rarely achieve real proficiency. Especially when their child is young, hearing parents mostly communicate with their deaf child using simple signs or gestures to refer to here-and-now objects (Vaccari & Marschark 1997; Moeller & Schick, 2006). Also, often only one person in the family – typically the mother – is the "designated" primary communicator and interactor for the child (Gregory et al., 1995). Deaf children in a hearing family – *late signers* – often begin life with little discourse about persons' inner states, thoughts and ideas, and generally have less access to the free-flowing, turn-taking, perspective-shifting interchange of social interactions.

Deaf children of hearing parents (but *not* native signers) are substantially delayed in understanding false belief, often as delayed as high-functioning children with autism (for a review, see Peterson, 2009). Again, however, a focus on sequences is more illuminating. When deaf children (of hearing parents) receive the theory of mind scale (ToM Scale) they too evidence a consistent sequence of progression, but one that is delayed at every step along the way. It takes deaf children 12 or more years to progressively achieve what hearing children (and deaf children of deaf parents) progressively achieve in 4 or 5 years (Wellman et al., 2011).

Scaling plus longitudinal data

Although patterns of success and failure, as revealed in developmental scales across children, have the promise of providing cross-sectional approximations to developmental sequences, such data cannot definitively indicate that individual children proceed longitudinally through the identified sequences. Thus, in recent research we addressed whether scale progressions and longitudinal progressions converge (e.g., Wellman et al., 2011). We did so by examining the scale progressions of children given the ToM Scale at two, three, or four times as they grew older and we did so for children from the USA, from China, and a group of children born deaf to hearing parents.

These longitudinal data showed that theory-of-mind progressions apparent in cross-sectional scaling data also characterized longitudinal sequences of understanding for individual children. Figure 1.2 presents those data graphically. Clearly, individuals consistently proceed in order up the scale. This match between cross-sectional and longitudinal sequences appeared for children who exhibited different progressions across cultural contexts (USA vs. China) and for children with substantial delays (deaf children of hearing parents). These data not only validate this scale as a good cross-sectional proxy for longitudinal sequences, they demonstrate the power of combining scaling data with longitudinal data as well.

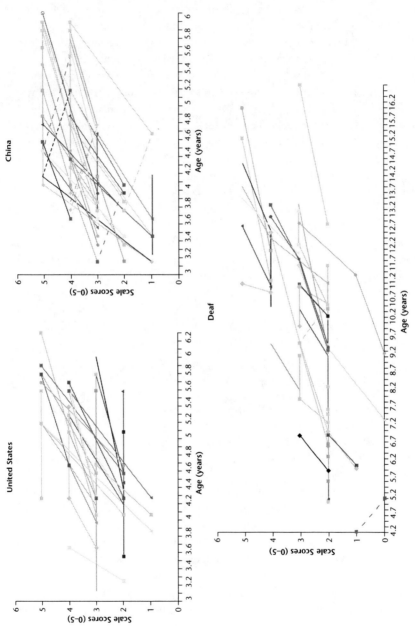

FIGURE 1.2 Longitudinal trajectories of theory-of-mind mastery derived by retesting children on the Theory of Mind Scale. Scores range from 0 to 5, where 0 means the child fails all five tasks, 1 means s/he passes diverse desires (DD), 2 means DD and diverse beliefs (DB), and so on.

It is also of note that the data in Figure 1.2 for the deaf children speak against any maturational, critical-period analysis of theory of mind. Potentially, there might be a critical period for achieving what are ordinarily preschool theory-of-mind milestones like false belief (Siegal & Varley, 2002). If not acquired early in development, appreciation of others' mistaken beliefs might become impossible to achieve. Thus, Morgan and Kegal (2006) suggested there would be "long-lasting deficits in false belief abilities" (p. 811) if these were not achieved by the age of 10 years. However, Figure 1.2 makes clear that deaf children of hearing parents continue to progress in these "preschool" theory-of-mind understandings as adolescents. Pyers and Senghas (2009) provide related data with still older deaf persons (see also O'Reilly et al., 2014). The data from Pyers and Senghas come from an intriguing longitudinal study of a unique group of Nicaraguan deaf adults who had grown up with no language other than a very restricted form of pidgin signing with no words or syntactic structures for expressing mental states. When first tested at a mean age of 22 years, most of these adults still could not pass standard false-belief tests. However, over the next several years, these adults joined a deaf social club and gained opportunities to converse and learn signs for mental states from a younger deaf cohort who had grown up using these terms. With this experience, the adults' false-belief performance improved substantially when tested 2 years later. Indeed, they improved enough to equal the younger cohort.

Microgenetic data

What is the basic nature of cognitive progress, or more specifically, of theory-of-mind progress? Although this progress is now well documented empirically for typically developing children, the research essentially documents "before" and "after" snapshots of development. Cross-sectional studies depict typical 3-year-olds who fail false belief followed by 4- and 5-year-olds who pass a variety of explicit, inferential tasks. And meta-analyses only partly and indirectly overcome this limitation. Longitudinal studies also, because retestings have employed intervals of 6 and 12 or more months (e.g., Dunn, 1995; Ruffman et al., 2002; Wellman et al., 2011), mostly capture performance before and after the preschool transition to false-belief success and fail to provide rich information about how the transition unfolds.

Scaling data provide one way to begin to overcome these shortcomings. But, an additional, powerful way to capture developmental change more richly is through multiple closely packed sessions with the same children over a protracted transition, thereby achieving a microgenetic record. To elaborate briefly, microgenetic studies are a special type of longitudinal study where one samples behavior very frequently, to get a fine-grained picture of developmental change. Further, to experimentally capture developmental learning, some microgenetic research involves not just measuring change but accelerating it, in designs where investigators "choose a task representative of the cognition in question, hypothesize the types of everyday experiences that lead to change, and then provide a higher concentration of these experiences than ordinary" (Siegler, 1995, p. 413).

Following this thinking, in an initial theory-of-mind microgenetic study, Jennifer Amsterlaw and I (2006) began with young 3-year-olds for whom a pretest showed that they systematically failed numerous false-belief tasks as well as several other false-belief-like tasks. Research of the kind I have already described shows that, in the course of everyday development, it takes such young children considerable time to go from consistent false-belief errors to consistent correct performance. Indeed, in Amsterlaw and Wellman (2006), in a control group that received only pre- and posttests, after 10–12 weeks children made virtually no progress in false-belief understanding. Moreover, when another group of 3-year-olds who consistently failed false belief at pretest received repeated false-belief tests over multiple weeks – not just a pre- and posttest – they made little progress.

Focally, however, in the Amsterlaw and Wellman study we took a comparable group of 12 young children who consistently failed false belief and required them to make both false-belief predictions and explanations again and again over many weeks. So, in two sessions a week for a total of 12 sessions, they had to predict what would happen in a false-belief scenario (say in Box 1.1, predict where Max would look for Band-Aids), then were shown what actually happens (Max looked in the Band-Aid box), and asked to explain the character's actions (Why did Max do that?). The rationale for providing a higher concentration of these "everyday" experiences rested on two things. First, data from earlier research have shown that parents and children frequently ask for explanations of persons' actions (e.g., Hickling & Wellman, 2001; Wellman, 2011) and that variability in the frequency of explanations during everyday family conversations predicts individual differences in children's social-cognitive understanding (Dunn & Brown, 1993; Bartsch & Wellman, 1995; Ruffman et al., 2002; Peterson & Slaughter, 2003).

A second rationale was more Bayesian. Children's microgenetic experiences required them to note their predictive failures and to explain them. In a Bayesian fashion, children were prompted to consider their priors (their failed prediction) and attempt to reconcile them with the evidence (via attempted explanations).

In this focal microgenetic group, there was significant improvement relative both to a pretest (that children consistently failed) and to two control groups (where consistent failure persisted). Children in the focal microgenetic group went from initially making consistent false-belief errors (being incorrect 88 percent of the time) to later being consistently correct (performing correctly 79 percent of the time). Moreover, on posttests these microgenetic children also improved on several other theory-of-mind tasks.

However, this initial study's assessment of children's theory-of-mind competence relied on all-or-none success on false-belief tests alone, assessments that leave much unknown. For example, first, how did children progress (e.g., through what steps)? And, second, why did some progress and others apparently did not? In Amsterlaw and Wellman's (2006) microgenetic study, the focal children who received scripted theory-of-mind experiences (over multiple sessions) indeed improved; nevertheless, there was considerable individual variation. Using a criterion of 75 percent or better performance on multiple false-belief tasks, nine of the 12 focal microgenetic children met this criterion at posttest, and seven scored perfectly. But this means that three (25 percent) or five (42 percent) of the 12 did not. Other training studies (e.g., Lohmann & Tomasello, 2003) show similar variability. Why do some children gain but others, exposed to the same conditions, do not? This question is fundamental to any theoretical account of the nature of cognitive change.

Two rough but importantly distinct possibilities could account for such variations. Perhaps general cognitive factors "external" to the domain of theory of mind – e.g., some children were more attentive, thoughtful, interested, or had better memory or executive functioning – account for why some children learned more. A complementary possibility, however, concerns factors "internal" to theory-of-mind conceptions themselves: although all children consistently failed at pretest, some may have had a more solid or advanced conceptual foundation about persons and minds to begin with and so progressed more by building upon these early insights. Bayesian analyses of development and learning (e.g., Tenenbaum et al., 2011) emphasize the relationship between new information (the evidence) and one's prior hypotheses. The result is incremental changes from prior to posterior probabilities. Piaget's classic constructivist position would also be an example of this sort of account (Piaget, 1983). Because cognitive change depends on accommodating to new information, and accommodation equally requires assimilation to existing cognitive structures, having a prior understanding "closer" to a target achievement would facilitate change over prior understandings that were more "distant." In such constructivist accounts, earlier conceptual status shapes later learning (beyond mere attention, executive skill, or general cognitive ability). By extension, consistent failure on false-belief tests at pretest in a training or microgenetic study may nonetheless mask relevant conceptual differences.

Scaling and microgenetic data

To address the steps that characterize children's progress and why progress varies across individuals, in our latest research we have merged our microgenetic and scaling approaches. We give children our ToM Scale at pre- and posttest; accelerate their understanding via prediction-explanation microgenetic experiences; and see how learning proceeds in terms of progressions of understanding.

In one recent study (Rhodes & Wellman, 2013) we included a larger sample of focal children – 29 (as opposed to 12 in Amsterlaw & Wellman, 2006) – to be better able to capture differences in how children change. Just as in the original Amsterlaw and Wellman study, when given prediction-explanation microgenetic experiences, most children progressed, but again in terms of false belief at the posttest, not all advanced. While almost 60 percent consistently passed false-belief tasks at posttest, essentially 40 percent did not. This expected variability allowed us to address the key questions because children not only varied at posttest; they also varied on their ToM Scale performance at pretest. While all children in the microgenetic group consistently failed false-belief tasks at the start, some were further along the ToM Scale than others. At pretest essentially half had gotten as far as passing the diverse belief task (DD and DB) and half had progressed as far as knowledge access (DD, DB, and KA). Call the first group the *Diverse-Belief* pretest group (*n* = 17) and the second the *Knowledge* pretest group (*n* = 12).

How did these two groups learn? For the Knowledge pretest group, 75 percent became consistent at false belief: they passed three or four of four false-belief tests at posttest. Indeed, 50 percent were perfect – they passed four of four. Of the Diverse-Belief pretest group, none became consistent false-belief passers (and thus none passed all four posttest false-belief tasks either). So, it was the Knowledge pretest children who progressed to false-belief understanding (given prediction-explanation microgenetic experiences) and Diverse-Belief pretest children did not, although they received the same microgenetic-enhancement experiences (Rhodes & Wellman, 2013).

Thus, in a constructivist manner, progress was dependent on the child's diet of experiences (because children in control groups without prediction-explanation experiences did not progress) but was also dependent on where a child was to begin with. Moreover, children achieved a progression of intermediate under-standings on the way to understanding false belief. This is clearest if we track what happened to the Diverse-Belief pretest children. Although all failed to understand false belief, on their posttest ToM Scale, many had progressed beyond Diverse Belief to understanding knowledge access; 43 percent of the Diverse-Belief chil-dren made such progress.

In a further utilization of this same approach, Candi Peterson and I (Wellman & Peterson, 2013) trained 13 deaf children of hearing parents who consistently failed false belief at pretest in extended microgenetic sessions over 6 weeks and ana-lyzed their progress. For deaf children we did not use explanations for our added, microgenetic experiences; we used thought bubbles. We did this because previous research shows that children with deafness may be more responsive to pictorial stimuli than hearing preschoolers (e.g., Peterson, 2002). Moreover, everyday media that feature pictures along with print – comics, storybooks, cartoons, and graphic novels (e.g., manga) – are very popular with deaf children in the age range we tested. Thought bubbles could thus provide a useful tool for helping deaf children to understand representational mental states and a helpful conversational forum for discussing such states, including differences among persons in the mental represen-tations they may hold.

An age-matched control group who simply received the pre- and posttests did not change over a 12-week period, confirming that without intervention these children make very little change over such a period. Yet the focal group who had multiple intervening microgenetic training sessions did change – they became correct on 69 percent of their false-belief tasks at posttest. Not only did they gain understanding of theory-of-mind concepts focal to their training (the exact sort of false-belief task used in their microgenetic training sessions), they also generalized to other novel false-belief tasks as well. Moreover, they progressed significantly on the broader ToM Scale of theory-of-mind concepts.

Once again, however, not all children in this focal group came to understand false belief or progressed equally. What accounted for this variation? Children who were further along the ToM Scale at pretest (e.g., DD, DB, and KA) were more likely to make greater false-belief progress than those less far along (e.g., DD or DD and DB instead). In regression analyses this influence of prior knowledge was by far the largest factor accounting for posttest gain and did so even after language competence and age were controlled.

Summary: a constructivist perspective on learning and on social context

In total, these data help address one of the most basic issues for understanding conceptual development: specifying the mechanisms of cognitive learning. To reiterate, some influences on conceptual progress undoubtedly concern factors external to theory-of-mind conceptions themselves – increases in memory or language or executive functioning, for example. But, conceptual progress also demonstrably depends on conceptual learning within a conceptual domain. And this learning integrates the prior conceptual infrastructure a child brings to the task of learning something new, coupled with his or her exposures to relevant environmental evidence.

This is a basic, constructivist proposal, yet direct evidence for it has been in surprisingly short supply. But, as I foreshadowed earlier, our data manifest three empirical signatures of such a process of constructivist learning and development: (1) learning proceeds in orderly conceptual progressions; (2) sequences and timetables are experience-dependent (and hence context-dependent); and, (3) prior conceptual knowledge influences the presence and nature of learning.

In our microgenetic research, children's prior understandings both enabled learning (for children closer to false belief on the ToM Scale at pretest) and constrained it (for those further away to begin with). Whether closer or further, however, children's progress proceeded through an ordered set of intermediate understandings. For those further from an understanding of false belief, being trained about false beliefs did not often engender an understanding of false belief, but it provoked other intermediate theory-of-mind understandings anyway.

These sorts of data underwrite the title of my chapter, "Learning a theory of mind." Theory of mind is a developmental achievement. It is early acquired (in the normal case) but is also dynamic – it changes during development. Both its early acquisition and its continuing changes reflect developmental learning. Indeed, theory of mind is learned on the basis of experiences and evidence in a learning dynamic that manifests three crucial hallmarks of constructivist, conceptual learning.

References

Amsterlaw, J., & Wellman, H. M. (2006). Theories of mind in transition: a microgenetic study of the development of false belief understanding. *Journal of Cognition and Development*, 7(2), 139–172. doi: 10.1207/s15327647jcd0702_1.

Astington, J. W., & Jenkins, J. M. (1995). Theory of mind development and social understanding. *Cognition and Emotion, 9*, 151–165.

Baron-Cohen, S. (1995). *Mindblindness: An Essay on Autism and Theory of Mind*. Cambridge, MA: MIT Press.

Bartsch, K., & Wellman, H. M. (1995). *Children Talk About the Mind*. New York: Oxford University Press.

Buttelmann, D., Carpenter, M., & Tomasello, M. (2009). Eighteen-month-old infants show false belief understanding in an active helping paradigm. *Cognition, 112*(2), 337–342. doi: 10.1016/j.cognition.2009.05.006.

Callaghan, T., Rochat, P., Lillard, A., Claux, M. L., Odden, H., Itakura, S., et al. (2005). Synchrony in the onset of mental-state reasoning. *Psychological Science, 16*(5), 378–384. doi: 10.1111/j.0956-7976.2005.01544.x.

Chomsky, N. (1975). *Reflections on Language*. New York: Pantheon Books.

Churchland, P. M. (1984). *Matter and Consciousness: A Contemporary Introduction to the Philosophy of Mind*. Cambridge, MA: MIT Press.

D'Andrade, R. (1987). A folk model of the mind. In D. Holland & N. Quinn (Eds.), *Cultural Models in Language and Thought* (pp. 112–148). Cambridge: Cambridge University Press.

Diesendruck, G., & Ben-Eliyahu, A. (2006). The relationships among social cognition, peer acceptance, and social behavior in Israeli kindergarteners. *International Journal of Behavioral Development, 30*(2), 137–147. doi: 10.1177/0165025406063628.

Dunn, J. (1995). Children as psychologists: the later correlates of individual differences in understanding of emotions and other minds. *Cognition & Emotion, 9*, 187–201.

Dunn, J., & Brown, J. R. (1993). Early conversations about causality: content, pragmatics and developmental change. *British Journal of Developmental Psychology, 11*(2), 107–123. doi: 10.1111/j.2044-835X.1993.tb00591.x.

Fink, E., Begeer, S., Hunt, C., & de Rosnay, M. (2014). False-belief understanding and social preference over the first 2 years of school: a longitudinal study. *Child Development, 85*(6), 2389–2403.

Fodor, J. A. (1987). *Psychosemantics: The problem of meaning in the philosophy of mind*. Cambridge, MA: Bradford Books/MIT Press.

Goodman, N. D., Ullman, T. D., & Tenenbaum, J. B. (2011). Learning a theory of causality. *Psychological Review, 118*(1), 110–119. doi: 10.1037/a0021336.

Gopnik, A., & Wellman, H. M. (1994). The theory theory. In L. Hirschfield, & S. Gelman (Eds.), *Mapping the Mind: Domain Specificity in Cognition and Culture* (pp. 257–293, xiv, 516). New York: Cambridge University Press.

Gopnik, A., & Wellman, H. M. (2012). Reconstructing constructivism: causal models, Bayesian learning mechanisms, and the theory theory. *Psychological Bulletin*, 1085–1108. doi: 10.1037/a0028044.

Gopnik, A., Glymour, C., Sobel, D. M., Schulz, L. E., Kushnir, T., & Danks, D. (2004). A theory of causal learning in children: causal maps and Bayes nets. *Psychological Review, 111*(1), 3–32. doi: 10.1037/0033-295X.111.1.3.

Griffiths, T. L., Chater, N., Kemp, C., Perfors, A., & Tenenbaum, J. B. (2010). Probabilistic models of cognition: exploring representations and inductive biases. *Trends in Cognitive Sciences, 14*(8), 357–364. doi: 10.1016/j.tics.2010.05.004.

Hickling, A. K., & Wellman, H. M. (2001). The emergence of children's causal explanations and theories: evidence from everyday conversation. *Developmental Psychology, 37*(5), 668–683.

Kristen, S., Thoermer, C., Hofer, T., Aschersleben, G., & Sodian, B. (2006). Skalierung von "theory of mind" aufgaben (Scaling of theory of mind tasks). *Zeitschrift fur*

Entwicklungspsychologie und Pädagogische Psychologie, 38(4), 186–195. doi: 10.1026/0049-8637.38.4.186.

Lederberg, A. R., Schick, B., & Spencer, P. E. (2013). Language and literacy development of deaf and hard-of-hearing children: successes and challenges. *Developmental Psychology, 49*(1), 15–30. doi: 10.1037/a0029558.

Lee, K. (2013). Little liars: development of verbal deception in children. *Child Development Perspectives, 7* (2), 91–96.

Leslie, A. M. (1994). ToMM, ToBy, and agency: core architecture and domain specificity in cognition and culture. In L. Hirschfeld & S. Gelman (Eds.), *Mapping the Mind: Domain Specificity in Cognition and Culture* (pp. 119–148). New York: Cambridge University Press.

Li, J. (2001). Chinese conceptualization of learning. *Ethos, 29*(2), 111–137. doi: 10.1525/eth.2001.29.2.111.

Liu, D., Wellman, H. M., Tardif, T., & Sabbagh, M. A. (2008). Theory of mind development in Chinese children: a meta-analysis of false-belief understanding across cultures and languages. *Developmental Psychology, 44*(2), 523–531. doi: 10.1037/0012-1649.44.2.523.

Lohmann, H., & Tomasello, M. (2003). The role of language in the development of false belief understanding: a training study. *Child Development, 74*(4), 1130–1144. doi: 10.1111/1467-8624.00597.

Luhrmann, T. (2011). Towards an anthropological theory of mind. *Journal of the Finnish Anthropological Society, 36,* 5–13.

Milligan, K., Astington, J. W., & Dack, L. A. (2007). Language and theory of mind: meta-analysis of the relation between language ability and false-belief understanding. *Child Development, 78*(2), 622–646. doi: 10.1111/j.1467-8624.2007.01018.x.

Moeller, M. P., & Schick, B. (2006). Relations between maternal input and theory of mind understanding in deaf children. *Child Development, 77,* 751–766. doi: 10.1111/j.1467-8624.2006.00901.x.

Morgan, G., & Kegal, J. (2006). Nicaraguan sign language and theory of mind: the issue of critical periods and abilities. *Journal of Child Psychology and Psychiatry, 47,* 811–819. doi: 10.1111/j.1469-7610.2006.01621.x.

Neumann, A., Thoermer, C., & Sodian, B. (2008). *Belief-based actions anticipation in 18-month-old infants.* Paper presented at the International Congress of Psychology, Berlin, Germany.

Nisbett, R. E. (2003). *The Geography of Thought: How Asians and Westerners Think Differently – and why.* New York: Free Press.

Onishi, K. H., & Baillargeon, R. (2005). Do 15-month-old infants understand false beliefs? *Science, 308*(5719), 255–258. doi: 10.1126/science.1107621.

O'Reilly, K., Peterson, C. C., & Wellman, H. M. (2014). Sarcasm and advanced theory of mind understanding in children and adults with prelingual deafness. *Developmental Psychology, 50*(7), 1862–1877. doi: 10.1037/a0036654.

Peskin, J., & Ardino, V. (2003). Representing the mental world in children's social behavior: playing hide-and-seek and keeping a secret. *Social Development, 12*(4), 496–512. doi: 10.1111/1467-9507.00245.

Peterson, C. C. (2002). Drawing insights from pictures: the development of concepts of false drawing and false belief in children with deafness, normal hearing and autism. *Child Development, 73,* 1442–1459. doi: 10.1111/1467-8624.00482.

Peterson, C. C. (2009). Development of social-cognitive and communication skills in children born deaf. *Scandinavian Journal of Psychology, 50*(5), 475–483. doi: 10.1111/j.1467-9450.2009.00750.x.

Peterson, C. C., & Siegal, M. (1995). Deafness, conversation and theory of mind. *Journal of Child Psychology and Psychiatry, 36*(3), 459–474. doi: 10.1111/j.1469-7610.1995.tb01303.x.

Peterson, C. C., & Slaughter, V. (2003). Opening windows into the mind: mothers' preferences for mental state explanations and children's theory of mind. *Cognitive Development*, *18*(3), 399–429. doi: 10.1016/s0885-2014(03)00041-8.

Peterson, C. C., Wellman, H. M., & Liu, D. (2005). Steps in theory-of-mind development for children with deafness or autism. *Child Development*, *76*(2), 502–517. doi: 10.1111/j.1467-8624.2005.00859.x.

Piaget, J. (1983). Piaget's theory. In P. H. Mussen (Ed.), *Handbook of Child Psychology*, 4th edition (Vol. 1). New York: John Wiley.

Pyers, J. E., & Senghas, A. (2009). Language promotes false-belief understanding: evidence from learners of a new sign language. *Psychological Science*, *20*(7), 805–812. doi: 10.1111/j.1467-9280.2009.02377.x.

Rhodes, M., & Wellman, H. (2013). Constructing a new theory from old ideas and new evidence. *Cognitive Science*, *37*(3), 592–604. doi: 10.1111/cogs.12031.

Ruffman, T., Slade, L., & Crowe, E. (2002). The relation between children's and mothers' mental state language and theory-of-mind understanding. *Child Development*, *73*(3), 734–751. doi: 10.1111/1467-8624.00435.

Saffran, J. R., Aslin, R. N., & Newport, E. L. (1996). Statistical learning by 8-month-old infants. *Science*, *274*(5294), 1926–1928. doi: 10.1126/science.274.5294.1926.

Scott, R. M., & Baillargeon, R. (2009). Which penguin is this? Attributing false beliefs about object identity at 18 months. *Child Development*, *80*(4), 1172–1196.

Shahaeian, A., Peterson, C. C., Slaughter, V., & Wellman, H. M. (2011). Culture and the sequence of steps in theory of mind development. *Developmental Psychology*, *47*(5), 1239–1247. doi: 10.1037/a0023899.

Shakespeare, W. (1597/1961). Romeo and Juliet. In C. Hardin (Ed.), *The Complete Works of Shakespeare* (pp. 393–424). Glenview, IL: Scott, Foresman.

Siegal, M., & Varley, R. (2002). Neural systems involved in 'theory of mind'. *Nature Reviews Neuroscience*, *3*(6), 463–471. doi: 10.1038/nrn844.

Siegler, R. S. (1995). Children's thinking: How does change occur? In W. Schneider & F. Weinert (Eds.), *Memory Performance and Competencies* (pp. 405–430). Hillsdale, NJ: Erlbaum.

Siegler, R. S. (2007). Cognitive variability. *Developmental Science*, *10*(1), 104–109. doi: 10.1111/j.1467-7687.2007.00571.x.

Slaughter, V., Imuta, K., Peterson, C. C., & Henry, J. D. (2015). Meta-analysis of theory of mind and peer popularity in the preschool and early school years. *Child Development*, *86*, 1159–174.

Southgate, V., Senju, A., & Csibra, G. (2007). Action anticipation through attribution of false belief by 2-year-olds. *Psychological Science*, *18*(7), 587–592.

Southgate, V., Chevallier, C., & Csibra, G. (2010). Seventeen-month-olds appeal to false beliefs to interpret others' referential communication. *Developmental Science*, *13*(6), 907–912. doi: 10.1111/j.1467-7687.2009.00946.x.

Surian, L., Caldi, S., & Sperber, D. (2007). Attribution of beliefs by 13-month-old infants. *Psychological Science*, *18*(7), 580–586. doi: 10.1111/j.1467-9280.2007.01943.x.

Tardif, T., & Wellman, H. M. (2000). Acquisition of mental state language in Mandarin- and Cantonese-speaking children. *Developmental Psychology*, *36*(1), 25–43. doi: 10.1037/0012-1649.36.1.25.

Tenenbaum, J. B., Griffiths, T. L., & Kemp, C. (2006). Theory-based Bayesian models of inductive learning and reasoning. *Trends in Cognitive Sciences*, *10*(7), 309–318. doi: http://dx.doi.org/10.1016/j.tics.2006.05.009.

Tenenbaum, J. B., Kemp, C., Griffiths, T. L., & Goodman, N. D. (2011). How to grow a mind: statistics, structure, and abstraction. *Science, 331*(6022), 1279–1285. doi: 10.1126/science.1192788.

Ullman, T. D., Goodman, N. D., & Tenenbaum, J. B. (2012). Theory learning as stochastic search in the language of thought. *Cognitive Development, 27*(4), 455–480. doi: 10.1016/j.cogdev.2012.07.005.

Vaccari, C., & Marschark, M. (1997). Communication between parents and deaf children: implications for social-emotional development. *Journal of Child Psychology and Psychiatry, 38*, 793–801.

Walker, C. M., & Gopnik, A. (2014). Toddlers infer higher-order relational principles in causal learning. *Psychological Science, 25*(1), 161–169. doi: 10.1177/0956797613502983.

Watson, A. C., Nixon, C. L., Wilson, A., & Capage, L. (1999). Social interaction skills and theory of mind in young children. *Developmental Psychology, 35*, 386–391. doi: 10.1037/0012-1649.35.2.386.

Wellman, H. M. (1990). *The Child's Theory of Mind.* Cambridge, MA: MIT Press.

Wellman, H. M. (2011). Reinvigorating explanations for the study of cognitive development. *Child Development Perspectives, 5*, 33–38.

Wellman, H. M. (2013). Universal social cognition: childhood theory of mind. In M. Banaji & S. Gelman (Eds.), *Navigating the Social World: A Developmental Perspective* (pp. 69–74). New York: Oxford University Press.

Wellman, H. M. (2014). *Making Minds: How Theory of Mind Develops.* New York: Oxford University Press.

Wellman, H. M., & Liu, D. (2004). Scaling of theory-of-mind tasks. *Child Development, 75*(2), 523–541. doi: 10.1111/j.1467-8624.2004.00691.x.

Wellman, H. M., & Peterson, C. C. (2013). Deafness, thought bubbles, and theory-of-mind development. *Developmental Psychology, 49*(12), 2357–2367. doi: 10.1037/a0032419.

Wellman, H. M., Cross, D., & Watson, J. (2001). A meta-analysis of theory-of-mind development: the truth about false belief. *Child Development, 72*(3), 655–684. doi: 10.1111/1467-8624.00304.

Wellman, H. M., Fang, F., Liu, D., Zhu, L., & Liu, G. (2006). Scaling of theory-of-mind understandings in Chinese children. *Psychological Science, 17*(12), 1075–1081. doi: 10.1111/j.1467-9280.2006.01830.x.

Wellman, H. M., Fang, F., & Peterson, C. C. (2011). Sequential progressions in a theory of mind scale: longitudinal perspectives. *Child Development, 82*(3), 780–792. doi: 10.1111/j.1467-8624.2011.01583.x.

PART I

Social contexts for development

2

CULTURE AND THE SEQUENCE OF DEVELOPMENTAL MILESTONES TOWARD THEORY OF MIND MASTERY

Candida C. Peterson and Virginia Slaughter

Culture and theory of mind development

The issue of whether or not there are cross-cultural differences in children's development of an understanding of others' minds (theory of mind: ToM) has important theoretical implications. It has the potential to shed light on the relative roles of biological maturation and social interactions via cultural participation in the growth of social cognition. If ToM mastery is culturally universal, with little variation from one cultural community to the next in either its timing or its form, this would favor biological maturation as the crucial developmental process. If, on the other hand, children in different cultural settings differ in their patterns and/or rates of ToM growth, this would give weight to the role of social and cultural experiences.

Proponents of a strong cultural influence model predict wide cultural differences not only in the timing of ToM acquisition but at a broader level in the very process of development itself. "The main wager of cultural psychology is that . . . few components of the human mental equipment are so inherently constrained [or] hard-wired . . . that their developmental pathway cannot be transformed through cultural participation" (Schweder et al., 2006, p. 716). In the case of ToM, two key aspects of the developmental pathway have so far been the primary focus of empirical research. One of these is the issue of universality: is there a culture where ToM never emerges? The second is the issue of rate or timetabling of ToM growth. For example, taking false-belief task mastery (Wellman, Cross, & Watson, 2001) as the marker of ToM, are children in some cultures slower than others to acquire ToM concepts? Here, "culture" refers to the set of rules, norms, and modes of interaction that are acquired and practiced by a distinct social group, often sharing a geographical locale, a common language as well as traditions, beliefs, and practices.

Avis and Harris' (1991) study was seminal in showing no cross-cultural difference in the timing of false-belief mastery between two highly disparate groups, namely British middle-class preschoolers versus children of a preliterate hunter-gatherer culture in West Africa. Using a standard false-belief task, the schooled British and unschooled African children passed at roughly the same age. This suggested universality not only of ToM as a construct but also of its timing across disparate cultures. A number of studies since Avis and Harris (1991) have likewise concluded that ToM is culturally universal in both manifestation and timing. For instance, Callaghan et al. (2005) used a single culturally friendly procedure in five distinct cultural groups to test the timing of false-belief acquisition. Children were tested in India, Peru, Samoa, Thailand, and Canada. There was no significant difference among these cultures in children's age at false-belief mastery. A majority of children in each culture passed the false-belief test at approximately 5 years of age.

Not all studies have agreed with this conclusion, however. Wellman et al. (2001) noted that, whereas a transition from below-chance false-belief performance at age 3 to significant success at some later point in development appeared to be culturally universal, there was some variation by locale in the point at which a majority of children made the transition. Those in the USA, Canada, and the UK, along with Koreans and African hunter-gatherers, all mastered false belief at approximately the same age. But Japanese children were notably slower to do so, as were Quechua-speaking Peruvian Indian children. More recently, Slaughter and Perez-Zapata's (2014) review also suggested cultural variability in the ages of false-belief mastery among children in different cultures. However, it is somewhat problematic to compare across a small number of imperfectly matched individual studies often of small samples and lacking in cross-cultural comparison groups.

Consequently, to achieve a wider synthesis, Liu, Wellman, Tardif, and Sabbagh (2008) conducted a meta-analysis of false-belief performance by several thousand children in four locales. There were Chinese preschoolers in Hong Kong and Beijing plus English-speaking Canadian and US children. The authors discovered an intriguing contrast that was not strictly cross-cultural. Whereas Canadian, US, and Beijing children all mastered false belief at about the same age, Chinese children in Hong Kong were approximately 2 years slower than these other groups. In other words, despite sharing a language (in different dialects), a culture, and similar familial lifestyles, the Hong Kong and Beijing children differed substantially in false-belief timing. Conversely, despite their widely disparate cultural backgrounds, English-speaking North Americans and Chinese-speaking children in Beijing displayed the same timing as one another.

It would seem that a more subtle and nuanced way of exploring cross-cultural variation may be needed in order to fully tease apart the specific social, microcultural, and general environmental influences that may play a role. Indeed, by closely examining the social-conversational features of the cultural settings their Hong Kong versus Beijing samples inhabited, two plausible hypotheses were suggested by Liu et al. (2008) about the role of social-environmental factors in the Beijing–Hong Kong differences in ToM development timing. For one thing, the

Hong Kong children were more likely than their Beijing peers to have siblings, given mainland China's one-child family policy. Yet, at least for Western children, having siblings often predicts faster ToM mastery (McAlister & Peterson, 2013; Perner, Ruffman, & Leekam, 1994), in direct opposition to what was observed in China.

If siblings are not the issue, another possibility is the fact that the Hong Kong children studied by Liu et al. (2008) were more likely to be bilingual than the Canadian, US, and Beijing samples. The role of bilingualism in ToM growth is unclear. Though a positive link was seen in one study (Goetz, 2003), it had methodological problems. The sampling procedure excluded bilinguals unless their command of *both* their languages was as high as or higher than monolinguals' command of their *sole* language. This selective sampling of exceptionally linguistically advanced bilingual children may have created an artifact. The linguistic skills of bilingual children in general may not have been fairly represented and since monolinguals were not selected for advanced language, this could explain the group difference in ToM. Nevertheless, bilingualism has been linked with certain cognitive and executive-function correlates of ToM (specifically, inhibitory control; Bialystok, 2001) and is likewise associated with pragmatic language skill (Siegal et al., 2010).

However, bilingualism could also be a potential disadvantage to early ToM growth, owing to bilingual language learners initially having relatively small vocabularies in each language compared to their monolingual peers (Poulin-Dubois, Bialystok, Blaye, Polonia, & Yott, 2012). This could limit ToM by restricting access to fluent and varied conversational input about subtle, non-obvious things like what another speaker is thinking. Thus, until the bilingual child attains an adequate mastery of *both* languages (including mental-state vocabulary and syntax), conversational access to other speakers' minds may be restricted. If so, limited conversation only about things that can be seen and pointed at, rather than abstract referents like people's thoughts and feelings, may limit ToM growth.

The case of late signing deaf children who are reared in the bilingual environment of joint exposure to spoken language (at home with parents and siblings), and a signed language (at school with teachers and peers), provides an example. These deaf children, unlike deaf native signers with monolingual exposure to signing from birth, are often seriously delayed in their ToM understanding (see Peterson, 2009, for a review). Furthermore, deaf children's ToM task performance correlates with the extent of their parents' abilities to communicate mental-state vocabulary in sign language (Moeller, 2007). This is consistent with the idea that until a bilingual child's command of mental-state terms in at least one of her languages is achieved, conversational access to ToM-promoting mental-state input may be delayed. At this stage in development, bilingualism would therefore delay rather than enhance ToM mastery. It is clear there is a need for further systematic study of ToM and bilingualism. Furthermore there are numerous other possible explanations besides bilingualism for the microcultural contrast in children's false-belief mastery in Beijing and Hong Kong (Liu et al., 2008), all requiring further investigation. The empirical study to be reported later in this chapter adds new evidence to this unfolding picture.

Developmental sequences across cultures

Looking beyond these data from specific studies, there is a more serious limitation to the body of past research on ToM and culture. This is the predominant focus on the false-belief test alone. Despite Astington's (2001) warning that "there is danger in allowing a single task to become a marker for complex development" (p. 687), most past cross-cultural studies have equated ToM with false-belief test success. This selective focus fails to address the broader question of whether or not cultures vary in the overall long-term developmental process of ToM growth. In the broader scheme of ToM, false-belief mastery is not an isolated event, but rather is just one of several key milestones in a continuous developmental process of coming to understand others' minds. The process has its roots in infancy and toddlerhood (e.g., O'Reilly & Peterson, 2014a; Wellman, Lopez-Duran, Labounty, & Hamilton, 2008) and extends through adolescence (Bosco, Gabbatore, & Tirassa, 2014) and even into adulthood (e.g., O'Reilly, Peterson, & Wellman, 2014).

Empirical evidence for a sequence of developmental milestones towards full ToM maturity emerged convincingly with Wellman and Liu's (2004) discovery of a statistically reliable five-step Guttman scale of ToM acquisition. They found that, with increasing age, the overwhelming majority of preschoolers from the USA mastered each of the five scale concepts in the same fixed order. First they understood diverse desires (DD: different people want different things), then diverse beliefs (DB: different people hold different (potentially true) opinions or beliefs), then knowledge access (KA: those who do not witness an event may not know about it), then false belief (FB: people act on what they think is true, not necessarily what is genuinely true) and, finally, hidden emotion (HE: people can hide their true feelings). Via Guttman scaling and Rasch modeling techniques, Wellman and Liu (2004) showed that the tasks obeyed a fixed developmental order with mastery of each task in the sequence contingent upon mastery of the previous one. Most children passed DD before any other task; those who passed two tasks passed DD and DB, and so on. The same sequence was confirmed for English-speaking Australian children both cross-sectionally (Peterson, Wellman, & Liu, 2005) and longitudinally (Wellman, Fang, & Peterson, 2011).

Cross-culturally, an intriguing question is whether or not this same developmental sequence applies to children growing up in different socio-cultural contexts. Cultural practices, including differences in parent–child conversation, parents' values and childrearing techniques, and different socialization pressures and patterns could conceivably cause children in different locales to construct their ideas about others' minds in varying ways. Alternatively, something inherent in the process of ToM development itself could possibly constrain the order of emergence of each of the concepts assessed by the ToM Scale; for instance, brain maturation (Leslie, Friedman, & German, 2004). Thus if developmental sequence of Wellman and Liu's ToM Scale is shown to vary across different cultural groups, this would strongly implicate cultural influence rather than modular neurocognitive maturation in the process of ToM acquisition.

To examine the ToM Scale progression cross-culturally, Wellman, Fang, Liu, Zhu, and Liu (2006) compared Chinese-speaking preschoolers in Beijing with English-speaking preschoolers in Australia and the USA. There were no significant differences between the groups in overall timing of ToM mastery, meaning that all three groups passed the same mean number of ToM Scale steps at equivalent ages. Yet there was a significant cultural contrast in the order of acquisition of the tasks within the scale. The two English-speaking groups passed the tasks in the order predicted by Wellman and Liu's (2004) Guttman sequence, whereas the Chinese children followed a different developmental ordering. They mastered KA reliably before DB, thus transposing the ordering of two steps for English-speaking Western children.

Further evidence of cross-cultural variation in the order of ToM Scale concepts emerged from a subsequent comparison between Farsi-speaking Iranian children and English-speaking Australians (Shahaeian, Peterson, Slaughter, & Wellman, 2011). Like the Chinese children, the Iranian children passed KA reliably before DB. The Australian comparison group matched to these Iranian children passed DB before KA. Importantly, though, neither Wellman et al. (2006) nor Shahaeian et al. (2011) found any significant differences between overall rates of ToM mastery (i.e., total scores on the ToM Scale) between their non-Western samples and English-speaking Western children.

Two important ideas are suggested by these findings. First they show that culture can shape not only how early individual ToM concepts like false belief are mastered but also, and independently, the overall pattern and shape of the process of ToM development itself. In Western, English-speaking cultures like the USA and Australia, children progress from the awareness that different people can want different things (DD) directly to the concept that beliefs are variable among different people (DB). Yet, in at least two non-Western cultures (China and Iran) the next ToM concept to emerge after DD is KA, or the awareness of the contrast between knowing versus ignorance. Second, the findings showed that the sequence difference can coexist with uniform rates of ToM progress.

Presumably, the culturally specific experiences children have while growing up shape these variations in the ToM Scale sequence. Parental values, philosophies of childrearing and day-to-day social practices may well contribute to the cultural contrast in the aspects of others' thought processes that children first notice and make sense of. In Western cultures, parents often value children's independence and encourage them to forthrightly assert their own opinions even at the risk of disagreeing with others. Yet, in both Iran and China, there is a strong emphasis on social harmony and on children's deference to adult views. Respect for traditional wisdom reinforces the view that children have a duty to acquire the knowledge that is collectively respected by society as a whole. Possibly these different parental values express themselves in culturally varied childrearing practices as well as via explicit and implicit conversation and modeling. This could help to explain the intriguing sequence variations observed.

Methodologically, these studies suggest that cross-cultural ToM research needs to add another key question to its repertoire. As noted earlier, the two main questions that have so far preoccupied the field are: (a) Is the ToM construct culturally universal? and (b) Are there cross-cultural differences in ages of ToM acquisition? Both are undeniably interesting and important. However, it now seems equally important to examine a third question: (c) How culturally variable is the sequence of conceptual ToM milestones leading up to and beyond false belief?

The evidence from Wellman et al. (2006) and Shahaeian et al. (2011) that developmental sequence and developmental timing are independent of one another highlights the value of further study of the former. While each deserves attention in the context of a full picture of culture's role, it will be especially useful to study ToM Scale sequences further. This issue has been researched less often than the issue of age at false-belief mastery. Furthermore, by examining the entire sequence of ToM concept development from toddlerhood through middle childhood, a more nuanced picture of culture's influence can be obtained. With this focus, a brief review of past studies of the ToM Scale in children from non-Western cultures is first presented, followed by a new empirical study.

ToM scale sequences in non-Western children

To date, ten known published studies have used Wellman and Liu's (2004) ToM Scale (in whole or in part) to examine orders of emergence of sequential ToM concepts in children from non-Western cultural backgrounds. Designs and outcomes of these are summarized in Table 2.1, including pass rates on individual ToM Scale concepts and statistical data on scale conformity, where available.

If, in place of full sequences, we were to look at Table 2.1 data in the traditional manner via false-belief success alone, there is a suggestion of cross-cultural variation. Setting aside two studies (O'Reilly & Peterson, 2014a; Wu & Su, 2014) that had samples younger than the norm, the mean sample age in most other studies (roughly 4.50–5.00 years) was similar across studies, yet false-belief success rates varied from below 20 percent to over 50 percent. However, another potential influence besides culture on false belief in these studies is socioeconomic status (SES). Although the meta-analysis by Hughes and Devine presented in Chapter 3 of this volume reveals SES to be a significant correlate of understanding, they also reported that the effect is small overall and was more pronounced in the UK compared to other samples. Thus, strikingly, Kuntoro, Saraswati, Peterson, and Slaughter (2013) found that 40 percent of their very-low-SES children living in a Jakarta slum with parents who had rarely completed primary school did not differ significantly from their middle-class Indonesian peers. Furthermore, their success rate was relatively high (54 percent) compared with other Table 2.1 studies. Indeed, in the Qu and Shen (2013) study, only 11 percent of bilingual Singaporean children passed at 4.50 years and only 21 percent at 5.50 years.

TABLE 2.1 Theory of Mind (ToM) Scale sequences in non-Western children

Study (chronogically)	Sample characteristics	Percent correct	Guttman Scale conformity
Wellman, Fang, Liu, Zhu, and Liu (2006)	92 Chinese-speaking preschoolers aged 3–5 years in Beijing	DD (89%) > KA (79%) > DB (71%) > FB (54%) > HE (37%)	Yes: 86% of sample match KA > DB sequence; Rep = 0.93
Toyama (2007)	120 Japanese-speaking children aged 3–6 years in Tokyo	DD (90%) > DB (64%) = KA (64%) > FB (40%) > HE (16%)	No: Reps for both DB > KA and KA > DB sequences are non-significant
Wellman, Fang and Peterson (2011)	31 Chinese-speaking preschoolers aged 4 and 5 years in Beijing	DD > KA > DB > FB > HE	Yes: 79% of sample match KA > DB sequence; Rep = 0.95
Shahaeian, Peterson, Slaughter, and Wellman (2011)	58 Farsi-speaking Iranian children aged 3–6 years in Shiraz, Iran (mean age = 4.79 years)	DD (86%) = KA (88%) > DB (47%) = FB (46%) > HE (22%)	Yes: Rep = 0.94; for KA > DB sequence
Kuntoro, Saraswati, Peterson, and Slaughter (2013)	101 Bahasa-Indonesian-speaking children aged 3–7 years in Jakarta	DD (86%) = DB (85%) > KA (44%) = FB (46%) > HE (22%)	Yes: Rep = 0.93 for DB > KA sequence

(continued)

TABLE 2.1 (continued)

Study (chronologically)	Sample characteristics	Percent correct	Guttman Scale conformity
Qu and Shen (2013)	120 English-speaking 3–5-year-olds of Chinese ethnicity in Singapore	DD (91%) > DB (43%) = KA (43%) > FB (17%)	N/A; cannot compute Rep as full ToM Scale was not administered
Wu and Su (2014)	74 Chinese-speaking preschoolers aged 2–4 years in Beijing (mean age = 3.21 years)	DD (95%) > DB (70%) > KA (38%) > FB (12%) > HE (3%)	No scaling statistics reported
Shahaeian, Nielsen, Peterson, and Slaughter (2014)	80 Farsi-speaking Iranian children aged 3–9 years in Shiraz (mean age = 6 years)	DD (86%) = KA (94%) > DB (45%) = FB (57%) > HE (48%) >	Yes: Rep = 0.91 for KA > DB sequence
Shahaeian, Nielsen, Peterson, and Slaughter (2014)	22 Farsi-speaking Iranian children aged 3–5 years in Shiraz (subset of Shahaeian et al., 2014, above)	DD (86%) = KA (86%) > DB (27%) > FB (18%) > HE (14%)	Yes: Rep = 0.91 for KA > DB sequence
O'Reilly and Peterson (2014a)	49 Indigenous Australian Aboriginal-English speakers (mean age = 4.27 years)	DD (82%) = DB (84%) > KA (24%) = FB (29%) > HE (4%)	Yes: 80% of sample match the original (DB > KA) sequence; Rep = 0.96 for DB > KA

DD, diverse desires; KA, knowledge access; DB, diverse beliefs; FB, false beliefs; HE, hidden emotion; Rep, reproducibility; N/A, not applicable.

While highlighting questions about possible influences of culture and other factors (e.g., bilingualism) on the timing of false-belief mastery, these data are also illustrative from a methodological viewpoint. If false-belief scores alone are considered, the Table 2.1 data suggest cultural variation. However, when the overall sequence of ToM development across all five sequential steps is examined instead, substantial cross-cultural uniformity is apparent. Table 2.1 shows pass rates on these five tasks by each sample. The consistency is impressive. The earliest emerging of these five tasks (highest proportions passing) is DD in all but one of the ten studies and it is equal first in the latter. Similarly, HE was the hardest task in all nine studies in which this task was administered and FB was next hardest in all ten studies. Not only is the consistency striking among all these non-Western studies, but these same patterns replicate those found in the vast majority of studies of Western cultural groups (e.g., Peterson, Wellman, & Slaughter, 2012; Wellman & Liu, 2004). Thus there is some uniformity in the overall developmental trajectory through successive steps of the ToM Scale across the varied non-Western cultures that have so far been studied. Yet, at the same time, there is also one intriguing cross-cultural variation, namely the ordering of DB relative to KA in the developmental sequence.

Understanding belief diversity versus knowledge access

The ToM Scale sequence for most Chinese and Iranian samples in Table 2.1 matches Wellman et al.'s (2006) initial observation that KA emerged ahead of DB in China, as subsequently replicated by Shahaeian et al. (2011) in Iran. This raises provocative questions about the basis for this cross-cultural difference relative to Western samples. Examining just these two tasks relative to one another in the Table 2.1 data, the pattern shows some consistency. Including the Wellman et al. (2006) original, four of the ten studies in Table 2.1 had Chinese samples. Eighty percent of these (four of five) displayed the KA > DB ordering. Furthermore, the one non-supportive study (Wu & Su, 2014) had a disproportionate number of young 2-year-olds who may not yet have had enough basic language skill to comprehend the ToM tasks and/or test and control questions. (Under such circumstances, random guessing is a strong possibility, making the DB task spuriously easier, with its 50 percent odds of chance success by guessing rather than 25 percent for KA with its control question.)

Similarly, all three of the studies of Iranian children in Table 2.1 revealed the KA > DB pattern consistently. Three other non-Western cultural groups are included in Table 2.1. Japanese-speaking preschoolers displayed equal performance on DB and KA, while Bahasa-Indonesian-speakers and Indigenous Australian speakers of Aboriginal English clearly showed the "Western" (DB > KA) ordering. This suggests that cultural influences that are shared by common China and Iran, but not these other three non-Western cultures, may be responsible for the sequence variation. What could these cultural factors be? No easy answer is possible at this stage, but further converging data from other cultural groups should eventually help to shed light on this question. The following empirical study is designed with this in mind.

ToM development in bilingual (Chinese-English) Singaporean preschoolers

The main aim of our study was to further explore the question of ToM Scale sequences cross-culturally in a population of theoretical interest. We elected to study children of Chinese ethnicity growing up in the multilingual, cosmopolitan city of Singapore, where there are four official languages (English, Chinese, Malay, and Tamil). In practice, Chinese and English are the dominant languages. Many Singaporean child-care centers use Chinese as the mother tongue, and this was true of the two we worked in. However, from primary school onwards English becomes the official language of instruction. Thus, as preparation, daily subsidiary exposure to English in these centers was normative and most teachers and other staff were fully bilingual in both English and Chinese.

Culturally, the family background of all children we tested was Chinese. Thus this sample provided an opportunity for a novel test of the sequencing of ToM Scale stages in a somewhat different linguistic and cultural setting than that of the Beijing preschools where most previous ToM Scale sequence data were gathered (see Table 2.1). Also of subsidiary interest was the question of bilingualism. As noted earlier, a previous study of Chinese-English bilingual Singaporean children indicated an unusually slow rate of false-belief mastery (Qu & Shen, 2013: Table 2.1), possibly owing to incomplete bilingualism. However, the full ToM Scale was not administered so further investigation of this population is clearly needed.

Sample and procedure

A total of 62 Singaporean children of Chinese ethnicity aged 3–6 years took part in our study. There were 39 boys. They were recruited from one of two branches of an education-oriented preschool/child-care center. All participating children were Chinese-Singaporean whose first language was Chinese (these children comprised the vast majority of the center's populations). According to teachers, the vast majority of their parents were also fluent in English. All children were being exposed to English-language instruction even though (as noted above) the primary language of their center was Chinese. Teachers selected children whom they believed had enough English-language skills to complete our tasks. This proved true in a large majority of cases (76 percent), as shown by these 47 children having passed at least 60 percent of false-belief control questions upon their initial presentation in English. However, for 15 children (24 percent), English-language skills were insufficient, as indicated by control question failure and/or inability to carry on a simple warm-up conversation with the researcher in English but ability to do so in Chinese. This researcher, a fully bilingual native-born Singaporean, gave the ToM tests in Chinese to these children.

Measures

ToM was assessed with a three-item false-belief test battery, plus Wellman and Liu's (2004) five-step ToM Scale. (See Appendix for procedural details of these

ToM assessments.) We also estimated children's verbal abilities in English using the Peabody Picture Vocabulary Test (PPVT). Since no norms for bilingual children were available, we used raw scores in all statistical analyses. We had no equivalent norm-reference standard tests of receptive vocabulary skills in the Chinese language available. Thus we attempted the English-language version of PPVT with all children. Eleven (18 percent) had missing PPVT data owing to either inability or unwillingness to take it.

Results

Table 2.2 shows performance on each of the five ToM Scale tasks. Notably, the success rate on KA (77 percent) was higher than on DB (55 percent). This is consistent with the non-Western sequence previously observed in Beijing-Chinese and Iranian preschoolers. There were 27 children who passed one or other of these two tasks but not both. Of these, 18 (67 percent) passed KA only, while just 33 percent passed DB only. Thus, the overall response pattern appears to match the sequence (KA > DB) originally observed by Wellman et al. (2006) in China.

In total, 41 children (66 percent) showed patterns across the full ToM Scale that were perfectly consistent with the Chinese-Iranian pattern (KA > DB). To test statistically whether this seemingly high frequency of passing and failing the five tasks in this exact order was significant, we used Green's (1956) methods. A Guttman sequence is strict, such that success on each earlier scale step is a prerequisite for passing the next step and no successes occur after the first failure. The statistic, called coefficient of reproducibility (or Rep), evaluates how closely observed data conform to this pattern. Values of 0.90 or higher are significant. Using the Chinese-Iranian (KA > DB) scale ordering, the Rep for our children was a statistically significant 0.93. It seems that the Chinese cultural background these Singaporean children shared with the Beijing preschoolers previously tested contributed importantly to the ordering of the ToM Scale sequence, despite the many other differences in their lifestyles and social experiences.

As well as sequence ordering, another question of interest was whether the rate of ToM development for these bilingual Singaporean children matched that of preschoolers in other cultures. One index of this is ToM Scale total scores. Our sample's mean was 2.63 (SD = 0.96). Australian preschoolers of similar age in Shahaeian et al. (2011) did not differ (t (137) = 1.60, $p = 0.11$). Their mean was 2.90. Similarly, the Iranian preschoolers (mean = 2.53) in that study scored equivalently to this Singapore group (t (118) < 1, $p = 0.58$). Thus previous findings that cultural variations in task sequencing can go hand in hand with cultural similarity in overall rate of ToM development are supported by these data. Using just the false-belief test as the rate index, similar results applied. Our Singaporean group's pass rate (23 percent) did not differ significantly from either Shahaeian et al.'s (2011) Australians (36 percent pass), (Chi square (1) = 2.48, $n = 139$, $p = 0.116$), or Iranians (16 percent pass), (Chi square (1) = 0.56, $n = 120$, $p = 0.453$). Thus the overall picture is one of cultural consistency in ToM timing. Both

TABLE 2.2 Background variables and performance on theory of mind (ToM) tests

| n | Background variables | | Percent passing (n) | | | | | Mean summed scores | |
	Mean age (in years; SD; range)	Mean PPVT (raw score)	Diverse desires	Diverse beliefs	Knowledge access	False beliefs	Hidden emotion	ToM Scale total (SD; range)	Total false belief (SD; range)
62	4.64 (0.85; 3–6.4)	46.96 (18.28; 14–85)	95% (59)	55% (34)	77% (48)	23% (14)	13% (8)	2.63 (0.96; 0–5)	0.55 (1.05; 0–3)

PPVT, Peabody Picture Vocabulary Test.

false-belief mastery and ToM Scale totals emerge at similar ages in these three quite different cultures.

Finally, we attempted a preliminary exploration of possible differences due to bilingualism in the Singapore group. ToM Scale totals for the 15 children in our sample who were effectively monolingual (i.e., could only pass ToM control questions in their Chinese mother tongue) were compared with the remainder of the sample (all tested in English, their less fluent language). Since the former subgroup was younger, we used analysis of covariance to statistically control for any age effects. With means of 2.07 and 2.85, respectively, the difference between the groups in ToM performance was non-significant ($F(1, 60) = 3.93, p = 0.052$). Nor was there a difference in passing the false-belief test (Chi square $(1) = 0.97, n = 62, p = 0.325$). However, further study of bilingualism is clearly needed to confirm and extend this tentative result. There were too few monolinguals in our study, and their selection was too *ad hoc,* for the findings about bilingualism to be taken as anything more than a promising hypothesis for future investigation.

The overall results of our empirical study of Singaporean Chinese children are consistent with most past studies of Chinese children in other locales (see Table 2.1) in showing an important cross-cultural difference from Western samples in ToM Scale sequences despite cross-culturally equivalent rates of ToM growth. This consistent support for the alternative KA > DB ordering for Chinese children in Singapore as well as Beijing strongly implicates cultural learning in the process of ToM mastery. Contrary to a simple biologically driven process of maturation, the steps children go through in constructing a ToM vary with experience, including the diverse social and cognitive experiences that membership in a particular cultural group supplies.

A Chinese cultural upbringing (whether in China itself or elsewhere, like Singapore) seems to foster earlier appreciation of the gaining of knowledge, coupled with later awareness of the diversity of people's beliefs, than in the West. Perhaps the contrast between Chinese and Anglo-Western values and beliefs (e.g., Peng & Nisbett, 1999) is influential. In Chinese culture, a strong emphasis on respect for elders and traditions, together with a collective interdependence among family members and society, may motivate parents to encourage their children's seeking of knowledge and to frown upon ignorance via parent–child conversation and other socialization efforts. This could foster early awareness of the process of knowledge acquisition, and of the contrast between knowing and not knowing, as needed to pass the KA task.

Western cultures, contrastingly, value independence of thinking and behavior and parents teach children to assertively express their own opinions even when these disagree with the views of others, including the parents themselves. Given these emphases and conversational practices, Western children may realize earlier that different people have different opinions, leading to success on the DB task before KA. Such an interpretation is consistent with data from Iran, where knowledge mastery is often encouraged and children's assertion of discordant personal opinions is often discouraged (consistent with the KA > DB scale sequence). Direct cross-cultural study of parenting practices and parent–child conversation in these cultures would be useful to explore these possibilities.

At a broader level, these cross-cultural data strongly support the suggestion by Schweder et al. (2006) that cultural participation influences virtually all aspects of the lifelong developmental pathway. Methodologically, they show that simple comparisons among cultures in age of false-belief mastery are not enough. As well, the sequence of steps leading up to and beyond false belief to a fully mature ToM is worthy of exploration. The present study and those in Table 2.1 clearly illustrate cross-cultural sequence variations that, intriguingly, can coexist with cultural uniformity in ToM timing.

Conclusion: universality, timetabling, and sequencing in theory of mind development

To return to this chapter's three central questions of universality, timetabling, and sequencing, it appears that ToM is universal (at least in all cultures so far studied). However, across diverse cultures, children may acquire its key concepts at different rates and in somewhat differing orders. The research reviewed here confirms that culture plays a key role in the developmental process of ToM mastery, although it is not yet fully clear what specific culturally determined features of a child's upbringing are influential. One obvious candidate is patterns of conversation. It is well established that in Western cultures children with restricted conversational access, such as deaf children in hearing families, are slow to develop ToM (see Peterson, 2009, for a review). Conversely, rich social and conversational input about thoughts and feelings from parents (e.g., Ruffman, Slade, & Crowe, 2002) and siblings (e.g., Peterson, 2000) appears to accelerate ToM growth for individuals within the same culture. Therefore cross-cultural variations in children's conversational experience, among other things, may plausibly shape the different patterns of ToM development reviewed in this chapter.

References

Astington, J. W. (2001). The future of theory-of-mind research: understanding motivational states, the role of language, and real-world consequences. *Child Development, 72*, 685–687.

Avis, J., & Harris, P. L. (1991). Belief-desire reasoning among Baka children. *Child Development, 62*, 460–467.

Bialystok, E. (2001). *Bilingualism in development: Language, literacy, and cognition.* New York: Cambridge University Press.

Bosco, F. M., Gabbatore, I., & Tirassa, M. (2014). A broad assessment of theory of mind in adolescence: the complexity of mindreading. *Consciousness and Cognition, 24*, 84–97. doi: 10.1016/j.concog.2014.01.003.

Callaghan, T., Rochat, P., Lillard, A., Claux, M. L., Odden, H., Itakura, S., et al. (2005). Synchrony in the onset of mental-state reasoning: evidence from five cultures. *Psychological Science, 16*, 378–384.

Goetz, P. J. (2003). The effects of bilingualism on theory of mind development. *Bilingualism: Language and Cognition, 6*, 1–15.

Green, B. F. (1956). A method of scalogram analysis using summary statistics. *Psychometrika*, *21*, 79–88.

Kuntoro, I., Saraswati, L., Peterson, C. C., & Slaughter, V. (2013). Micro-cultural influences on theory of mind development: a comparative study of middle-class and Pemulung children in Jakarta, Indonesia. *International Journal of Behavioral Development*, *37*, 266–273.

Leslie, A., Friedman, O., &. German, T. (2004). Core mechanisms in 'theory of mind.' *Trends in Cognitive Sciences*, *8*, 528–533.

Liu, D., Wellman, H. M., Tardif, T., & Sabbagh, M. A. (2008). Theory of mind development in Chinese children: a meta-analysis of false-belief understanding across cultures and languages. *Developmental Psychology*, *44*, 523–531.

McAlister, A. R., & Peterson, C. C. (2013). Siblings, theory of mind, and executive functioning in children aged 3–6 years: new longitudinal evidence. *Child Development*, *84*(4), 1442–1458.

Moeller, M. P. (2007). Current state of knowledge: psychosocial development in children with hearing impairment. *Ear and Hearing*, *28*, 729–739.

O'Reilly, J., & Peterson, C. C. (2014a). Scaling theory of mind development in Indigenous- and Anglo-Australian toddlers and older children. *Journal of Cross-Cultural Psychology*, *45*, 1459–1501.

O'Reilly, J. & Peterson, C. C. (2014b). Theory of mind at home: linking authoritative and authoritarian parenting styles to children's social understanding. *Early Child Development and Care*, *184*, 1934–1947.

O'Reilly, K., Peterson, C. C., & Wellman, H. M. (2014). Sarcasm and advanced theory of mind understanding in children and adults with prelingual deafness. *Developmental Psychology*, *50*, 1862–1877.

Peng, K., & Nisbett, R. (1999). Culture, dialectics, and reasoning about contradiction. *American Psychologist*, *54*, 741–754.

Perner, J., Ruffman, T., & Leekam, S. R. (1994). Theory of mind is contagious: you catch it from your sibs. *Child Development*, *65*(4), 1228–1238.

Peterson, C. C. (2000). Influence of siblings' perspectives on theory of mind. *Cognitive Development*, *15*, 435–455.

Peterson, C. C. (2009). Development of social-cognitive and communication skills in children born deaf. *Scandinavian Journal of Psychology*, *50*, 475–483.

Peterson, C. C., Wellman, H., & Liu, D. (2005). Steps in theory of mind development for children with deafness, autism or typical development. *Child Development*, *76*, 502–517.

Peterson, C. C., Wellman, H., & Slaughter, V. (2012). The mind behind the message: advancing theory of mind scales for typically developing children, and those with deafness, autism, or Asperger syndrome. *Child Development*, *83*, 469–485.

Poulin-Dubois, D., Bialystok, E., Blaye, A., Polonia, A., & Yott, J. (2012). Lexical access and vocabulary development in very young bilinguals. *International Journal of Bilingualism*, April 20, 1367006911431198.

Qu, L., & Shen, P. (2013). Development of children who grow up in two conflicting unbalanced cultures. *Child Studies in Diverse Contexts*, *3*, 123–127.

Ruffman, T., Slade, L., & Crowe, E. (2002). The relation between child and mothers' mental state language and theory-of-mind understanding. *Child Development*, *73*, 734–751.

Schweder, R., Goodnow, J. J., Hatano, G., Levine, R., Markus, H., & Miller, P. (2006). The cultural psychology of development: one mind, many mentalities. In W. Damon & R. Lerner (Eds.), *Handbook of child psychology*, 6th edition (pp. 716–792). New York: John Wiley.

Shahaeian, A., Peterson, C. C., Slaughter, V., & Wellman, H. (2011). Culture and the sequence of steps in theory of mind development. *Developmental Psychology*, *47*, 1239–1247.

Shahaeian, A., Nielsen, M., Peterson, C., & Slaughter, V. (2014). Cultural and family influences on children's theory of mind development: A comparison of Australian and Iranian school-age children. *Journal of Cross-Cultural Psychology, 45*, 555–568.

Siegal, M., Surian, L., Matsuo, A., Geraci, A., Iozzi, L., Okumura, Y., & Itakura, S. (2010). Bilingualism accentuates children's conversational understanding. *PloS One, 5*(2), e9004.

Slaughter, V., & Perez-Zapata, D. (2014). Cultural variations in the development of mindreading. *Child Development Perspectives, 8*, 237–241.

Toyama, K. (2007). Examining theory-of-mind tasks with Japanese children: the Wellman and Liu tasks. *Japanese Journal of Educational Psychology, 55*, 359–369.

Wellman, H. M., Cross, D., & Watson, J. (2001). Meta-analysis of theory-of-mind development: the truth about false belief. *Child Development, 72*(3), 655–684.

Wellman, H. M., Fang, F., Liu, D., Zhu, L., & Liu, G. (2006). Scaling of theory-of-mind understandings in Chinese children. *Psychological Science, 17*, 1075–1081.

Wellman, H. M., Fang, F. X., & Peterson, C. C. (2011). Sequential progressions in a theory-of-mind scale: longitudinal perspectives. *Child Development, 82*(3), 780–792.

Wellman, H. M., & Liu, D. (2004). Scaling of theory-of-mind tasks. *Child Development, 75*(2), 523–541.

Wellman, H. M., Lopez-Duran, S., LaBounty, J., & Hamilton, B. (2008). Infant attention to intentional action predicts preschool theory of mind. *Developmental Psychology, 44*, 618–623.

Wu, Z., & Su, Y. (2014). How do preschoolers' sharing behaviors relate to their theory of mind understanding? *Journal of Experimental Child Psychology, 120*, 73–86.

3

FAMILY INFLUENCES ON THEORY OF MIND

A review

Claire Hughes and Rory T. Devine

A quarter of a century ago, Dunn, Brown, Slomkowski, Tesla, and Youngblade (1991) conducted a seminal observational study of 50 33-month-olds and their mothers, which showed that variation in the frequency of talk about feelings predicted individual differences (7 months later) in the children's ability to explain a character's mistaken beliefs. This pioneering study led to a dramatic growth in research on potential social influences upon children's developing understanding of mind. Another study, conducted by Peterson and Siegal (1995), was an important catalyst for this expanding field of research. This second study showed that deaf children born to hearing parents (but not those born to deaf parents) displayed delays in understanding that were equivalent in magnitude to those reported for children with autism spectrum disorders (e.g. Baron-Cohen, Leslie, & Frith, 1985). It is thus very fitting that this volume, born of a celebration of Candi Peterson's work, should coincide with the field's 25th birthday.

In this chapter we synthesise two recently conducted reviews: a detailed narrative review focusing on social influences on theory of mind (Hughes & Devine, 2015) and a subsequent meta-analytic study in which we investigated family correlates of false-belief understanding in early childhood (Devine & Hughes, submitted). Our meta-analysis of the available literature revealed sufficient comparable studies to examine four family-based predictors of individual differences in false-belief understanding: (i) family socioeconomic status (SES); (ii) family size (i.e. number of siblings); (iii) parental mental-state talk; and (iv) parental mind-mindedness.

Briefly, to be included in the meta-analysis, studies had to meet five key inclusion criteria: (i) the study had to be available in English; (ii) the report had to contain findings from an empirical study; (iii) the sample had to include typically developing children; (iv) the study had to include at least one false-belief task; and (v) the study had to include at least one of the four measures of family influence.

Systematic searches of electronic bibliographic databases yielded 72 relevant data-sets (from 76 publications). Key features of these studies were recorded (e.g. year of publication; country of origin; number of participants; mean age of participants) alongside details of the measures used to index false-belief understanding and the different family variables. Crucially, we noted any reported correlation between false-belief understanding and any of the four family variables.

We analysed the effect sizes (i.e. Fisher-transformed r values) using an inverse-variance weighted random-effects model and calculated the mean effect size (r) and 95 per cent confidence intervals (CI). We analysed the effects of continuous moderators using inverse-variance weighted linear regression and the effects of categorical moderators using the Q statistic (Wilson & Lipsey, 2001).

In the first part of this chapter we provide a summary of conclusions from each of these four areas and briefly review the findings related to three further cor-relates (elaborative talk, attachment and parental style), for which fewer studies were available.

Through its focus on positive family influences on one aspect of theory of mind – false-belief understanding – we hope that this summary will provide a useful counterpoint to Luke and Banerjee's (2013) review of the literature on parental maltreatment and impairments in theory of mind (including the under-standing of emotion and belief). In the second part of this chapter we outline methodological advances in the field. Finally, we consider how future studies might further increase the rigour of this research field.

Four family predictors of false belief understanding: an outline of meta-analytic findings

Socioeconomic status

The association between family SES and children's cognitive development has received considerable attention within the scientific literature (e.g. Hackman & Farah, 2009). SES is a multifaceted construct that is often indexed by parental or family income, occupation or educational attainment or some combination of these measures (Bradley & Corwyn, 2002; Conger & Donnellan, 2007). Early theory-of-mind research involved relatively small and homogenous groups of middle-class preschool children such that the potential influence of SES on false-belief task performance was largely overlooked (Hughes, 2005). Since the 1990s there has been a growing interest in the ways in which family SES might relate to children's false-belief task performance. Supporting this relation, children from lower-SES families have been shown to lag behind those from higher-SES fami-lies in language ability (Hoff, 2006) and executive function (Noble, Norman, & Farah, 2005), two key correlates of individual differences in false-belief task per-formance (Devine & Hughes, 2014; Milligan, Astington, & Dack, 2007).

In our systematic review, we identified 34 effect sizes related to links between SES and false-belief understanding, based on data from of just under 5,000 3–5-year-olds

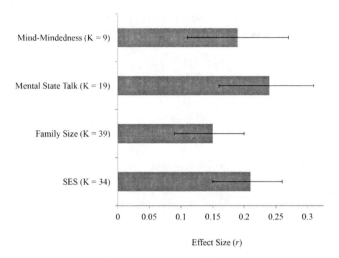

FIGURE 3.1   Mean effect sizes (*r*) and 95 per cent confidence intervals for each family correlate of children's false-belief understanding. K, number of effect sizes included in each analysis; SES, socioeconomic status. Error bars represent 95 per cent confidence intervals for point estimates.

living in nine different countries (Figure 3.1). The weighted mean effect size ($r = 0.21$) and the 95 per cent CI (0.15, 0.26) supported the overall reliability and statistical significance of this association between SES and false-belief understanding. As one might expect, stronger results emerged from studies that used aggregate measures of SES than from studies that relied on a single indicator ($\beta = 0.34$, $p = 0.03$). Interestingly, the correlation between family SES and children's false-belief understanding was stronger for UK studies than for studies in other countries ($\beta = 0.38$, $p = 0.03$). This intriguing result suggests that SES-related contrasts in home environment quality may be especially strong for UK samples.

How should the association between SES and false-belief understanding be explained? One possibility, which we can call the 'social selection' account, is that individual characteristics (e.g. IQ) result in lower levels of attainment, occupational prestige and income (Conger & Donnellan, 2007). Against this view, however, heritability estimates for individual differences in theory of mind are modest (e.g. Hughes et al., 2005; Ronald, Viding, Happe, & Plomin, 2006). Another possibility, which we can call the 'social causation' account, is that the limited resources and stressful conditions associated with lower SES hinder children's cognitive development (Bradley & Corwyn, 2002). This account fits neatly with many of the findings reported in other chapters in this volume. However, perhaps the most compelling evidence that parent–child interactions play a mediating role in the link between SES and children's cognitive development comes from Peterson and Siegal's (1995) seminal study (and subsequent research) with deaf children. Specifically, this work showed that deaf children born to hearing parents are much slower to master the concept of false belief than are (native signing) deaf children born to deaf parents.

Family size

In their study of family correlates of early individual differences in false-belief understanding, Dunn et al. (1991) found a positive correlation between the frequency with which 33-month-old children engaged in co-operative play with an older sibling and success on a false-belief task 7 months later. This association provided the first evidence that sibling relationships might play an important role in the emergence of false-belief understanding. Taking this idea forward, Perner, Ruffman, and Leekam (1994) reasoned that children with siblings would have more opportunities to learn about others' minds through conversations and play. Consistent with this hypothesis, family size (as indexed by number of siblings) was a strong predictor of false-belief task performance. These findings, however, have sometimes been difficult to replicate (e.g., Cole & Mitchell, 2000) and subsequent researchers have begun to revise the so-called 'siblings effect' (Ruffman, Perner, Naito, Parkin, & Clements, 1998, p. 161) by focusing specifically on the influence of older siblings or 'child-aged' siblings (Peterson, 2000).

Building on Vygotskian theory, Ruffman et al. (1998) argued that children would learn more about mental states from their more skilled older siblings than from younger siblings. Extending this, Peterson (2000) hypothesised that sibling interactions would only benefit false-belief understanding within specific age boundaries. Specifically, interactions with infant siblings (<12 months) and teenage or adult siblings (aged over 12) might not provide the linguistic or social opportunities for preschool children to reflect on or reason about mental states.

In our systematic review, we identified 39 separate studies with data on the correlation between false-belief understanding and the total number of siblings (or family size), the number of *older* siblings or the number of *child-aged* siblings. These datasets came from a total of 3,934 3–5-year-olds living in 14 different countries and showed: (i) a weak but significant weighted mean effect size ($r = 0.15$, 95 per cent CI 0.09–0.20); (ii) marked heterogeneity between study findings, with both positive and negative correlations being reported (range $= -0.29$ to 0.58); and (iii) a moderation effect for the way in which the number of siblings was measured. That is, consistent with the prediction made by Peterson (2000), the positive effect of siblings was stronger for studies that focused on child-aged siblings ($\beta = 0.36$, $p = 0.004$) than for studies that tallied either the total number of siblings or the number of older siblings.

Mental-state talk

From a Vygotskian perspective, children's emerging understanding of mind is underpinned not by individualistic cognitive development (e.g. in the capacity for meta-representation) but rather by socially mediated processes, described by Nelson

(2004, p. 119) as entering a 'community of minds'. In particular, it is through talking about mental states that thoughts, memories, and beliefs are brought to a child's attention. Unsurprisingly, then, despite the effort involved in transcribing and coding family conversations, numerous studies have examined parental reference to mental states as a predictor of children's performance on tests of theory of mind. Links between parental mental-state talk and children's false-belief understanding have been examined in 19 separate studies, involving a total of 1,174 3–5-year-olds, with a modest weighted mean effect size ($r = 0.24$, 95 per cent CI 0.16–0.31). These studies were almost all from Anglo-Saxon countries and yet, despite this cultural homogeneity, the strength of correlation between parental mental-state talk and children's false-belief understanding varied considerably between studies, with a range of −0.14 to 0.52. A key factor underpinning this variability was that some (but not all) of the studies controlled for variation in total frequency of parental talk (i.e. 'verbosity'). Other key contrasts between studies, such as sample characteristics, or use of structured versus unstructured observations conducted at home versus in a lab setting, did not contribute to the variation in effect size. This is important, as the convergence in results across different methodological approaches supports the reliability of study findings.

Note, however, that predictive links between parental mental-state talk and children's later understanding of mind do not necessarily demonstrate causality. For example, mental-state talk may simply act as a readily quantifiable marker of other dimensions of difference, such as level of elaboration. In our systematic review, we identified four separate studies that examined false-belief talk in relation to parental elaboration (Lazaridis, 2013; Reese & Sutcliffe, 2006; Taumoepeau & Reese, 2013; Welch-Ross, 1997), with effect sizes that ranged from 0.15 to 0.36. To our knowledge, the few studies to assess both mental-state reference and elaborative talk demonstrate that it is the combination of these two characteristics that is particularly helpful (Symons, Peterson, Slaughter, Roche, & Doyle, 2005). Likewise, Ensor and Hughes (2008) have reported that mental-state talk that occurs within connected conversational turns is particularly predictive of children's later false-belief understanding. Together these findings highlight the need to attend to the quality as well as the content of parent–child interactions.

Mind-mindedness

This term is defined as the propensity to view the infant as a psychological agent (termed 'mind-mindedness') and appears to be an independent predictor of later success on tasks that test preschoolers' understanding of mistaken beliefs and emotion (Meins et al., 2002). There are two prominent approaches to measuring parental mind-mindedness. Observations of parent–infant interactions can be coded for both the frequency and attunement of mind-related comments (e.g., Meins, Fernyhough, Fradley, & Tuckey, 2001). Alternatively interviews in which parents describe their children can be coded for the proportion of mentalistic (as opposed to physical, behavioural or general) attributions offered (e.g., Meins,

Fernyhough, Russell, & Clark-Carter, 1998). More recent work by Demers, Bernier, Tarabulsy, and Provost (2010) has refined this approach to distinguish between positive and negative mentalistic attributions.

From a theoretical perspective, by providing new perspectives on understanding attachment security and parental sensitivity (Meins, 2013), the construct of parental mind-mindedness has had a significant impact on research on social-cognitive development. Interestingly, there were only nine separate datasets, with data from 620 children, of whom three-quarters were British. This lack of heterogeneity in study samples may contribute to the relative consistency across studies observed in the correlation between children's false-belief understanding and parental mind-mindedness (which ranged from 0.02 to 0.37, with a weak but significant weighted mean effect size ($r = 0.19$, 95 per cent CI 0.11–0.27). Given that the studies varied in how mind-mindedness was measured, this lack of heterogeneity is reassuring in that, as noted above in regard to the literature on mental-state talk, it indicates convergent validity across different methodological approaches.

Strikingly, just one study to date has included both mind-mindedness and mental-state talk as predictors of children's false-belief understanding (Laranjo, Bernier, Meins, & Carlson, 2014). Unfortunately, this study did not examine either the relative independence or the interplay between these two predictor variables. Addressing this gap is therefore an obvious avenue for future research. In many ways, mind-mindedness and relative frequency of mental-state talk are complementary constructs. The former captures parental cognitions, which are increasingly recognised as a key influence on parental style. In contrast, mental-state talk captures a key feature of parents' actual interactions with children. However, as discussed elsewhere (Hughes, 2011), within close relationships, the literal content of a conversation is often only a small part of what is communicated between the speakers, such that the frequency of direct reference to mental states provides only a rough estimate of the extent to which their discourse has a mentalistic focus.

What underpins individual differences in mind-mindedness? One possibility is that the quality of the parent–child relationship (e.g. attachment security) is a key predictor of mind-mindedness. Another view is that parental characteristics (e.g. education, wellbeing) determine mind-mindedness. In a series of studies, Meins, Fernyhough and Harris-Waller (2014) examined the relations between adults' descriptions of individuals of varying degrees of closeness (e.g. partners, children, friends, celebrities) and inanimate objects (e.g. works of art). The authors found that, while mind-minded comments about friends, partners and children correlated across the different relationships, there was no relation between mind-minded comments about close individuals and famous people or inanimate objects. Rather than being a trait-like quality, Meins et al. (2014) have argued that mind-mindedness is related to relationship quality. Arguably, however, this conclusion is somewhat premature, given the lack of sample diversity in existing studies – for example, it is possible that there are striking cultural variations in parents' views of their children (e.g. Lillard, 1999), but cross-cultural comparisons remain scarce.

If, as Meins et al. (2014) argue, individual differences in mind-mindedness reflect variations in relationship quality, then one would predict that contrasts in attachment security would also predict children's false-belief understanding. However, researchers seeking to test this hypothesis face at least two challenges. First, numerous studies (e.g. Van Ijzendoorn, Dijkstra, & Bus, 1995) have reported predictive links between attachment security and children's general cognitive development, such that the specificity of links between attachment security and false-belief understanding requires testing. Second, these studies have adopted a variety of measures of attachment security: the three most commonly used methods are the Strange Situation paradigm, the Separation Anxiety Test and a variety of Q-sort procedures. Eight independent studies (in five different countries) have tested the hypothesis that securely attached children show a specific advantage in their understanding of other minds. The results from these studies highlight the importance of method effects, in that the three studies that employed the Strange Situation (McElwain & Volling, 2004; Meins et al., 1998, 2002) produced the clearest correlations with false-belief understanding (ranging from 0.16 to 0.51).

Evidence relating to the alternative view (in which mind-mindedness reflects parental rather than relationship characteristics) comes from four other studies (McElwain & Volling, 2004; Meins, Fernyhough, Arnott, Leekam, & DeRosnay, 2013; Meins, Fernyhough, Wainwright, & Clark-Carter, 2003; Symons & Clark, 2000) that have examined individual differences in children's false-belief understanding in relation to parental sensitivity. Again, however, the results from these studies have been mixed, with correlations ranging from −0.01 to 0.31.

Methodological progress in the study of environmental influences

At least two positive features of the studies in this field deserve note. First, between-study comparisons were only possible because so many studies had adopted similar measures of false-belief understanding. While this may seem a very simple point, it is nevertheless important. For example, within related areas of research (e.g. individual differences in early executive function) there is much less consensus over which tasks should be used and, as a result, integrating findings is much more difficult. Yet being able to combine data from different studies is valuable for improving the methods used in future studies. For example, consistent with Peterson's (2000) hypothesis that interactions with similarly aged siblings provide children with a training ground for theory-of-mind development, the moderator analyses confirmed that false-belief task performance was more strongly related to the number of child-aged siblings than to the total number of siblings. In other words, it matters how one studies the 'sibling effect'.

Moving beyond the focus on the number of siblings, other researchers have begun to elucidate the ways in which siblings might promote false-belief understanding through studying the quality of sibling interactions and relationships (e.g. Hughes & Ensor, 2005). While obviously more time consuming than simply asking about the number of siblings in a household, this focus on interaction quality is needed in order to understand *why* child-aged siblings matter for preschool children's theory-of-mind development. For example, in a recent study of 385 sibling pairs, Prime and Jenkins (2015) found that children's cognitive sensitivity towards their younger sibling in a Duplo-based teaching task (indexed by the frequency of 'scaffolding' behaviours, such as praise, clarification and articulation of subgoals) moderates the association between number of child-age siblings and false-belief understanding – to the extent that this association is actually negative in the context of low cognitive sensitivity.

Second, unlike early research, which relied heavily on single task indicators of false-belief understanding, the majority of studies in the meta-analysis (79 per cent) had employed aggregate task batteries, such that the study findings were likely to be quite reliable (cf., Hughes et al., 2000).

Reflections and future directions

Alongside the positive features of existing studies noted above (e.g. consensus regarding tasks, widespread adoption of an aggregate approach), a number of avenues open for further improvement also deserve note. The first of these is sample size. More than 60 of the 80 datasets included in this analysis were based on a sample of fewer than 100 participants. This is problematic because small samples can provide only imprecise effect size estimates. Moreover, the mean effect size for the relations between false-belief understanding and the four different aspects of family influence were modest, such that failure to use large sample sizes presents a real danger of false negatives. In addition, future research needs to adopt study designs that have the power to: (i) elucidate causal mechanisms; (ii) establish the specificity and independence of family influences on children's false-belief understanding; and (iii) increase the developmental and conceptual scope of existing research.

Addressing questions of causality

Our review of existing research on conversational influences upon children's developing understanding of mind highlighted the scarcity of studies that control for child-driven effects. This is surprising as there is now a consensus within the wider field of parenting research that child-driven effects are too powerful to ignore (e.g. Pardini, 2008). Findings from our own longitudinal work tracking the development of a socially diverse sample of toddlers highlight the importance of this omission. For example, as described elsewhere (Hughes, 2011), between the first (age 2) time point and a later (age 6) time point, the mean frequency of conversational reference to mental states (expressed as a proportion of total talk) increased 4-fold for the study children, but 18-fold for their mothers. This remarkable increase in the proportion of mental-state reference within mothers' talk is a testimony to the powerful influence of child characteristics upon mothers' talk.

Thus, any analysis of conversational influence upon children's understanding of mind must take children's own contributions to these conversations into account.

For example, cross-lagged designs could shed light on whether early parental mental-state talk predicts later false-belief understanding or whether parents of children with advanced false-belief understanding use more mental-state terms in response to children's interest or skill in mindreading. This would involve measuring *both* constructs at more than one time point (e.g. time 1 and time 2) and comparing regression coefficients (controlling for stability in each construct) to establish whether the links between each construct are reciprocal or asymmetric. Adopting this approach in a lab-based study, Ruffman, Slade, and Crowe (2002) found that maternal mental-state talk contributed to the development of later theory of mind, but individual differences in children's theory-of-mind performance did not predict later maternal mental-state talk. Given that rates of mental-state talk also vary by social context – with higher levels reported in families with older siblings (Jenkins, Turrell, Kogushi, Louis, & Ross, 2003) or in dyads engaged in shared picture book reading (Symons, Peterson, Slaughter, Roche, & Doyle, 2005) – it would be useful to extend this work to more naturalistic longitudinal research. Furthermore, to establish a causal connection between the frequency of parental mental-state talk and children's theory-of-mind development, parent-mediated intervention studies are also required. Combined, these two sources of evidence could elucidate whether mental-state talk is both necessary and sufficient for the development of children's theory of mind.

Adopting a finer grain of analysis

Another gap in existing research that emerged from our review was a paucity of research examining the specificity or independence of effects. For example, researchers have yet to investigate whether individual differences in false-belief understanding are particularly strongly related to specific markers of SES (e.g. parental education versus material wealth). This lack of fine-grained analysis reflects the situation in more general research on SES and cognitive development (e.g. Conger & Donnellan, 2007), such that there is little foundation for specific hypotheses That said, it is tempting to speculate on what processes might underpin any contrast in the salience of education and wealth as predictors of false-belief understanding. For example, if parental income is a much stronger predictor of false-belief understanding than parental education, one might infer that factors outside the home (e.g., access to high-quality schooling or playgrounds providing opportunities for playing with peers) are pivotal; conversely, if parental education is a much stronger predictor of false-belief understanding than parental income, one might infer that factors within the home (e.g. shared reading, conversational quantity and quality) are most important.

Likewise, although most investigations of conversational predictors of theory of mind have focused on frequency of mental-state talk, there is evidence that other aspects of parent–child conversations (e.g. elaborative talk, causal talk, connected talk) might also predict individual differences in false-belief understanding (e.g. Slaughter, Peterson, & Mackintosh, 2007). Moreover, echoing the specific temporal associations reported for frequencies of family talk about different mental states (Jenkins et al., 2003), both the study by Slaughter et al. (2007) and a more recent study (Ensor, Devine, Marks, & Hughes, 2014) have shown that parental use of cognitive terms is more strongly related to false-belief understanding than is parental use of desire or emotion terms. These detailed investigations of the content and quality of parent–child talk are helpful in elucidating the specific aspects of talk that are related to theory-of-mind development.

In addition, while individual differences in young children's understanding of mind showed modest associations with SES, family size, parental mind-mindedness, and family conversations, the independence or overlap of these associations is not yet clear. Likewise, it has yet to be established whether 'proximal' correlates such as family conversations might mediate the links between false-belief performance and 'distal' correlates such as SES. To establish which of these diverse predictors plays a primary role in fostering children's social understanding, future studies should embrace a multi-method approach in which several different facets of children's social environments are examined in tandem as predictors of individual differences in theory of mind.

Finally, it is important to remember that effects of nurture and nature often go hand in hand and, as illustrated by the growing literature on differential susceptibility, may show important interactions (for a recent theoretical review, see Bjorklund & Ellis, 2014). In recent years, investigations of genetic effects have gone beyond simple twin designs (e.g. Hughes et al., 2005) to compare false-belief understanding in children with allelic variations on specific genes, such as the dopamine transporter gene (DRD4: Lackner, Sabbagh, Hallinan, Liu, & Holden, 2012) and the oxytocin receptor gene (OXTR: Wu & Su, 2015). To date, however, studies in this field have been limited by small sample sizes. Moreover, the role of potential confounds (such as verbal ability) has yet to be examined. However these studies offer promising results for future work that integrates genetic and social factors in attempting to understand individual differences in theory of mind.

Expanding the developmental and conceptual scope of research

In the past decade, the developmental scope of theory-of-mind research has extended beyond the narrow confines of the preschool years, but this has largely been achieved by a growth of interest in infancy. A corresponding effort is needed to take theory-of-mind research beyond the preschool period. In one example of this approach, Ensor et al. (2014) showed that mothers' references to cognitive states within their conversations with their toddlers predicted the children's mental state reasoning 8 years later (as measured by the vignette-based Strange Stories task: Happé, 1994). Moreover, this predictive effect remained significant even when the stability of maternal mental-state talk and children's prior performances on tests of false-belief understanding were taken into account. This finding highlights the extended temporal reach of early family conversations as an influence upon children's growing understanding of mental states.

Alongside increasing the developmental scope of existing research, it would also be valuable to include a broader range of measures of social understanding. Luke and Banerjee's (2013) review of studies assessing the links between parental maltreatment and children's social understanding included a diverse array of outcome measures. To date, however, research with normative samples (our own included) has focused heavily on children's understanding of cognitive states (thoughts, beliefs, knowledge, memories). More work is needed to compare the overlap between social influences on children's understanding of both cognition and emotion.

A third direction in which future studies might usefully expand the scope of existing research is the variety of sources of social influence examined. As noted elsewhere (Hughes, White, & Ensor, 2014), the almost exclusive focus on talk with mothers is rather surprising because, by the age of 4 years, children engage in talk about thoughts and feelings more often with siblings than with mothers (Brown, Donelan-McCall, & Dunn, 1996; Hughes, Lecce, & Wilson, 2007). The sustained focus on mothers also fails to keep abreast of demographic changes in family life. For example, it is estimated that in the UK 21 per cent of fathers of under-5s have sole responsibility for child care at some point in the working week (EHRC, 2009). Yet, with few exceptions (e.g. LaBounty, Wellman, Olson, Lagattuta, & Liu, 2008; Lundy, 2013), there is a dearth of research on the links between children's understanding of mind and their interactions with fathers. This is an important gap as fathers and mothers might offer distinct forms of social support to their children's socio-cognitive development (e.g., LaBounty et al., 2008). Future studies that involve both mothers and fathers should also take child gender into account, as the match in gender between parents and children may play a moderating role (e.g. Johnson, Caskey, Rand, Tucker, & Vohr, 2014).

Finally, the lack of geographical variation in study sites precluded analysis of how the associations reported in this review might vary by culture, such that addressing this gap is another important direction for future theory-of-mind research. In particular, several conclusions from this field of research may be culturally specific. For example, with regard to sibling influences, the one-child policy means that Chinese children are likely to draw on contact with other groups of children to refine their understanding of mind. Interestingly, existing research involving Chinese children suggests that, while attending mixed-age classrooms is associated with accelerated understanding of false belief (Wang & Su, 2009), the frequency of contact with cousins is inversely related to false-belief performance (Lewis, Huang, & Rooksby, 2006). Clearly, more work is needed to replicate these findings and to elucidate the mechanisms underpinning this apparent contrast.

Similarly, with regard to mental-state talk, it should be noted that direct mental-state talk is much less commonplace in some languages and cultures than others. For example, Wang and Fivush (2005) have shown that Chinese-American mothers use more emotion attribution but fewer explanations than their European-American counterparts when talking with their children about past events. Differences in both the frequency and correlates of parents' emotion talk have also been reported between African-American and non-African-American families (Garrett-Peters, Mills-Koonce, Adkins, Vernon-Feagans, & Cox, 2008), while both cultural and education-related contrasts have been reported in mothers' perceptions of infant intentionality (Reznick, 1999).

There is now a rich literature on ethnic contrasts in parenting and their impact upon infant development. Future research on family influences upon theory of mind should therefore capitalise on the theoretical and empirical progress that has already been made in this field. For example, a growing body of research has confirmed the hypothesis that the contrast in parenting in rural/traditional versus industrial/Western cultures can be characterised as a contrast between (non-verbal) proximal parenting versus (verbally mediated) distal parenting (e.g. Greenfield, Keller, Fuligni, & Maynard, 2003; Keller et al., 2004, 2009). Moreover, within distal forms of parenting, others (e.g. Tamis-LeMonda, Song, Leavell, Kahana-Kalman, & Yoshikawa, 2012) have highlighted the contrast in infant outcomes associated with regulatory versus referential modes of speech. Yet only distal and referential modes of interaction have been examined within existing research on family influences upon theory of mind. There are thus several open avenues for future research.

As a final point, it is worth noting that *similarities* across cultures in family influences on theory of mind are also interesting. For example, despite marked contrasts in baseline levels of mothers' mental-state talk during a picture book task, predictive links with understanding of emotion appear similar for Chinese-American and European-American children (Doan & Wang, 2010). Likewise, recent data from matched samples recruited in the UK and in Hong Kong indicate that the predictive relation between parental mind-mindedness and preschool children's false-belief understanding is consistent across these very different cultures (Hughes, Devine, & Wang, 2015). The challenge for future studies is therefore to tease apart culturally universal and culturally specific influences of family interaction upon children's developing understanding of mind.

Acknowledgement

Rory T. Devine was funded by a grant from the Isaac Newton Trust, Cambridge.

References

Baron-Cohen, S., Leslie, A. M., & Frith, U. (1985). Does the autistic child have a "theory of mind"? *Cognition, 21*, 37–46.

Bjorklund, D., & Ellis, B. (2014). Children, childhood, and development in evolutionary perspective. *Developmental Review, 34*, 225–264.

Bradley, R. H., & Corwyn, R. F. (2002). Socioeconomic status and child development. *Annual Review of Psychology, 53*, 371–399.

Brown, J. R., Donelan-McCall, N., & Dunn, J. (1996). Why talk about mental states? The significance of children's conversations with friends, siblings, and mothers. *Child Development, 67*, 836.

Cole, K., & Mitchell, P. (2000). Siblings in the development of executive control and a theory of mind. *British Journal of Developmental Psychology, 18*, 279–295.

Conger, R. D., & Donnellan, M. B. (2007). An interactionist perspective on the socio-economic context of human development. *Annual Review of Psychology, 58*, 175–199.

Demers, I., Bernier, A., Tarabulsy, G. M., & Provost, M. A. (2010). Maternal and child characteristics as antecedents of maternal mind-mindedness. *Infant Mental Health Journal, 31*, 94–112.

Devine, R. T., & Hughes, C. (2014). Relations between false belief understanding and executive function in early childhood: a meta-analysis. *Child Development, 85*, 1777–1794.

Devine, R.T., & Hughes, C. (in press). *Family influences on false belief understanding: a meta-analysis*. Unpublished manuscript.

Doan, S. N., & Wang, Q. (2010). Maternal discussions of mental states and external behaviors: relations to children's emotion situation knowledge in European American and immigrant Chinese children. *Child Development, 81*, 1490–1503.

Dunn, J., Brown, J., Slomkowski, C., Tesla, C., & Youngblade, L. (1991). Young children's understanding of other people's feelings and beliefs: individual differences and their antecedents. *Child Development, 62*, 1352–1366.

EHRC. (2009). *Working better: Fathers, family and work contemporary perspectives*. London: Equality and Human Rights Commission.

Ensor, R., & Hughes, C. (2008). Consent or connectedness? Mother–child talk and early social understanding. *Child Development, 79*, 201–216.

Ensor, R., Devine, R. T., Marks, A., & Hughes, C. (2014). Mothers' cognitive references to 2-year-olds predict theory of mind at ages 6 and 10. *Child Development, 85*, 1222–1235.

Garrett-Peters, P., Mills-Koonce, R., Adkins, D., Vernon-Feagans, L., & Cox, M. (2008). Early environmental correlates of emotion talk. *Parenting, Science and Practice, 8*, 117–152.

Greenfield, P. M., Keller, H., Fuligni, A., & Maynard, A. (2003). Cultural pathways through universal development. *Annual Review of Psychology, 54*, 461–490.

Hackman, D. A., & Farah, M. J. (2009). Socioeconomic status and the developing brain. *Trends in Cognitive Sciences, 13*, 65–73.

Happé, F. G. E. (1994). An advanced test of theory of mind: understanding of story characters' thoughts and feelings by able, mentally handicapped and normal children. *Journal of Autism and Developmental Disorders, 24*, 129–154.

Hoff, E. (2006). How social contexts support and shape language development. *Developmental Review, 26*, 55–88.

Hughes, C. (2005). Genetic and environmental influences on individual differences in language and theory of mind: common or distinct? In J. W. Astington & J. A. Baird (Eds.), *Why language matters for theory of mind* (pp. 319–338). Oxford: Oxford University Press.

Hughes, C. (2011). *Social understanding and social lives: From toddlerhood through to the transition to school*. London: Psychology Press.

Hughes, C., Adlam, A., Happé, F., Jackson, J., Taylor, A., & Caspi, A. (2000). Good test–retest reliability for standard and advanced false-belief tasks across a wide range of abilities. *Journal of Child Psychology and Psychiatry, 41*, 483–490.

Hughes, C., & Devine, R. T. (2015). A social perspective on theory of mind. In M. Lamb (Ed.), *Handbook of child psychology and developmental science (Volume III): Social, emotional and personality development*, 7th edn. Hoboken, NJ: Wiley.

Hughes, C., Devine, R. T., & Wang, Z. (2015). *Mental-state awareness in pre-schoolers and parents: A cross-cultural comparison of the UK and Hong Kong*. Paper presented at the International Convention of Psychological Science. Amsterdam, the Netherlands: Beurs van Berlage.

Hughes, C., & Ensor, R. (2005). Executive function and theory of mind in 2 year olds: a family affair? *Developmental Neuropsychology, 28,* 645–668.

Hughes, C., Jaffee, S., Happe, F., Taylor, A., Caspi, A., & Moffitt, T. E. (2005). Origins of individual differences in theory of mind: from nature to nurture? *Child Development, 76,* 356–370.

Hughes, C., Lecce, S., & Wilson, C. (2007). "Do you know what I want?" Preschoolers' talk about desires, thoughts and feelings in their conversations with sibs and friends. *Cognition and Emotion, 21,* 330–350.

Hughes, C., White, N., & Ensor, R. (2014). How does talk about thoughts, desires and feelings foster children's socio-cognitive development? Mediators, moderators and implications for intervention. In K. H. Lagattuta (Ed.), *Children and emotion: New insights into developmental affective science* (pp. 95–105). London: Karger.

Jenkins, J. M., Turrell, S. L., Kogushi, Y., Louis, S., & Ross, H. S. (2003) A longitudinal investigation of the dynamics of mental state talk in families. *Child Development, 74,* 905–920.

Johnson, K., Caskey, M., Rand, K., Tucker, R., & Vohr, B. (2014). Gender differences in adult–infant communication in the first months of life. *Pediatrics, 134,* 1603–1610.

Keller, H., Borke, J., Staufenbiel, T., Yovsi, R. D., Abels, M., Papaligoura, Z., et al. (2009). Distal and proximal parenting as alternative parenting strategies during infants' early months of life: a cross-cultural study. *International Journal of Behavioral Development, 33,* 412–420.

Keller, H., Yovsi, R. D., Borke, J., Kartner, J., Jensen, H., & Papaligoura, Z. (2004). Developmental consequences of early parenting experiences: self-regulation and self-recognition in three cultural communities. *Child Development, 75,* 1745–1760.

LaBounty, J., Wellman, H. M., Olson, S., Lagattuta, K., & Liu, D. (2008). Mothers' and fathers' use of internal state talk with their young children. *Social Development, 17,* 757–775.

Lackner, C., Sabbagh, M., Hallinan, E., Liu, X., & Holden, J. (2012). Dopamine receptor D4 gene variation predicts preschoolers' developing theory of mind. *Developmental Science, 15,* 272–280.

Laranjo, J., Bernier, A., Meins, E., & Carlson, S. (2014). The roles of maternal mind-mindedness and infant security of attachment in predicting preschoolers' understanding of visual perspective taking and false belief. *Journal of Experimental Child Psychology, 125,* 48–62.

Lazaridis, M. (2013). The emergence of a temporally extended self and factors that contribute to its development: from theoretical and empirical perspectives. *Monographs of the Society for Research in Child Development, 78,* 1–120.

Lewis, C., Huang, Z., & Rooksby, M. (2006). Chinese preschoolers' false belief understanding: is social knowledge underpinned by parental styles, social interactions or executive functions? *Psychologia, 49,* 252–266.

Lillard, A. (1999). Developing a cultural theory of mind: the CIAO approach. *Current Directions in Psychological Science, 8,* 57–61.

Luke, N., & Banerjee, R. (2013). Differentiated associations between childhood maltreatment experiences and social understanding: a meta-analysis and systematic review. *Developmental Review, 33,* 1–28.

Lundy, B. (2013). Paternal and maternal mind-mindedness and preschoolers' theory of mind: the mediating role of interactional attunement. *Social Development, 22,* 58–74.

McElwain, N. L., & Volling, B. L. (2004). Attachment security and parental sensitivity during infancy: associations with friendship quality and false-belief understanding at age 4. *Journal of Social and Personal Relationships, 21,* 639–667.

Meins, E. (2013). Sensitive attunement to infants' internal states: operationalizing the construct of mind-mindedness. *Attachment and Human Development, 15,* 524–544.

Meins, E., Fernyhough, C., Arnott, B., Leekam, S. R., & DeRosnay, M. (2013). Mind-mindedness and theory of mind: mediating roles of language and perspectival symbolic play. *Child Development, 84,* 1777–1790.

Meins, E., Fernyhough, C., Fradley, E., & Tuckey, M. (2001). Rethinking maternal sensitivity: mothers' comments on infants' mental processes predict security of attachment at 12 months. *Journal of Child Psychology and Psychiatry, 42,* 637–648.

Meins, E., Fernyhough, C., & Harris-Waller, J. (2014). Is mind-mindedness trait-like or a quality of close relationships? Evidence from descriptions of significant others, famous people and works of art. *Cognition, 130,* 417–427.

Meins, E., Fernyhough, C., Russell, J., & Clark-Carter, D. (1998). Security of attachment as a predictor of symbolic and mentalising abilities: a longitudinal study. *Social Development, 7,* 1–24.

Meins, E., Fernyhough, C., Wainwright, R., & Clark-Carter, D. (2003). Pathways to understanding mind: construct validity and predictive validity of maternal mind-mindedness. *Child Development, 74,* 1194–1211.

Meins, E., Fernyhough, C., Wainwright, R., Das Gupta, M., Fradley, E., & Tuckey, M. (2002). Maternal mind-mindedness and attachment security as predictors of theory of mind understanding. *Child Development, 73,* 1715–1726.

Milligan, K., Astington, J. W., & Dack, L. A. (2007). Language and theory of mind: meta-analysis of the relation between language ability and false-belief understanding. *Child Development, 78*(2), 622–646.

Nelson, K. (2004). Toward a collaborative community of minds. *Behavioral and Brain Sciences, 27,* 119–120.

Noble, K. G., Norman, M. F., & Farah, M. J. (2005). Neurocognitive correlates of socioeconomic status in kindergarten children. *Developmental Science, 8,* 74–87.

Pardini, D. A. (2008). Novel insights into longstanding theories of bidirectional parent–child influences. *Journal of Abnormal Child Psychology, 36,* 627–631.

Perner, J., Ruffman, T., & Leekam, S. R. (1994). Theory of mind is contagious: you catch it from your sibs. *Child Development, 65,* 1228–1238.

Peterson, C. C. (2000). Kindred spirits: influences of siblings' perspectives on theory of mind. *Cognitive Development, 15,* 435–455.

Peterson, C. C., & Siegal, M. (1995). Deafness, conversation and theory of mind. *Journal of Child Psychology and Psychiatry, 36,* 459–474.

Prime, H. J., & Jenkins, J. (2015). Sibling cognitive sensitivity as a moderator of the relationship between sibship size and children's theory of mind. Paper presented at the *Society for Research in Child Development Biennial Conference,* Philadelphia, PA.

Reese, E., & Sutcliffe, E. (2006). Mother–child reminiscing and children's understanding of mind. *Merrill-Palmer Quarterly, 52,* 17–43.

Reznick, J. (1999). Influences on maternal attribution of infant intentionality. In P. D. Zelazo, J. W. Astington, & D. R. Olson (Eds.), *Developing theories of intention: Social understanding and self control* (pp. 243–268). Mahwah, NJ: Lawrence Erlbaum.

Ronald, A., Viding, E., Happe, F., & Plomin, R. (2006). Individual differences in theory of mind ability in middle childhood and links with verbal ability and autistic traits: a twin study. *Social Neuroscience, 1,* 412–425.

Ruffman, T., Perner, J., Naito, M., Parkin, L., & Clements, W. A. (1998). Older (but not younger) siblings facilitate false belief understanding. *Developmental Psychology, 34,* 161–174.

Ruffman, T., Slade, L., & Crowe, E. (2002). The relation between children's and mothers' mental state language and theory-of-mind understanding. *Child Development, 73*(3), 734–751.

Slaughter, V., Peterson, C. C., & Mackintosh, E. (2007). Mind what mother says: Narrative input and theory of mind in typical children and those on the autism spectrum. *Child Development, 78,* 839–858.

Symons, D. K., & Clark, S. E. (2000). A longitudinal study of mother–child relationships and theory of mind in the preschool period. *Social Development, 9,* 3–23.

Symons, D. K., Peterson, C. C., Slaughter, V., Roche, J., & Doyle, E. (2005). Theory of mind and mental state discourse during book reading and story-telling tasks. *British Journal of Developmental Psychology, 23,* 81–102.

Tamis-LeMonda, C. S., Song, L., Leavell, A. S., Kahana-Kalman, R., & Yoshikawa, H. (2012). Ethnic differences in mother–infant language and gestural communications are associated with specific skills in infants. *Developmental Science, 15,* 384–397.

Taumoepeau, M., & Reese, E. (2013). Maternal reminiscing, elaborative talk, and children's theory of mind: An intervention study. *First Language, 33*(4), 388–410.

Van Ijzendoorn, M. H., Dijkstra, J., & Bus, A. G. (1995). Attachment, intelligence and language: a meta-analysis. *Social Development, 4,* 115–128.

Wang, Q., & Fivush, R. (2005). Mother–child conversations of emotionally salient events: exploring the functions of emotional reminiscing in European-American and Chinese families. *Social Development, 14,* 473–495.

Wang, Y., & Su, Y. (2009). False belief understanding: children catch it from classmates of different ages. *International Journal of Behavioral Development, 33,* 331–336.

Welch-Ross, M. K. (1997). Mother–child participation in conversation about the past: relationships to preschoolers' theory of mind. *Developmental Psychology, 33,* 618–629.

Wilson, D. B., & Lipsey, M. W. (2001). The role of methods in treatment effectiveness research: Evidence from meta-analysis. *Psychological Methods, 6*(4), 413–429. doi: 10.1037/1082-989X.6.4.413.

Wu, N., & Su, Y. (2015). Oxytocin receptor gene relates to theory of mind and prosocial behavior in children. *Journal of Cognition and Development, 16,* 302–313.

4

WHY MONTESSORI IS A FACILITATIVE ENVIRONMENT FOR THEORY OF MIND

Three speculations

Angeline S. Lillard and Sierra Eisen

French biologist François Jacob (2002) drew a distinction between day science and night science. Day science is how we usually present discoveries: we have a hypothesis, we test it, we obtain clear results, we come up with a further hypothesis, we test it, we obtain clear results, and finally we publish them. In day science, everything proceeds in a neat, linear fashion. Night science works the other way around. It is

> where thought proceeds along sinuous paths, winding streets, most often blind alleys. At the mercy of chance, the mind frets in a labyrinth, deluged with messages, in its quest for a sign, a wink, an unexpected connection. One is surprised by a finding, and develops the hypothesis from there.
>
> *(Jacob, 2002, p. 12)*

The research described in this chapter is more akin to night than day science. The Montessori environment is based on a complex curriculum with no obvious connection to theory of mind (ToM) development. Thus, the findings presented here were not initially expected, but they have led to hypotheses, which we will present at the end of the chapter, rather than in the initial section where day science would place them.

We begin by describing Montessori education and our findings that suggest it is a facilitative environment for ToM. Then we speculate on three possible reasons for this Montessori advantage: multi-aged classrooms, encouraging mindfulness, and high demands on executive function.

What is Montessori education?

Montessori is an educational program for children from birth to adolescence; it is most often employed for children ages 3–6 in what is termed Primary classrooms. In the 1890s, Dr. Maria Montessori was the first woman to enroll as a medical student at the University of Rome (O'Donnell, 2007). Her initial interest in neuropsychology and mentally handicapped children ultimately led her to the study of typically developing children. While others were amazed that the mentally handicapped children with whom she worked passed state examinations for typically developing children, she was instead amazed that typically developing children weren't doing better than their mentally handicapped peers. She concluded that there must be something seriously awry in the conventional educational program and she set about studying children, trying to determine their *true* nature, and how they really learn (Montessori, 1964). She had the imaginative scope to re-evaluate educational methods and come up with a program that was markedly different.

The Montessori approach involves, at each age level, a tightly organized, interconnected curriculum using dozens of carefully selected hands-on materials designed to convey specific learning. For example, young children in Primary classrooms are introduced to the Pink Tower, a set of ten cubes, which gradually increase in size by 1 cm on all sides; the sides of the smallest cube are all 1 cm and those of the largest cube are 10 cm. Children build a tower, starting with the largest block at the base. The Pink Tower embodies the decimal system and cubing, and focuses attention on volume. The next material in this sequence is the Brown Stair, which is similar but changes only in two dimensions, not three; this is followed by the Red Rods, which vary in only one dimension, and then the number rods, which begin the concept of attaching symbols to the materials ("This is one, this is two," and so on). Following a one-on-one or small-group lesson with each material, children use it on their own until they master it, whereupon they get a lesson on the next material in the sequence. Children have tremendous choice over what they do each day, with the caveat that their activities must be constructive, in the sense of helpful to the child's development. A teacher's task is to determine that a child's activity is constructive, and to be sure that every child masters all the materials in the classroom during the 3 years the child spends in that classroom.

Dr. Montessori founded an organization, the Association Montessori Internationale, to continue her work after her death in 1952. This organization certifies experienced Montessori teachers to train new teachers, following a rigorous program of credentialing that includes apprenticing for many years with a certified teacher trainer and writing a series of papers on Montessori pedagogy that are approved by a credentialing committee. In these training programs, the teacher trainers learn to teach others how to present these materials to children. They therefore know well the set of materials that Dr. Montessori considered important.

Lillard (2005) explored how Montessori educational practices align with current models of human learning. A major conclusion of this study was that Dr. Montessori anticipated the findings of current research on how children learn and develop. Some of these findings are discussed in the conclusion.

Based on the broad alignment between Montessori and current developmental theory and research, Lillard undertook a series of empirical tests to examine whether the Montessori approach promotes child development more than other educational systems. This research compared young children in Montessori schools with children in other school settings for several outcomes that were thought to be important to human functioning, including ToM. Initially a wide net was cast, in order to bring to light whether Montessori education could be linked to any strong indicators of children's development. Intriguingly, across three studies, children attending the Montessori schools performed consistently better on standard ToM tasks than their counterparts in other school systems. In this chapter, we describe the initial study in which this association emerged and two subsequent studies designed to clarify the link between Montessori education and children's understanding of mind. We conclude by reflecting on the reasons for this association.

Three studies linking Montessori education to ToM

Since 2005, Lillard has conducted three studies addressing the outcomes of Montessori education: two at low-income public schools (one longitudinal and still in progress), and a third at middle-income private schools. Each of these studies is described below in relation to the link between Montessori education and children's ToM development.

Study 1: Public Montessori in Milwaukee (Lillard & Else-Quest, 2006)

In this study, parents who had listed a Montessori school as their first choice in a randomized public school lottery were invited to have their children participate in a study on the cognitive, academic, and social outcomes of children who attended Montessori versus other schooling options. Thirty 5-year-olds who were randomly selected by the lottery for Montessori education participated in the study. The *control* group consisted of 25 participants who had lost the lottery and ended up in a variety of school settings, mainly public, but also including a few private and charter schools. Most of the participants in both the Montessori and control groups were from low-income families and were ethnic minorities.

A variety of social and academic outcomes were assessed, including early reading and math skills, executive function, and social and behavioral skills; here we focus on those that concerned social understanding and behavior.

First, children were administered a standard *Maxi* false-belief task to access their ToM abilities (see Appendix). In contrast to the control group, which passed this test at chance levels, 80 percent of the Montessori children (significantly above chance) passed the test. Given the positive correlations between passing false-belief and social competence (e.g., Newton & Jenvey, 2011), this is clearly an interesting result.

Second, to test social problem-solving skills, children were given five stories about social problems and asked how they would resolve them (Rubin, 1988). For example, they were shown a picture of two children, one of whom had been on a swing for a long time and another who wanted to swing. Children were asked what the second child could say or do to gain access to the swing, and what the child him/herself would do. Children's performance on this task in kindergarten has been related to sociometric status in first grade (Rubin & Daniels-Beirness, 1983) and to teacher ratings of social skills (Rubin & Clark, 1983). Although children often gave conventional responses (e.g., "Say 'please'"), children from the Montessori group were significantly more likely than control children to use higher-level moral reasoning in their responses, such as explicitly considering fairness. Such other-oriented arguments have been related to children's performance on social cognitive tasks (Foote & Holmes-Lonergan, 2003; Slomkowski & Dunn, 1992).

Third, 10-minute playground observations were coded for children's activities, to determine whether children's social behavior differed across school settings. Montessori children were significantly more likely to engage in positive shared peer play, and significantly less likely to engage in ambiguous rough play – clearly a desirable pattern for playground behavior.

Overall, this first study showed positive effects of Montessori education on ToM as well as two behaviors that suggest application of a ToM: social problem solving and engagement in positive free play. Therefore, Montessori education appeared to create a facilitative environment for ToM development.

Study 2: Private Montessori with classic versus supplemented implementations

A second study was again concerned with Montessori versus conventional schooling, but also tested two different implementations of Montessori, designated as classic Montessori and supplemented Montessori (Lillard, 2012). Classic Montessori classrooms were those that adhered to the traditional Montessori philosophy and materials described earlier. Supplemented Montessori classrooms were those that used both Montessori materials and supplementary materials that are not part of the standardized Montessori curriculum. The conventional classrooms were just that – ordinary conventional kindergarten classrooms. In an effort to at least partially address the problem of self-selection, the conventional programs were selected by asking the Montessori parents where they would send their child to school if Montessori were not available; their top private school choices were used as sites of conventional classrooms.

This study involved 172 children between the ages of 3 and 6. The children were largely Caucasian and came from middle-class families, and all were tested both in the fall and in late spring on ToM, social problem solving, and several other tasks so we could examine school-year change based on classroom type.

Specifically, children were given items from the ToM scale (Wellman & Liu, 2004) and one object acquisition story from the same social problem-solving task as Study 1. For this task, children were again scored for considering the other's interests in their response.

We used three items from the Theory of Mind Scale: knowledge access, false belief, and hidden emotion (see Appendix). Because of the ages of children in this study, we started with the knowledge access task. To minimize testing time, the false-belief task was always presented first, hidden emotion was presented only if a child passed false belief, and knowledge access was presented only if a child failed false belief.

An object acquisition story from the social problem-solving task (Rubin, 1988) used in Study 1 was also used here; only one story was used because in Study 1 children responded similarly on each of three tasks. For this task, children were shown a picture of two children of their same race and gender and were told that the children were their same age. One of the children in the picture was reading and the other looking on. Children were told, "[The reading child] has been looking at this book for a long time and [the onlooker child] really wants to look at the book. What could [onlooker] do or say so he/she could have a look at the book?" Children's responses were recorded by hand, and then children were asked, "What else could he/she do or say?" and finally, "What if it was you? What could you do or say so you could have a look at the book?" The number of references to sharing or fairness, for example, references to how they might trade items, or how the reader had had 10 minutes with the book and now could the other person have 10 minutes, were coded and summed.

Results indicated that the classic Montessori children showed the highest level of social reasoning at posttest, controlling for pretest scores. They made particularly strong gains in the third year in the Montessori primary classroom, when children in the other classrooms remained essentially flat from fall to spring. Hence children in classic Montessori were more likely to learn, across the course of the school year, to offer fair solutions such as sharing and taking turns when a social problem arose. Although no difference between groups was found with a standard analysis of covariance on ToM tasks, the Kruskal–Wallis non-parametric test did show group differences. Although the three groups were equal at beginning of year, children in classic Montessori had the highest scores on the Theory of Mind Scale items at the end of the school year. Hence again in this study, children attending high-fidelity Montessori programs did particularly well on tests relating to ToM.

Study 3: Public Montessori in Hartford, Connecticut

The third, ongoing study concerning Montessori education and ToM used a lottery design, like that described for Study 1. One difference was that the Montessori schools in this study were *magnet schools*, meaning 25 percent of their population was from wealthy outlying suburbs of Hartford; these children were bused or driven in. Wealthier families whose children did not get into the Montessori through the lottery were perhaps less likely to be interested in the study than lower-income families (for whom the stipend offered might have more meaning), so the available Montessori families were somewhat wealthier than the families who lost the lottery. For this reason we matched children in the Montessori and non-Montessori samples for income as well as for parent education, ethnicity, age (born within 2 months of each other), and gender.

Another differentiating feature of Study 3 is the 3-year longitudinal design: children were assessed in their first few months of school as a baseline, and then followed up in the subsequent three springs. Recruitment for the study extended over several years; the data here includes the complete 3-year datasets (from age 3 to age 6) for 24 children, 2 years of data for 61 children, and just 1 year of data for another 79 children.

Although data collection is still underway, we can report preliminary results here. The sample is ethnically diverse (28 percent Hispanic, 16 percent African American, 22 percent mixed ethnicity), and the income range broad ($0–250,000, mean $64,000), but children in the two samples are well matched and their baseline scores did not differ.

In this study, ToM was measured with four items from the Theory of Mind Scale: knowledge access, diverse beliefs, false belief, and hidden emotion. A single social problem-solving task was also administered. The data from the first 84 participants (all tested at age 3, but fewer at age 4 and just 30 at age 5) showed that, controlling for the baseline scores, Montessori children performed significantly better overall across the test points. Both groups performed similarly at baseline, and with each advancing year a larger difference emerged; this difference was significant at age 4 (and likely will be at age 5 with the full sample). Likewise, the social problem-solving task did not show a difference between groups, but is trending in the expected direction; this is to be expected since in the earlier study this difference particularly emerged at age 5.

Why might Montessori education create an advantage in ToM?

Across three studies we have seen that Montessori, particularly classic Montessori, is consistently associated with better ToM than conventional schooling. This is the case even when the comparison group's parents also chose Montessori and children were randomly assigned to the school program, and when the Montessori and comparison children performed equally well in the first months of schooling. Why would Montessori education lead to better performance on ToM and social problem-solving tasks than conventional or supplemented Montessori? In an effort to shed light on this night science, we theorize here about three possible explanations: multi-aged classrooms, encouraging mindfulness, and executive function.

Multi-aged classrooms

Whereas conventional classrooms are often composed of children of a single age, authentic Montessori classrooms are composed of 3-year groupings: 3–6, 6–9, and so on. These particular levels represent key stages in Montessori's four "planes of development" (Montessori, 1971), which are four 6-year periods spanning 0–24. In the first 3 years of these periods, children are moving to a nadir, and in the next 3 they are rising. Montessori believed children in these bisections of each developmental plane were particularly suited to live and work together, with older ones helping younger ones along, while younger ones admire and look up to their elders.

Evidence that interacting with other ages assists ToM development is seen in research on family composition. Perner, Ruffman, and Leekam (1994) showed a linear relationship between family size and false-belief (but not knowledge) performance among 3- and 4-year-olds. Experiment 2 addressed whether siblings being older or younger made a difference by testing a sample of children with just one sibling, and found that it did not matter if the sibling was older or younger. Several further studies confirmed this finding (Jenkins & Astington, 1996; Lewis, Freeman, Kyriakidou, Maridaki-Kassotaki, & Berridge, 1996; McAlister & Peterson, 2006, 2007; Peterson, 2000). Sometimes only older siblings conferred the advantage (Ruffman, Perner, Naito, Parkin, & Clements, 1998). A possible reason for this could be the ages of the siblings involved, a point raised by Peterson, who suggested that siblings between the ages of 1 and 12 are likely to be especially relevant.

Peterson's reasoning was that the sibling advantage was likely to stem both from conversation about others' minds and pretend play, and that these activities would be less apt to occur with children under age 1 or over age 12. With younger siblings, the advent of walking leads to cascading changes in social interaction (Karasik, Tamis-LeMonda, & Adolph, 2014) and is associated with numerous developments (Campos et al., 2000) that might lead to increases in parent mental-state talk. On the other hand, teenagers might be too far out of the sphere of preschoolers for much mental-state discussion to occur. Peterson also thought that having siblings of a variety of ages was most likely to assist in the development of social understanding, and she created a "sibling variety score" in which having more siblings who were just a few years older or younger awarded more points than having a twin or siblings distant in age (Peterson, 2000). This served as a good predictor of ToM, a finding reiterated by Cassidy and her colleagues, who found no ToM benefit for being a twin (Cassidy, Fineberg, Brown, & Perkins, 2005). Moving from families to classrooms, a Chinese study involving urban children who are "onlies," meaning they have no siblings, found that those in multi-aged preschool classrooms from 8 a.m. to 5.30 p.m. each day performed better on false-belief tasks than did those in single-aged classrooms (Wang & Su, 2009).

In the family literature, there have been some important non-replications of these findings. Peterson and Slaughter (2003) found no sibling advantage, but their sample had a restricted range in terms of number of, and age differences to, siblings: the vast majority of children in the two samples had one or two siblings who were close in age. Three other studies with largely low-income samples also did not replicate the sibling advantage (Cole & Mitchell, 2000; Cutting & Dunn, 1999; Hughes & Ensor, 2005), suggesting it might be specific to middle- and higher-income families.

The sibling advantage findings point to the possible importance of two other factors that might go along with sibling variety: conversation and pretend play. Others have suggested that both of these factors could undergird earlier ToM performance (Wellman, 2014).

Regarding pretend play, there are three reasons to suspect that it might not be the source of the Montessori advantage seen here: children are unlikely to pretend more in Montessori classrooms, twins are likely to pretend more than nontwins (but they lack the ToM advantage), and the research showing that pretend play leads to ToM is weak.

First, Montessori classrooms are not set up for pretend play. Initially they were – in her very first classroom, Dr. Montessori had a special dollhouse and other toys inviting pretense – but when children showed a preference for the other materials and no interest in the pretend play toys, she removed them (Montessori, 1912/1965). Thus, it is unlikely that children in multi-age Montessori classrooms are getting more pretend-play experience than are those in single-aged classrooms.

Second, the twin finding might also work against this, because it seems likely that preschool children engage in pretend play as much with twins as with siblings just older or younger. Unless children actually pretend less with a twin (we know of no relevant data), frequency of pretend play seems unsupported by the twin data.

The third reason to doubt that pretend play holds the key is our recent review of the literature on the impact of pretend play on preschoolers' development (Lillard et al., 2013). Although there are some notable studies showing that social pretend play is associated with ToM, results from training studies are harder to interpret, with some inconsistent results, and methodological issues in those that delivered clear findings. A persistent problem in the literature on the benefits of pretend play is failure to use blind experimenters; replication studies that did use them failed to replicate those effects. This suggests that experimenter bias, more so than true training effects, might contribute to children's posttest scores. Lillard et al. (2013) proposed that the associations seen could result from a reverse direction of effects, whereby children with more developed social cognition are better at engaging their peers in social pretend play (Dore, Smith, & Lillard, 2015).

The alternate explanation for the sibling variety effect, and one that we think holds much more promise, is adult and older peer conversation about mental states. Several studies have pointed out that when there are siblings close in age, parents engage in rich mental-state discourse (Dunn, Bretherton, & Munn, 1987; Dunn, Brown, & Beardsall, 1991; Dunn & Hughes, 1998). These and other studies suggest that parents who focus on mental states have children who learn about them earlier. Ruffman and his colleagues showed this in the context of discipline: mothers who said they would discipline their children's wrong-doings by asking them to consider how another child would feel had children with more advanced mental-state reasoning (Ruffman, Perner, & Parkin, 1999). In addition, Meins finds that children whose mothers are more apt to describe their children with reference to their mental states (thoughts, emotions, perceptions) are also advanced in ToM (Meins et al., 2002). Causal mental-state language appears to be particularly important to helping children's false-belief understanding (Garner, Carlson Jones, Gaddy, & Rennie, 1997; Ruffman, Slade, & Crowe, 2002), a point also made clear in Wellman's research (see Chapter 1, this volume). Interestingly, it has been suggested that mothers engage in less of this discourse with twins (Cassidy et al., 2005).

Our speculation is that Montessori classrooms also encourage more of this discourse because there are children of different ages whose behaviors and motivations must be discussed. For example, while visiting a Primary classroom in Dallas, Lillard saw a 3-year-old girl take out the puzzle map of Europe. This is rather difficult work for a 3-year-old, and after a time, she gave up and asked for help from a 5-year-old girl who was working with another child on a long skip-counting bead chain. The 5-year-old left the bead chain momentarily to help her, but then the 3-year-old withdrew entirely and got out some shoe-polishing work. This left the 5-year-old in a quandary, which she discussed at length with the other 5-year-old. The classroom had a rule that one could only have one material out at a time, and the 3-year-old by her actions had made it such that the 5-year-old appeared to have two materials out. I overheard the older girls talking about what the 3-year-old wanted, their fears concerning how the teacher would perceive things, how they might discuss this with the younger girl and get her to follow the rules, and so on. The classroom situation thus inspired a great deal of talk concerning states of mind.

Such conversation, which likely occurs more often in mixed-age settings (because one is perhaps more likely to need to explain the behaviors of those just older and younger) could be the reason for the ToM advantage. Paul Harris has argued cogently that the very act of conversation alerts one to the fact that others have minds (Harris, 2005), and many studies have shown that it is vital to developing a ToM (Cutting & Dunn, 2006; Peterson & Siegal, 1995; Siegal & Peterson, 1994). In sum, mixed-age classrooms (with three age levels) might be a reason for advanced ToM in Montessori children, possibly because there is increased conversation related to the mental states of other children in such situations.

Mindfulness

One of the distinctive elements of Montessori education that sets it apart from conventional classrooms is its alignment with the practice of mindfulness (Lillard, 2011). Mindfulness is a focused awareness of the present moment along with a non-judgmental frame of mind. Many studies have shown that people who engage in mindfulness practices become more compassionate and empathic (e.g., Cameron &

Frederickson, 2015; Schonert-Reichl et al., 2015). Similarities to mindfulness practices can be found in several areas of Montessori education, including its emphasis on sensory experiences, practical work, and deep concentration.

One similarity between mindfulness and Montessori education is a focus on sensory engagement. Mindfulness training privileges attention to sensory experiences, encouraging attention on all of one's senses and movements (Kabat-Zinn, 1990). For example, people are urged to eat slowly, noticing the texture and feel of the food, even taking 20 minutes to eat a single raisin. As another example, in the practice of walking meditation, people move slowly, noticing how their foot raises and lowers, and the feeling of pressure as they step.

The integration of mind and body through sensory engagement is also evident in Montessori education. For example, children are taught through "The Silence Game" to tune the auditory sense to notice sounds. In contrast, conventional classrooms may encourage silence during work times but rarely use silence as its own learning experience. Mindfulness of the physical self in Montessori education also extends to how children are taught to move. In Montessori classrooms, children are given the opportunity to practice careful conscious movement. Even the simple act of setting up class materials is done very carefully, with children expected to pay attention to both their own movements and to how those movements affect those around them (Lillard, 2011). This expectation likely creates sensorimotor awareness in even very young children, similar to the sensorimotor awareness that is central to mindfulness practice. Montessori also has explicit materials (the "sensorial exercises") to develop sense awareness for all the senses. Children practice discriminating ever-finer differences across all the sense modalities with specific materials, for example with musical bells, baric tablets, and smelling bottles.

Both mindfulness and Montessori also share a focus on the importance of everyday work. Simple chores such as cleaning, cooking, and gardening are necessary to daily life, and can be rewarding as well. Montessori classrooms teach children to engage in such activities through the "exercises of practical life." Children are taught to carefully engage in daily tasks like clearing the table, cleaning furniture, and polishing silver. Dr. Montessori saw these activities as instrumental in showing children the relationship between their own actions and a practical goal. Through practical life tasks, children would be expected to gain a sense of themselves as independent agents, capable of their own accomplishments (Lillard, 2011). The direct relationship between the steps of the task and the end goal are highly evident, which contrasts with conventional schooling, where the objectives of the work in which children engage tend to be relatively abstract. Learning to pay attention to each step in the tasks also would be expected to train attention.

A third similarity between mindfulness training and Montessori is their focus on concentrated attention; this underpins executive function, which is the next potential reason for advanced ToM to be discussed, but it is worth touching on here as an aspect of mindfulness. Montessori education emphasizes deep concentration, in this case as crucial to learning (Lillard, 2011). During 3-hour work periods, children are encouraged to immerse themselves in a task of their choosing.

This is in stark contrast to conventional education, where children are typically taught in a lecture format and for shorter periods of time. The traditional teaching model assumes that young children have short attention spans, yet Montessori methods have shown that children are capable of sustained attention when the task is engaging and self-directed (Montessori, 1917/1965).

Executive function

A third possible reason why Montessori children are advanced in ToM is that they are advanced in executive function. The first two studies described here showed this to be the case; results are not yet clear for the third study. In the first study (Lillard & Else-Quest, 2006), children in the Montessori programs performed significantly better on the dimensional change card sort test of executive function. Although it was not statistically significant, they also waited a full minute and a half longer (out of 6 minutes) on a delay of gratification (standard marshmallow) task. In the second study, although they scored equally at baseline, children in classic Montessori advanced the most over the school year on the Head-Toes-Knees-Shoulders task, ending with the highest scores (Lillard, 2012).

Why might Montessori be associated with improved executive function? There are many potential reasons. One is that every Montessori exercise involves a specific set of steps that children must re-enact. The work is very precise, and children are expected to execute the steps exactly, and then return the work neatly to its place on a shelf. In executing these steps, children must inhibit all the other steps they might want to take. As mentioned above, this ties into mindfulness: Mindfulness training has been linked to better executive function in many correlational studies, and experimental (training) studies suggest the relationship is causal, with mindfulness practices increasing executive function (Holzel et al., 2011; Tang, Ma, & Posner, 2007).

Many studies have shown strong relationships between executive function and ToM (Frye, Zelazo, & Palfai, 1995; for a more recent review, see Muller & Kerns, 2015). One possible reason for this is quite direct: children have to inhibit the incorrect (but prepotent) response of where an object really is, or which object is really hidden, in order to say what is falsely believed. Children also must flexibly shift sets, from the "reality set" to the "belief set," to answer such questions. But the influence could also be indirect. For example, children who have stronger executive control might be better at considering others' thoughts and feelings separately from their own, and thereby might learn about others' mental states; this knowledge could then enable them to respond correctly on false-belief tasks.

We have considered three potential reasons for the better ToM performance we have observed in Montessori children in three different studies: (1) multi-aged classrooms, and the attendant discussion of mental states that might occur there; (2) mindfulness of the environment and thus others (and one's own) mental states; and (3) executive function, which could both directly and indirectly influence performance on ToM tasks.

Further research should aim to tease apart these possibilities by, for example, exploring relationships between executive function and ToM within Montessori classrooms, or examining whether engaging in practical life and other mindfulness activities does predict increased empathy in Montessori or conventional classrooms. Regardless of the reasons, the findings themselves are intriguing and important. A better ToM is related to numerous positive outcomes (Wellman, 2014), and that a century-old alternative method of education appears to reliably improve ToM is important to know and understand.

Acknowledgments

Writing of this manuscript was supported by NSF grant 1024293 and grants from the Sir John Templeton Foundation and the Brady Education Foundation to Angeline Lillard.

References

Cameron, C. D., & Fredrickson, B. L. (2015). Mindfulness facets predict helping behavior and distinct helping-related emotions. *Mindfulness, 6*(5), 1–8.

Campos, J. J., Anderson, D. I., Barbu-Roth, M. A., Hubbard, E. M., Hertenstein, M. J., & Witherington, D. (2000). Travel broadens the mind. *Infancy, 1*, 149–219.

Cassidy, K. W., Fineberg, D. S., Brown, K., & Perkins, A. (2005). ToM may be contagious, but you don't catch it from your twin. *Child Development, 76*, 97–106. doi: 0009-3920/2005/7601-0007.

Cole, K., & Mitchell, P. (2000). Siblings in the development of executive control and a ToM. *British Journal of Developmental Psychology, 18*, 279–295.

Cutting, A. L., & Dunn, J. (1999). ToM, emotion understanding, language, and family background: individual differences and interrelations. *Child Development, 70*, 853–865. doi: 0009-3920/99/7004-0004.

Cutting, A. L., & Dunn, J. (2006). Conversations with siblings and with friends: links between relationship quality and social understanding. *British Journal of Developmental Psychology, 24*, 73–87. doi: 10.1348/026151005x70337.

Dore, R. A., Smith, E. D., & Lillard, A. S. (2015). How is ToM useful? Perhaps to enable social pretend play. *Frontiers in Psychology: Cognitive Science, 6*. doi: 10.3389/fpsyg.2015.01559.

Dunn, J., Bretherton, I., & Munn, P. (1987). Conversations about feeling states between mothers and their young children. *Developmental Psychology, 23*, 132–139.

Dunn, J., Brown, J., & Beardsall, L. (1991). Family talk about feeling states and children's later understanding of others' emotions. *Developmental Psychology, 27*, 448–455.

Dunn, J., & Hughes, C. (1998). Young children's understanding of emotions within close relationships. *Cognition and Emotion, 12*, 171–190.

Foote, R., & Holmes-Lonergan, H. (2003). Sibling conflict and theory of mind. *British Journal of Developmental Psychology, 21*, 45–58.

Frye, D., Zelazo, P., & Palfai, T. (1995). The cognitive basis of ToM. *Cognitive Development, 10*, 483–527.

Garner, P. W., Carlson Jones, D., Gaddy, G., & Rennie, K. M. (1997). Low-income mothers' conversations about emotions and their children's emotional competence. *Social Development, 6*, 37–52.

Harris, P. L. (2005). Conversation, pretense, and ToM. In J. W. Astington & J. A. Baird (Eds.), *Why language matters for ToM* (pp. 70–83). New York: Oxford University Press.

Holzel, B. K., Lazar, S. W., Gard, T., Schuman-Olivier, Z., Vago, D. R., & Ott, U. (2011). How does mindfulness meditation work? Proposing mechanisms of action from a conceptual and neural perspective. *Perspectives on Psychological Science, 6,* 537–559.

Hughes, C., & Ensor, R. (2005). Executive function and ToM in 2 year olds: a family affair? *Developmental Neuropsychology, 28,* 645–648.

Jacob, F. (2002). From night bustle to printed quietness. *Treballs de la Societat Catalana de Biologia, 51,* 11–13.

Jenkins, J. M., & Astington, J. W. (1996). Cognitive factors and family structure associated with ToM development in young children. *Developmental Psychology, 32,* 70–78.

Kabat-Zinn, J. (1990). *Full catastrophe living.* New York: Delta.

Karasik, L. B., Tamis-LeMonda, C. S., & Adolph, K. E. (2014). Crawling and walking infants elicit different verbal responses from mothers. *Developmental Science, 17,* 388–395.

Lewis, C., Freeman, N., Kyriakidou, C., Maridaki-Kassotaki, K., & Berridge, D. (1996). Social influences on false belief access: specific sibling influences or general apprenticeship? *Child Development, 67,* 2930–2947. doi: 10.1111/j.1467-8624.1996.tb01896.x.

Lillard, A. S. (2005). *Montessori: The science behind the genius,* 1st edn. New York: Oxford University Press.

Lillard, A. S. (2011). Mindfulness practices in education: Montessori's approach. *Mindfulness, 2,* 78–85. doi: 10.1007/s12671-011-0045-6.

Lillard, A. S. (2012). Preschool children's development in classic Montessori, supplemented Montessori, and conventional programs. *Journal of School Psychology, 50,* 379–401. doi: 10.1016/j.jsp.2012.01.001.

Lillard, A. S., & Else-Quest, N. (2006). Evaluating Montessori education. *Science, 313*(5795), 1893–1894.

Lillard, A. S., Lerner, M. D., Hopkins, E. J., Dore, R. A., Smith, E. D., & Palmquist, C. M. (2013). The impact of pretend play on children's development: a review of the evidence. *Psychological Bulletin, 139,* 1–34. doi: 10.1037/a0029321.

McAlister, A., & Peterson, C. C. (2006). Mental playmates: siblings, executive functioning and ToM. *British Journal of Developmental Psychology, 24,* 733–751.

McAlister, A., & Peterson, C. C. (2007). A longitudinal study of child siblings and ToM development. *Cognitive Development, 22,* 258–270.

Meins, E., Fernyhough, C., Wainwright, R., Gupta, M. D., Fradley, E., & Tuckey, M. (2002). Maternal mind-mindedness and attachment security as predictors of ToM understanding. *Child Development, 73,* 1715–1726. doi: 10.1111/1467-8624.00501.

Montessori, M. (1912/1965). *The Montessori method.* New York: Schocken.

Montessori, M. (1917/1965). *Spontaneous activity in education: The advanced Montessori method* (F. Simmonds, trans.). New York: Schocken.

Montessori, M. (1964). *The Montessori method* (A. George, trans.). New York: Schocken.

Montessori, M. (1971). *The four planes of education.* Amsterdam, Netherlands: Association Montessori Internationale.

Muller, U., & Kerns, K. (2015). The development of executive function. In L. S. Liben & U. Mueller (Eds.), *Handbook of child psychology and developmental science: Cognitive processes* (7th edn, Vol. 2). New York: Wiley-Blackwell.

Newton, E., & Jenvey, V. (2011). Play and theory of mind: associations with social competence in young children. *Early Child Development and Care, 181,* 761–773.

O'Donnell, M. (2007). *Maria Montessori* (Vol. 7). London: Continuum.

Perner, J., Ruffman, T., & Leekam, S. R. (1994). ToM is contagious: you catch it from your sibs. *Child Development, 65,* 1228–1238. doi: 10.2307/1131316.

Peterson, C. C. (2000). Kindred spirits: influences of siblings' perspectives on ToM. *Cognitive Development, 15*, 435–455.

Peterson, C. C., & Siegal, M. (1995). Deafness, conversation, and ToM. *Journal of Child Psychology and Psychiatry, 36*, 459–474. doi: 0.1111/j.1469-7610.1995.tb01303.x.

Peterson, C. C., & Slaughter, V. (2003). Opening windows into the mind: mothers' preferences for mental state explanations and childrens' ToM. *Cognitive Development, 18*, 399–429.

Rubin, K. H. (1988). *The social problem-solving test-revised*. Waterloo, Ontario: University of Waterloo.

Rubin, K. H., & Clark, M. L. (1983). Preschool teachers' ratings of behavioral problems: observational, sociometric, and social-cognitive correlates. *Journal of Abnormal Child Psychology, 11*, 273–286.

Rubin, K. H., & Daniels-Beirness, T. (1983). Concurrent and predictive correlates of socio-metric status in kindergarten and grade 1 children. *Merrill-Palmer Quarterly, 29*, 337–351.

Ruffman, T., Perner, J., Naito, M., Parkin, L., & Clements, W. (1998). Older (but not younger) siblings facilitate false belief understanding. *Developmental Psychology, 34*, 161–174. doi: 10.1037//0012-1649.34.1.161.

Ruffman, T., Perner, J., & Parkin, L. (1999). How parenting style affects false belief under-standing. *Social Development, 8*, 395–411. doi: 10.1111/1467-9507.00103.

Ruffman, T., Slade, L., & Crowe, E. (2002). The relation between children's and mothers' mental state language and theory-of-mind understanding. *Child Development, 73*, 734–751.

Schonert-Reichl, K. A., Oberle, E., Lawlor, M. S., Abbott, D., Thomson, K., Oberlander, T. F., & Diamond, A. (2015). Enhancing cognitive and social–emotional development through a simple-to-administer mindfulness-based school program for elementary school children: a randomized controlled trial. *Developmental Psychology, 51*, 52–66.

Siegal, M., & Peterson, C. C. (1994). Children's ToM and the conversational territory of cognitive development. In C. Lewis & P. Mitchell (Eds.), *Children's early understanding of mind: Origins and development*. Hillsdale, NJ: Erlbaum.

Slomkowski, C. L., & Dunn, J. (1992). Arguments and relationships within the family: dif-ferences in young children's disputes with mother and sibling. *Developmental Psychology, 28*, 919–924.

Tang, Y., Ma, Y., & Posner, M. I. (2007). Short-term meditation training improves attention and self-regulation. *Proceedings of the National Academy of Sciences, 104*, 17152–17156.

Wang, Y., & Su, Y. (2009). False belief understanding: children catch it from classmates of different ages. *International Journal of Behavioral Development, 33*, 331–337. doi: 10.1177/0165025409104525.

Wellman, H. M. (2014). *Making minds: How ToM develops*. New York: Oxford.

Wellman, H. M., & Liu, D. (2004). Scaling of theory-of-mind tasks. *Child Development, 75*, 523–541.

5

BEHAVIOUR TO BELIEFS

Ted Ruffman and Mele Taumoepeau

We begin our chapter with a question: when does insight into mental states first begin? Over the past 10 years, researchers have carried out a series of experiments indicating a surprising competence in young infants, with consistent claims that a theory of mind (ToM) is present in infancy (e.g. Baillargeon, Scott, & He, 2010; Surian & Geraci, 2012). This view is sometimes termed *mentalism*. A very strong form of mentalism is that infants' ToM is innate (e.g. Baron-Cohen, 1997; Carruthers, 2013; He, Bolz, & Baillargeon, 2011; Luo, 2011; Poulin-Dubois & Chow, 2009; Scott, Baillargeon, Song, & Leslie, 2010; Song & Baillargeon, 2008; Surian & Geraci, 2012). In contrast to such "rich" claims, others have argued that young infants might not understand mental states, and instead, pass ToM tasks through an understanding of behaviour, sometimes termed *minimalism* (Heyes, 2014; Perner, 2010; Perner & Ruffman, 2005; Ruffman & Perner, 2005). Indeed, both mentalism and minimalism require infants to understand behaviour. In the former case, the behaviour stems from underlying mental states. In the latter case, infants' insight does not go beyond the behaviour. One of the challenges for the minimalist view is, if infants don't understand mental states, how might they learn about behaviours? We begin to answer this question in the present chapter.

From behaviours to beliefs

Over the past few years we have presented arguments for how children might acquire an understanding of behaviour (Ruffman, 2014; Ruffman, Perkins, & Taumoepeau, 2012). Our version of minimalism is sketched in Figure 5.1. It assumes some innate or early developing abilities in infants, including attention to the face, interest in motion and the capacity for statistical learning. Infants' attention to the face is helpful because the face expresses mental states such as attention and emotion, and the same is true for motion. For instance, I walk to and open the freezer because

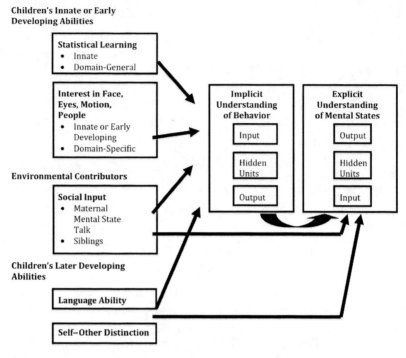

Children's Innate or Early Developing Abilities

FIGURE 5.1 Model: from behaviour to mental states. Reproduced from Ruffman, T. (2014). To belief or not belief: children's theory of mind. *Developmental Review, 34,* 265–293, with permission from Elsevier.

I *want* ice cream and *believe* it is there. Statistical learning helps infants to recognise patterns of behaviour, for instance, that one reaches continually for one object as opposed to another, or for an object in a particular place rather than another place. It is very difficult to say exactly when a child understands mental states rather than behaviour, although we have argued that there are signs such an understanding is in place by around 2 years (see Ruffman, 2014, and below).

This account provides an alternative to the idea that mental-state insight is innate by providing infants with the means to learn about behaviour as well as links between perception (e.g. what one sees) and behaviour. It is likely that initial insight into behaviour is likely unconscious (Clements & Perner, 1994; Garnham & Ruffman, 2001; Low, 2010; Wang, Low, Jing, & Qinghua, 2012). Thus, although 3-year-olds look to the correct location in a false-belief task when anticipating a story character's return, they give the wrong answer to a direct, verbal question. Crucially, they show no awareness of the knowledge manifest in their eye gaze, even when the measure of awareness is shown to be a sensitive index of their certainty (Ruffman, Garnham, Import, & Connolly, 2001).

Subsequently, an explicit understanding of mental states emerges through parallel development in other of children's abilities. One such ability is language understanding, a reliable correlate of ToM (e.g., Milligan, Astington, & Dack, 2007; San Juan & Astington, 2012). General language ability provides children with the means for thinking about and reflecting upon implicit knowledge to make it explicit. Learning of mental-state terms provides them with a deepening understanding of what such terms mean, evolving from an understanding of behaviour to an understanding of mental states (see below).

We have also found that self-awareness relates to ToM development (see below). Self-awareness is not an all-or-nothing process. For instance, Rochat (2003) identifies five levels of self-awareness that evolve through the lifespan, although a key step is the ability to recognise oneself in a mirror, which occurs around 18–24 months of age (Amsterdam, 1972). Nevertheless, it is unclear what exactly this insight entails. Is it awareness of the bodily self on its own, or is mirror self-recognition accompanied by some form of awareness of one's own mental states? If the latter, then the mirror task, as well as measuring bodily awareness, would measure ToM. Indeed, there is some evidence that this might be the case, because mirror self-recognition correlates with self-conscious emotions such as embarrassment (Lewis, Sullivan, Stanger, & Weiss, 1989) as well as increased empathy (Bischof-Koehler, 1991). When children recognise themselves in a mirror, does this also imply some immediate distinction between self and other? If so, does it imply some awareness of the distinction between self and others' mental states or does this insight evolve thereafter? If it evolves thereafter, how gradual is the process and how deep is the initial level of insight into own and others' mental states? While some have attempted to answer such questions (Morin, 2011), it seems that no definitive answers can be provided. All one can say is that mirror self-recognition allows for the possibility (immediate or eventual) of recognition of own and others' mental states.

Children's social environments also play an important role in helping children to learn about mental states. Language develops through participation in social encounters as parents and siblings speak to a child. The presence of siblings correlates with children's ToM (McAlister & Peterson, 2007, 2013; Perner, Ruffman, & Leekam, 1994; Ruffman, Perner, Naito, Parkin, & Clements, 1998) and children with greater self-awareness are more able to take advantage of sibling input (Taumoepeau & Reese, 2014). Likewise, connected talk with parents (Ensor & Hughes, 2008) and parental talk about mental states is helpful to children's subsequent ToM in typical development (Dunn, Brown, Slomkowski, Tesla, & Youngblade, 1991; Meins et al., 2003; Ruffman, Slade, & Crowe, 2002; Taumoepeau & Ruffman, 2006, 2008), in deaf children (Moeller & Schick, 2006), and in children with autism (Slaughter, Peterson, & Mackintosh, 2007).

Environmental influences

Environment is crucial to understanding individual differences in children's explicit ability to reason about mental states (Carpendale & Lewis, 2004; Hughes et al., 2005). In this section we propose ways in which the seemingly intractable problem of learning about mental states can be made tractable through the consideration of key features in children's social environment. Specifically, we discuss how children's understanding evolves from an implicit understanding of behaviour to an explicit understanding of mental states. We do not suggest that this is a definitive account of this process, but rather a pointer towards a balanced position on how children's understanding might develop.

Scaffolding a theory of mind

Wood and Middleton (1975) demonstrated that scaffolding a child's learning by providing instruction that is targeted just beyond the child's capability is most effective in helping children complete tasks they couldn't complete on their own. This is consistent with Vygotsky's (1978) zone of proximal development. Scaffolding is also useful for understanding how the environment can shape development from an implicit understanding of behaviour to an explicit understanding of mental states. We propose that conversation with significant caregivers, specifically conversation about mental states, plays a significant role in describing behaviours observed, for example, in many social routines in which children engage (Nelson, 2010). This doesn't occur as an all-or-nothing process, but rather parents engage in infant- and child-directed speech in a scaffolded fashion. Although parents of children of all ages tend to engage in all kinds of mental-state talk, the emphasis changes as children age. Thus, early conversational exchanges in infancy and toddlerhood tend to focus on infants' perceptions, then developing joint attention, then commenting on children's desires, then commenting on cognitions.

Evidence for this scaffold comes from several studies. First, mothers are more likely to use terms that refer to infants' perceptual states rather than their mental states (Beeghly, Bretherton, & Mervis, 1986; Slaughter, Peterson, & Carpenter, 2008). Moreover, mothers decreased their comments and references to their infants' perceptual states after children had acquired the capacity to engage in joint visual attention (Slaughter et al., 2008). Parents also are sensitive to gesture cues from infants in that they will increase references to infants' desires and intentions when children begin to engage in imperative pointing gestures (Slaughter et al., 2008). References to children's perceptual experiences are also differentially effective in predicting children's mental-state vocabulary in that mothers' references to infants' but not toddlers' perceptual states following children's pointing gestures are related to their acquisition of mental-state terms (Taumoepeau & Ruffman, in preparation). Commenting on infants' visual experiences, especially within the context of social routines, is a first step in helping children attend to a component of early subjective experiences, highlighting that people notice and attend to objects.

Children's volitional acts also provide fertile ground for mothers to comment on the child's subjective experience. Thus, Taumoepeau and Ruffman (2006, 2008) found that mothers talked more about the child's desires at 15 months of age, whereas the same mothers talked increasingly about their own thoughts and knowledge when the child was 24 months of age. These different kinds of maternal talk are also differentially effective. Maternal talk about the child's desires at 15 months of age is the most consistent correlate of 24-month-olds' ToM, whereas maternal talk about the child's desires as well as talk about her own thoughts and knowledge are both correlates of 33-month-olds' ToM. We argue that maternal talk about the child's desires helps young children focus on their salient internal experiences of desire, which then helps them to understand such states in other persons. Then, when they are older and possess a nascent understanding of desire as well as a more intact distinction between self and other, mothers up the ante and talk more about other people's cognitions. Indeed, a number of studies have shown that older children, who have consolidated their understanding of desires and emotions, are in a better position to benefit from talk that contrasts and explains cognitions (Adrián, Clemente, & Villanueva, 2007; Peterson & Slaughter, 2003; Slaughter et al., 2007).

A key question is: what triggers change in the way mothers talk to children? This question is difficult to answer because longitudinal studies typically employ a relatively lengthy gap of several months between time points, which constitutes a substantial portion of young children's life and in which many child abilities might evolve and influence maternal input.

One idea would be that children's acquisition of mental-state terms influences the way mothers talk. To this end, children begin to talk about desires before they talk about cognitions, with 68 per cent of 26-month-olds using "wanna" and only 22 per cent using "think" (Dale & Fenson, 1996). Leaving aside the issue of a potentially confounding third variable, this finding raises a chicken-and-egg problem as to what causes what: does the trend in maternal talk (talk about desires, then cognitions) stem from the language they observe in their children, or does the input from parents create the trend in children? Our findings are consistent with the latter possibility in that maternal mental-state talk predicted children's subsequent mental-state talk but not the reverse (Ruffman et al., 2002). If so, children's mental-state talk cannot be a trigger for the changes in maternal talk.

Another possibility is that children's use of personal pronouns (e.g., "I", "me") triggers mothers to up the ante, reducing their talk about the child and instead talking more about themselves. We obtained preliminary data to this end (Taumoepeau & Ruffman, 2008), but a replication and further exploration would be helpful.

A third possibility is that parents pick up on subtle indications of understanding in children and change their input as a result. One potential change might be children's growing independence at this time. In particular, there is evidence that mothers who use questions, suggestions or comments that relate to the activity in which 2-year-olds are engaged have children who are more independent at 4 years (Landry, Smith, Swank, & Miller-Loncar, 2000). Our suggestion is that this relation is likely in place earlier in development, such that mothers of 15-month-olds who comment on the child's current activity, including the child's desires, have children who are more independent at 2 years of age, and that because the children are more independent, the mother no longer feels the need to comment on the child or the child's desires, and so talks more about herself, including her own thoughts and knowledge. Further, because the mother has helped the child to understand her own desires at 15 months of age, the child is now in a better position to learn from talk about the mother's thoughts and knowledge at 2 years of age. Thus, growing independence might be one factor contributing to the change in maternal talk, although we suspect that there are other currently unidentified contributors.

Maternal mental-state talk in multiple contexts

Learning the meaning of mental-state terms is likely to be gradual. Bartsch and Wellman (1995) argued that initially children used such terms conversationally and then five months later use them to refer to mental states. We propose that children's initial use of mental-state terms is to refer to behaviours. This would be consistent with the idea that infants have an implicit theory of behaviour, as well as with research on children's general language acquisition, which shows that children tend to learn typical uses of words before they learn less typical uses. For instance, they learn that a family car is a more typical instance of "car" than a race car (Meints, Plunkett, & Harris, 1999; Meints, Plunkett, Harris, & Dimmock, 2002). Likewise, Nelson and Kessler-Shaw (2002) examined children's understanding of "know" and "think". Use of each verb occurs in distinct lexical frames. For instance, for "think", a mother might say "I think that X" or "Do you think that X?", whereas for "know" she might say "I don't know" or "Do you know . . .?" Nelson and Kessler-Shaw argue that restrictions in the use of such terms means that only *some* uses clearly refer to mental states. Subsequently, preschoolers learn primarily "*how* the terms are used in embedded discourse contexts rather than *what* the terms denote conceptually" (p. 50).

Thus, mere acquisition of a term does not mean that children understand everything about the concept denoted by that term, and the same is true of mental-state terms. Just as it is possible that infants' initial success on ToM tasks is underpinned by an understanding of behaviour rather than an understanding of mental states, it is possible that children's first use of mental-state terms is restricted to an understanding of the behaviours typically described but does not include full insight into the underlying mental states. Consistent with this idea, behaviours are salient even for 3–5-year-old children (Papafragou, Cassidy, & Gleitman, 2007). When given a false-belief scenario and asked to explain the meaning of a novel verb (e.g., *gorp*), children are more likely to infer it refers to an agent's action rather than a desire or belief. Thus, even if children can reflect on mental states by this age, their tendency to reflect on behaviours is well entrenched.

Children's early experiences of hearing and using terms such as "want" may be restricted to very limited behavioural contexts that are driven by the child's own social experiences. As children's language skills and social experiences evolve, their exposure to language that ascribes mental states to behaviour will also broaden. The idea is that initial understanding of a term such as "want" is likely to be piecemeal; children hear the term used to describe different behaviours and roughly associate it with each. However, the behaviours described can be very different (e.g., reaching for something: "He wants it"; a baby crying and pushing away food: "He doesn't want it"). Children might tolerate these inconsistencies initially by thinking of "wanting" as referring to a collection of different behaviours, without properly integrating the underlying meaning of "want" as referring to the mental state of desire.

Indeed, studies of children's scientific reasoning indicate that children initially disregard inconsistent data while maintaining prior beliefs and vacillating in their reasoning. Only later, as evidence piles up regarding inconsistencies in data, are they compelled to arrive at a new understanding that is in line with all data (Zimmerman, 2000). Likewise, the same is true of adult scientists (Kuhn, 1962), and we argue that acquisition of the meaning of mental-state terms might be similar. Multiple uses of "want" speed the process by eventually compelling children to look for a deeper link (the underlying mental state) that underlies the range of different behaviours. Having gained an insight into mental states, this would then likely help to bootstrap learning of other mental-state terms and the sign of such bootstrapping would be a more rapid onset in the acquisition of many mental-state terms in addition to "want". An older child's better general language ability and better social understanding (e.g. ability to benefit from maternal talk about the child's own desires) will help to scaffold learning, enabling the recognition of a deeper link entailing the underlying mental state of *wanting*.

Now consider the alternative espoused by most infancy researchers, that infants already understand mental states. Regardless of the context in which mothers use the term "want" – the child's "wanting", someone reaching, someone's display of positive or negative affect – the mental state should be salient. If so, using the term "want" in different contexts should be helpful, but no more than labelling similar actions in similar contexts, since in all cases the agent's mental state should be salient. On this account, one might predict that the total number of uses of "want" will be most helpful to the child rather than use of "want" in multiple contexts because each instance of using "want" should be equally helpful in assisting children to learn to apply the term to the salient mental state.

To explore this idea, we examined two age groups – 9–15 months (mean = 12 months) and 21–27 months (mean = 24 months) – at two time points, with Time 2 being 6 months later (Ruffman & Taumoepeau, submitted). Mothers could use the mental-state term "want" in five different contexts: to describe their own desires, to describe the child's desires, or to describe three different contexts in a picture book (people reaching for things, people reacting negatively toward something or people reacting positively toward something). As the dependent measure, we examined children's mental-state vocabulary at both time points because mental-state talk acts as a precursor to successful task performance (Pyers & Senghas, 2009) and because there are dozens of mental-state terms to provide a sensitive index of their social understanding, whereas ToM tasks are typically pass or fail.

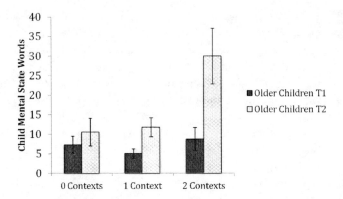

FIGURE 5.2 The relation of younger and older children's mental-state language to maternal use of *want* in 0, 1 or 2 contexts.

Our findings were *not* consistent with the view that infants already understand mental states (Figure 5.2). Independently of children's Time 1 language ability and the total number of times mothers used "want", older children benefitted most between Times 1 and 2 from maternal use of "want" in multiple contexts compared to a single context. Furthermore, we controlled for total number of maternal uses of "want", demonstrating that it is not simply that "want" in multiple contexts is associated with more talking about desire, but that it is use of "want" in different contexts that is most important. On average, children's mental-state terms grew from 7.95 to 27.45 when mothers used "want" in multiple contexts, whereas children's mental-state terms grew from 5.17 to 12.75 terms when mothers used "want" in a single context. This represents a gain of 19.50 terms versus 5.17 terms, that is, more than 2.5 times as many terms. In contrast, mothers' total use of "want" did not correlate with gains in children's mental-state vocabulary independently of use of "want" in multiple contexts.

To reiterate, we think this is because use of "want" in multiple contexts helped children to realise that "want" could not refer specifically to the act of reaching, or to the positive or negative affect displayed, because the behaviours described are so diverse. This would compel older children to infer that "want" must refer to something more general, that is, an underlying mental state. Further, it would bootstrap learning of additional mental-state terms as children then look for underlying mental states when hearing such terms used to describe different behaviours.

Intervening to facilitate ToM

Recently, we carried out an intervention study to examine further findings that certain kinds of talk are helpful for children's ToM (Taumoepeau & Ruffman, 2016). As described above, our longitudinal study found that maternal talk about the child's desires is most helpful for a 15-month-old child's subsequent ToM, whereas at 24 months, maternal talk about their own thoughts and knowledge also becomes important for children's subsequent ToM (Taumoepeau & Ruffman, 2006, 2008). Longitudinal studies are helpful for establishing whether a particular variable plays a causal role in facilitating children's ToM, but even better evidence is provided by intervention studies because potential confounding variables can be better controlled.

We examined 96 children aged 20–26 months old (mean = 21 months), assigning children to one of two conditions. In each condition mothers read a book to children several times a week over a 4-week period, on average, about 17 times. In one condition the book allowed mothers several opportunities to talk about their children's desires, and in the other condition the book allowed mothers opportunities to talk about their own thoughts and knowledge. Our children fell in between the two Time 1 ages – 15 and 24 months – in our longitudinal studies (Taumoepeau & Ruffman, 2006, 2008), and since mother talk about the child's desires was consistently beneficial in both studies (whereas mother talk about others' cognitions was only beneficial at 24 months), we expected the desire-training book would be most beneficial in the present study.

There have been several previous training studies that have intervened to increase children's exposure to mental-state talk. For instance, Lohmann and Tomasello (2003) showed 3-year-olds misleading objects, and highlighted their properties using terms such as "know" and "think". Ornaghi, Brockmeier, and Grazzani (2011) trained 3- and 4-year-olds using stories enriched with a variety of mental-state terms referring to emotions, desires and cognitions. In contrast, our children were much younger (mean = 1.83 years) and we specifically contrasted talk about the child's desires with talk about the mother's cognitions. Our aim was not simply to show that general mental-state talk is helpful, but to demonstrate that specific types of talk are most helpful at different times. Further, because previous intervention studies were conducted with 3- and 4-year-olds, they were not concerned with how insights such as self-recognition might mediate the benefits of maternal talk.

Before and after the intervention we assessed children's non-mental-state and mental-state language using mother report. We also examined children's ability to recognise themselves in a mirror. Mirror self-recognition will assist understanding that maternal talk about the child's own mental state refers unambiguously to herself. That is, recognition of a mirror image as "me" should assist recognition of an internal experience as belonging to "me", enabling greater benefit from maternal talk about the child's internal experiences. In contrast, a child who cannot identify herself in a mirror will have internal experiences without necessarily understanding that others may refer to these internal experiences and thus, will not gain as readily from maternal talk. Further, because what is likely to be salient to a young child is his or her internal state of wanting, it will help if a mother talks about the child's *desires* as opposed to some other mental state (e.g. knowing or thinking).

As anticipated, children benefitted more from maternal talk about the child's desires, and this was particularly so when they passed the mirror task (Figure 5.3). In contrast, children's gain when mothers talked about their own cognitions was

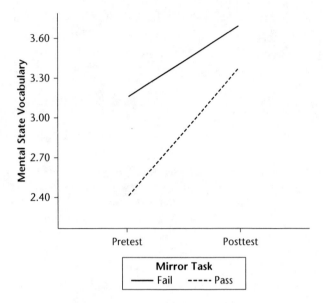

FIGURE 5.3   Children's pre- and posttest mental-state verbs in the desire condition as a function of self-awareness status, covarying for age in months, intervention period, and MacArthur Communicative Development Inventory (MCDI) vocabulary at pretest.

significantly less and there was no hint that mirror task performance affected the gain. We then removed all desire terms from the Time 2 measure of children's mental-state vocabulary in order to ensure that maternal reporting was not related to being placed in the desire condition (thereby highlighting the salience of desires and inflating their reporting of desire terms when reporting children's vocabulary). Still, children in this condition gained substantially more mental-state terms than children in the cognition condition. This suggests that maternal talk about the child's desires scaffolds children's general acquisition of mental-state terms (i.e. emotion and cognitive terms), rather than just their acquisition of the desire terms (*want, like*) that were used in training or desire terms generally.

A final finding was that children's acquisition of *non*-mental-state terms was unaffected by the desire training. This pattern of results is interesting because it suggests that maternal talk about the child's desires did not scaffold children's general language acquisition, or simply their acquisition of desire terms. Instead, maternal desire talk scaffolded children's knowledge about their own mental states (provided they had a self-concept demonstrated through passing the mirror task), which then helped children to understand that other mental-state terms referred to mental states, facilitating acquisition of these terms.

Overall, these findings provide specific information about *how* children learn about mental states, that is, the precise way in which scaffolding works. They demonstrate that at particular points in the child's development, specific types of mental-state talk are more efficacious than others, and that parental talk does not work in a vacuum. Rather, the efficacy of parental talk depends on the child's current point of development – a fine-tuning between parent and child.

Where to from here?

We can see at least two broad lines of research that follow from the findings we have obtained thus far. First, almost no one has studied the ways in which very young children (i.e. infants and toddlers) might learn about behaviours and mental states. Instead, mentalists have simply argued that it is implausible that infants could learn about such things. For instance, Surian, Caldi, and Sperber (2007) argued that, "evidence of where people last saw an object is not easily tracked in everyday experience" (p.585). Likewise, when considering infants' reasoning about unfair agents, Meristo and Surian (2014) argued that, "the detection of environmental regularities plays a minor role, if any at all". In our view, it is highly premature to dismiss the possibility of learning and conclude that infants understand mental states without careful examination of how infants' exposure to regularities in their environment and parental input might combine to help them learn (see also Hunnius & Bekkering, 2014). We are currently examining such phenomena.

Second, the role that mental-state conversations play in creating a scaffold between implicit and explicit mental-state understanding requires more attention. We have provided some pointers as to how the implicit understanding of behaviour can develop into an explicit understanding of mental states, through developmentally scaffolded talk. Further work, however, needs to take place in cultures that do not privilege the use of mental-state language in interactions with their children. For example, ethnographic work in certain Pacific cultures reveals a different style of parent–child interaction that is more directive than European/American communication style, and less child-centred and mind-oriented (Fonua, 2004; Morton, 1996; Ochs, 1982). A recent longitudinal study of ours conducted with a sample of families who identified with a range of Pacific cultures demonstrated that change in the trajectories of mental-state talk over the toddlerhood period was predicted by the extent to which the parents identified with their Pacific identity, with parents who identified strongly as Pacific using less cognitive talk over time (Taumoepeau, 2015). These types of studies are important because they provide information that might begin to explain cross-cultural differences in the age of acquisition on explicit ToM tasks (Callaghan et al., 2005; Lecce & Hughes, 2010; Liu, Wellman, Tardif, & Sabbagh, 2008; Mayer & Träuble, 2013; Shahaeian, Peterson, Slaughter, & Wellman, 2011; Wellman, Cross, & Watson, 2001), including a recent study of Samoan children showing that the majority of children under 8 years did not pass the false-belief task (Mayer & Träuble, 2013). Indeed, Heyes and Frith (2014) recently proposed that explicit mind-reading capability is a culturally specific skill and thus likely to reflect substantial variation.

Thus, further studies of the kind described above are needed to test the specific impact that conversations about mental states from toddlerhood to school age have on individual differences in ToM development. Future studies could specifically test how conversation about mental states bridges development from implicit understanding to explicit understanding, and if this bridge is consistently shown across cultures.

In summary, we started this chapter with a critique of studies that interpret infants' performance on implicit ToM tasks as reflecting innate understanding of mental states, and ended with a question regarding the role that culture plays in this development. We think it is right to consider this breadth of research because we cannot ignore the opportunity for learning within the intensely social experiences that human infants are exposed to from birth. We simply cannot rule out the possibility that infants reason about behaviour when succeeding in such tasks without recourse to a deeper understanding of the mental states that motivate this behaviour. We have proposed that understanding the role of the environment, and especially the experiences that infants have in listening to and using language within that environment, is key to understanding our fundamental capacity to engage with others at a mental level.

References

Adrián, J. E., Clemente, R. A., & Villanueva, L. (2007). Mothers' use of cognitive state verbs in picture-book reading and the development of children's understanding of mind: a longitudinal study. *Child Development, 78*, 1052–1067. doi: 10.1111/j.1467-8624.2007.01052.x.

Amsterdam, B. (1972). Mirror self-image reactions before age two. *Developmental Psychobiology, 5*, 297–305. doi: 10.1002/dev.420050403.

Baillargeon, R., Scott, R. M., & He, Z. (2010). False-belief understanding in infants. *Trends in Cognitive Sciences, 14*, 110–118. doi: 10.1016/j.tics.2009.12.006.

Baron-Cohen, S. (1997). *Mindblindness: An essay on autism and theory of mind.* Cambridge, MA: MIT Press.

Bartsch, K., & Wellman, H. (1995). *Children talk about the mind.* Oxford: Oxford University Press.

Beeghly, M., Bretherton, I., & Mervis, C. B. (1986). Mothers' internal state language to toddlers. *British Journal of Developmental Psychology, 4*, 247–261. doi: 10.1111/j.2044-835X.1986.tb01016.x.

Bischof-Koehler, D. (1991). The development of empathy in infants. In M. E. Lamb & H. Keller (Eds,), *Infant development: Perspectives from German speaking countries* (pp. 245–273). Hillsdale, NJ: Erlbaum.

Callaghan, T., Rochat, P., Lillard, A., Claux, M. L., Odden, H., Itakura, S., et al. (2005). Synchrony in the onset of mental-state reasoning: evidence from five cultures. *Psychological Science, 16*, 378–384. doi: 10.1111/j.0956-7976.2005.01544.x.

Carpendale, J. I. M., & Lewis, C. (2004). Constructing an understanding of mind: the development of children's social understanding within social interaction. *Behavioral and Brain Sciences, 27*, 79–96. doi: 10.1017/S0140525X04000032.

Carruthers, P. (2013). Mindreading in infancy. *Mind and Language, 28*, 141–172. doi: 10.1111/mila.12014.

Clements, W. A., & Perner, J. (1994). Implicit understanding of belief. *Cognitive Development, 9*, 377–395. http://dx.doi.org/ 10.1016/0885-2014(94)90012-4.

Dale, P. S., & Fenson, L. (1996). Lexical development norms for young children. *Behavioral Research Methods, Instruments, and Computers, 28,* 125–127. http://dx.doi.org/10.3758/BF03203646.

Dunn, J., Brown, J., Slomkowski, C., Tesla, C., & Youngblade, L. (1991). Young children's understanding of other peoples' feelings and beliefs: individual differences and their antecedents. *Child Development, 62,* 1352–1366. http://dx.doi.org/10.2307/1130811.

Ensor, R., & Hughes, C. (2008). Content or connectedness? Mother–child talk and early social understanding. *Child Development, 79,* 201–216. http://dx.doi.org/10.1111/j.1467-8624.2007.01120.x.

Fonua, S. (2004). '*Ko E Ako Lea 'a E Fanau Ta'u Nima 'i Tonga': Five-year old children's learning language practices at home and school in Tonga.* Unpublished PhD thesis, Victoria University.

Garnham, W. A., & Ruffman, T. (2001). Doesn't see, doesn't know: Is anticipatory looking really related to understanding of belief? *Developmental Science, 4,* 94–100. http://dx.doi.org/10.1111/1467-7687.00153.

He, Z., Bolz, M., & Baillargeon, R. (2011). False-belief understanding in 2.5-year-olds: evidence from violation-of-expectation change-of-location and unexpected-contents tasks. *Developmental Science, 14,* 292–305. doi: 10.1111/j.1467-7687.2010.00980.x.

Heyes, C. M. (2014). False belief in infancy: a fresh look. *Developmental Science, 17,* 647–659. doi: 10.1111/desc.12148.

Heyes, C. M., & Frith, C. D. (2014). The cultural evolution of mind reading. *Science, 20,* 1357–1363. doi: 10.1126/science.1243091.

Hughes, C., Jaffee, S. R., Happé, F., Taylor, A., Caspi, A., & Moffitt, T. E. (2005). Origins of individual differences in theory of mind: from nature to nurture? *Child Development, 76,* 356–370. doi: 10.1111/j.1467-8624.2005.00850_a.x.

Hunnius, S., & Bekkering, H. (2014). What are you doing? How active and observational experience shape infants' action understanding. *Philosophical Transactions of the Royal Society B, 369,* 20130490. doi: 10.1098/rstb.2013.0490.

Kuhn, T. S. (1962). *The structure of scientific revolutions.* Chicago, IL: University of Chicago Press.

Landry, S. H., Smith, K. E., Swank, P. R., & Miller-Loncar, C. L. (2000). Early maternal and child influences on children's later independent cognitive and social functioning. *Child Development, 71,* 358–375. doi: 10.1111/1467-8624.00150.

Lecce, S., & Hughes, C. (2010). The Italian job? Comparing theory of mind performance in British and Italian children. *British Journal of Developmental Psychology, 28,* 747–766. doi: 10.1348/026151009X479006.

Lewis, M., Sullivan, M. W., Stanger, C., & Weiss, M. (1989). Self development and self-conscious emotions. *Child Development, 60,* 146–156. doi: 10.2307/1131080.

Liu, D., Wellman, H. M., Tardif, T., & Sabbagh, M. A. (2008). Theory of mind development in Chinese children: a meta-analysis of false-belief understanding across cultures and languages. *Developmental Psychology, 44,* 523–531. doi: 10.1037/0012-1649.44.2.523.

Lohmann, H., & Tomasello, M. (2003). The role of language in the development of false belief understanding: a training study. *Child Development, 74,* 1130–1144. doi: 10.1111/1467-8624.00597.

Low, J. (2010). Preschoolers' implicit and explicit false-belief understanding: relations with complex syntactical mastery. *Child Development, 81,* 597–615. http://dx.doi.org/10.1111/j.1467-8624.2009.01418.x.

Luo, Y. (2011). Do 10-month-old infants understand others' false beliefs? *Cognition, 121,* 289–298. doi: 10.1016/j.cognition.2011.07.011.

Mayer, A., & Träuble, B. E. (2013). Synchrony in the onset of mental state understanding across cultures? A study among children in Samoa. *International Journal of Behavioral Development, 37*, 21–28. doi: 10.1177/0165025412454030.

McAlister, A. R., & Peterson, C. C. (2007). A longitudinal study of child siblings and theory of mind development. *Cognitive Development, 22*, 258–270. doi: 10.1016/j.cogdev. 2006.10.009.

McAlister, A. R., & Peterson, C. C. (2013). Siblings, theory of mind, and executive functioning in children aged 3–6 years: new longitudinal evidence. *Child Development, 84*, 1442–1458. doi: 10.1111/cdev.12043.

Meins, E., Fernyhough, C., Wainwright, R., Clark-Carter, D., Das Gupta, M., Fradley, E., et al. (2003). Pathways to understanding mind: construct validity and predictive validity of maternal mind-mindedness. *Child Development, 74*, 1194–1211. http://dx.doi.org/10.1111/1467-8624.00601.

Meints, K., Plunkett, K., & Harris, P. L. (1999). When does an ostrich become a bird? The role of typicality in early word comprehension. *Developmental Psychology, 35*, 1072–1078. doi: 10.1037//0012-1649.35.4.1072.

Meints, K., Plunkett, K., Harris, P. L., & Dimmock, D. (2002). What is 'on' and 'under' for 15-, 18-, and 24-month-olds? Typicality effects in early comprehension of spatial prepositions. *British Journal of Developmental Psychology, 20*, 113–130. doi: 10.1348/026151002166352.

Meristo, M., & Surian, L. (2014). Infants distinguish antisocial actions directed towards fair and unfair agents. *PLoSOne, 9*, e110553. doi: 10.1371/journal.pone.0110553.

Milligan, K., Astington, J. W., & Dack, L. A. (2007). Language and theory of mind: Meta-analysis of the relation between language ability and false-belief understanding. *Child Development, 78*, 622–646. doi: 10.1111/j.1467-8624.2007.01018.x.

Moeller, M. P., & Schick, B. (2006). Relations between maternal input and theory of mind understanding in deaf children. *Child Development, 77*, 751–766. http://dx.doi.org/10.1111/j.1467-8624.2006.00901.x.

Morin, A. (2011). Self-recognition, theory-of-mind, and self-awareness: what side are you on? *Laterality, 16*, 367–383. doi: 0.1080/13576501003702648.

Morton, H. (1996). *Becoming Tongan: An ethnography of childhood*. Honolulu: University of Hawaii Press.

Nelson, K. (2010). *Young minds in social worlds: Experience, meaning and memory*. Cambridge, MA: Harvard University Press.

Nelson, K., & Kessler-Shaw, L. (2002). Developing a socially shared symbolic system. In E. Amsel and J. P. Byrnes (Eds.), *Language, literacy and cognitive development: The development and consequences of symbolic communication* (pp. 27–57). Mahway, NJ: Erlbaum.

Ochs, E. (1982). Talking to children in Western Samoa. *Language in Society, 11*, 77–104. doi: 10.1017/S0047404500009040.

Ornaghi, V., Brockmeier, J., & Grazzani, I. (2011). The role of language games in children's understanding of mental states: a training study. *Journal of Cognition and Development, 12*, 239–259. doi: 10.1080/15248372.2011.563487.

Papafragou, A., Cassidy, K., & Gleitman, L. (2007). When we think about thinking: the acquisition of belief verbs. *Cognition, 105*, 125–165. doi: 10.1016/j.cognition.2006.09.008.

Perner, J. (2010). Who took the cog out of cognitive science? In P. A. Frensch & R. Schwarzer (Eds.). *Perception, attention, and action: International perspectives on psychological science* (Vol. 1, pp. 241–261). Hove, UK: Psychology Press.

Perner, J., & Ruffman, T. (2005). Infants' insight into the mind: how deep? *Science, 308*, 214–216. doi: 10.1126/science.1111656.

Perner, J., Ruffman, T., & Leekam, S. R. (1994). Theory of mind is contagious: you catch it from your siblings. *Child Development, 65,* 1228–1238. http://dx.doi.org/10.1111/j.1467-8624.1994.tb00814.x.

Peterson, C. C., & Slaughter, V. (2003). Opening windows into the mind: mothers' preferences for mental state explanations and children's theory of mind. *Cognitive Development, 18,* 399–429. doi: 10.1016/S0885-2014(03)00041-8.

Poulin-Dubois, D., & Chow, V. (2009) The effect of a looker's past reliability on infants' reasoning about beliefs. *Developmental Psychology, 45,* 1576–1582. doi: 10.1037/a0016715.

Pyers, J., & Senghas, A. (2009). Language promotes false-belief understanding: evidence from learners of a new sign language. *Psychological Science, 20,* 805–812. 10.1111/j.1467-9280.2009.02377.x.

Rochat, P. (2003). Five levels of self-awareness as they unfold early in life. *Consciousness and Cognition, 12,* 717–731. doi: 10.1016/S1053-8100(03)00081-3.

Ruffman, T. (2014). To belief or not belief: children's theory of mind. *Developmental Review, 34,* 265–293. doi: 10.1016/j.dr.2014.04.001.

Ruffman, T., Garnham, W., Import, A., & Connolly, D. (2001). Does eye gaze indicate implicit knowledge of false belief? Charting transitions in knowledge. *Journal of Experimental Child Psychology, 80,* 201–224. doi: 10.1006/jecp.2001.2633.

Ruffman, T., Perkins, C., & Taumoepeau, M. (2012). Statistical learning as a basis for social understanding in children. *British Journal of Developmental Psychology, 30,* 87–104. doi: 10.1111/j.2044-835X.2011.02045.x.

Ruffman, T., & Perner, J. (2005). Do infants really understand false belief? *Trends in Cognitive Sciences, 9,* 462–463. doi: 10.1016/j.tics.2005.08.001.

Ruffman, T., Perner, J., Naito, M., Parkin, L., & Clements, W. A. (1998). Older (but not younger) siblings facilitate false belief understanding. *Developmental Psychology, 34,* 161–174. http://dx.doi.org/10.1037//0012-1649.34.1.161.

Ruffman, T., Slade, L., & Crowe, E. (2002). The relation between children's and mothers' mental state language and theory-of-mind understanding. *Child Development, 73,* 734–751. http://dx.doi.org/10.1111/1467-8624.00435.

Ruffman, T., & Taumoepeau, M. (in press). *Maternal talk about desires in multiple contexts and children's acquisition of mental state terms.* University of Otago.

San Juan, V., & Astington, J. W. (2012). Bridging the gap between implicit and explicit understanding: how language development promotes the processing and representation of false belief. *British Journal of Developmental Psychology, 30,* 105–122. doi: 10.1111/j.2044-835X.2011.02051.x.

Scott, R. M., Baillargeon, R., Song, H.-J., & Leslie, A. M. (2010). Attributing false beliefs about non-obvious properties at 18 months. *Cognitive Psychology, 61,* 366–395. doi: 10.1016/j.cogpsych.2010.09.001.

Shahaeian, A., Peterson, C. C., Slaughter, V., & Wellman, H. M. (2011). Culture and the sequence of steps in theory of mind development. *Developmental Psychology, 47,* 1239–1247. doi: 10.1037/a0023899.

Slaughter, V., Peterson, C. C., & Carpenter, M. (2008). Maternal talk about mental states and the emergence of joint visual attention. *Infancy, 13,* 640–659. doi: 10.1080/15250000802458807.

Slaughter, V., Peterson, C. C., & Mackintosh, E. (2007). Mind what mother says: narrative input and theory of mind in typical children and those on the autism spectrum. *Child Development, 78,* 839–858. http://dx.doi.org/10.1111/j.1467- 8624.2007.01036.x.

Song, H., & Baillargeon, R. (2008). Infants' reasoning about others' false perceptions. *Developmental Psychology, 44,* 1789–1795. doi: 10.1037/a0013774.

Surian, L., Caldi, S., & Sperber, D. (2007). Attribution of beliefs by 13-month-old infants. *Psychological Science, 18,* 580–586. doi: 10.1111/j.1467-9280.2007.01943.x.

Surian, L., & Geraci, A. (2012). Where will the triangle look for it? Attributing false beliefs to a geometric shape at 17 months. *British Journal of Developmental Psychology, 30,* 30–44. doi: 10.1111/j.2044-835X.2011.02046.x.

Taumoepeau, M. (2015). From talk to thought: strength of ethnic identity and caregiver mental state talk predict social understanding in preschoolers. *Journal of Cross-Cultural Psychology 46,* 1169–1190.

Taumoepeau, M., & Reese, E. (2014). Understanding the self through siblings: self-awareness mediates the sibling effect on social understanding. *Social Development, 23,* 1–18. doi: 10.1111/sode.12035.

Taumoepeau, M., & Ruffman, T. (2006). Mother and infant talk about mental states relates to desire language and emotion understanding. *Child Development, 77,* 465–481. doi: 10.1111/j.1467-8624.2006.00882.x.

Taumoepeau, M., & Ruffman, T. (2008). Stepping stones to others' minds: maternal talk relates to child mental state language and emotion understanding at 15, 24, and 33 months. *Child Development, 79,* 284–302. doi: 10.1111/j.1467- 8624.2007.01126.x.

Taumoepeau, M., & Ruffman, T. (2016). Self-awareness moderates the relation between maternal mental state language and children's mental state vocabulary. *Journal of Experimental Child Psychology, 144,* 114–129.

Taumoepeau, M., & Ruffman, T. (in press). *Maternal mental state talk within gesture contexts scaffolds children's knowledge of mental state vocabulary.* University of Otago.

Vygotsky, L. (1978). *Mind in society.* Cambridge, MA: Harvard University Press.

Wang, B., Low, J., Jing, Z., & Qinghua, Q. (2012). Chinese preschoolers' implicit and explicit false-belief understanding. *British Journal of Developmental Psychology, 30,* 123–140. http://dx.doi.org/10.1111/j.2044-835X.2011.02052.x.

Wellman, H. M., Cross, D., & Watson, J. (2001). Meta-analysis of theory-of-mind development: the truth about false belief. *Child Development, 72,* 655–684. doi: 10.1111/ 1467-8624.00304.

Wood, D., & Middleton, D. (1975). A study of assisted problem-solving. *British Journal of Psychology, 66,* 181–191. doi: 10.1111/j.2044-8295.1975.tb01454.x.

Zimmerman, C. (2000). The development of scientific reasoning skills. *Developmental Review, 20,* 99–149. doi: 10.1006/drev.1999.0497.

PART II

Atypical developmental contexts

6

THE ROLE OF INSTITUTIONALIZATION IN THEORY OF MIND

Bilge Selcuk and N. Meltem Yucel

To know what is atypical we must have knowledge of what is typical, and to understand what is typical, we must examine the atypical; these are the basic premises in developmental psychology and developmental psychopathology (Cicchetti, 2013). The literature on theory of mind (ToM) is rooted in both. Questions that gave rise to this book started with the work of Premack and Woodruff, published in 1978, which revealed that chimpanzees had an understanding of goal-directed behavior. At a similar time, the discovery that people with autism have deficits in mental-state understanding also increased scientific interest in ToM (Baron-Cohen, Leslie, & Frith, 1985; Rutter, 1983). Developmental psychopathology emerged as a new discipline (Cicchetti, 1984) that aims to unravel the pathways toward typical and atypical outcomes, by focusing on biological, environmental, social, and cognitive influences. Numerous research followed these early pioneering studies in the next decades; and among these, the work of Candi Peterson sped ahead with its focus on different populations, including children with typical development from different cultures (Shahaeian, Nielsen, Peterson, & Slaughter, 2014) as well as children with blindness (Peterson, Peterson, & Webb, 2000) and autism (Peterson, 2002; Peterson & Siegal, 2000; Peterson, Slaughter, Peterson, & Premack, 2013). And, most importantly, to unravel the processes of development in mind reading, Peterson conducted various studies on ToM in deaf children who were native signers, late signers, or who had cochlear implants (Peterson & Siegal, 2000). These studies emphasized the role of environment and social interaction, particularly exposure to conversation, in ToM development (Peterson & Siegal, 1999).

In this chapter, we focus on ToM in another atypical development context, that is, child-rearing institutions. As we describe in detail in the following pages, child-rearing institutions (sometimes called orphanages) provide a distinct, non-normative environment due to the lack of a stable caregiver, lack of stimulating materials (e.g., educational materials and toys), and differences in composition of the rearing context (e.g., characterized mainly by many similar-aged children living together with few adults) and conversational interactions with caregivers (Hakimi-Manesh, Mojdehi, & Tashakkori, 1984; Muhamedrahimov, 1999). For many decades, research which investigated development of institution-reared children helped us better understand the mechanisms of normative development and developmental psychopathology (e.g., Beckett et al., 2006; Kreppner et al., 2007; Lawler, Hostinar, Mliner, & Gunnar, 2014; MacLean, 2003; Rutter et al., 1999; Stellern, Esposito, Mliner, Pears, & Gunnar, 2014). Although at first sight the two literatures look distinct, the findings in the above-mentioned literature on children with physical disabilities and autism are also relevant for elucidating the mechanisms of influence in development of institution-reared children. Another literature which is helpful to understand the development of institution-reared children is the one on maltreated children (e.g., Cicchetti & Ng, 2014). In this chapter, we have a look at these literatures to better understand the mind-reading abilities of institution-reared children. But first, we briefly focus on another relevant literature, the literature on sibling and adult influences on ToM development in normative populations, and then give a summary of the literature on ToM development in children with physical disabilities and maltreated children. And then we provide information about child-rearing institutions and review the limited literature that investigates mental-state understanding in this child population. Despite having some commonalities with maltreated, deaf, and autistic children, institution-reared children have other, unique experiences which make them distinct, so that studies in this field provide valuable information on the influence of early context in the development of mental-state understanding.

Importance of sibling and adult interaction for ToM development

The importance of early environment and relationships for child development has been shown for many decades. Children's understanding of the mind is formed through the social interactions they are involved in (Carpendale & Lewis, 2004). The rate of acquisition of mental-state understanding is linked with variations in social circumstances and experiences. The literature, in general, suggests that the presence of siblings (McAlister & Peterson, 2013; Ruffman, Perner, Naito, Parkin, & Clements, 1998) predicts higher ToM scores for young children, over and above the influence of chronological age and language abilities. It is thought that sibling relations include certain experiences that increase children's access to others' minds, such as engaging in pretend play, disputing and cooperating, and overhearing parental talk with siblings (Harris, 2005; Randell & Peterson, 2009; Ruffman, Perner, & Parkin, 1999).

Studies have also underlined the importance of parent characteristics (e.g., education, verbal fluency), behaviors, and mother–child interaction for ToM development. Specifically it was found that mothers' responsivity (Fónagy, Redfern, & Charman, 1997; Symons & Clark, 2000), discussion of situations by referring to desires, feelings (Ruffman et al., 1999), and mental states (Ensor & Hughes, 2008; Peterson & Slaughter, 2003; Ruffman, Slade, & Crowe, 2002) were related to increased ToM in children.

For optimal development, one key factor in the environment is, without a doubt, linguistic input and stimulation. These studies, which mostly include typically developing children, highlight the importance of engaging in conversations with the child for the early development of understanding other people's minds and emotions (de Rosnay & Hughes, 2006; Dunn & Brophy, 2005; Peterson & Siegal, 1999; Taumoepeau & Ruffman, 2008). Another line of research in the ToM literature explores the mechanisms of ToM acquisition in children with atypical or non-normative characteristics.

Studying atypically developing children to understand the role of environment on ToM

Research with special groups of children has made a substantial contribution to our understanding of child development, including ToM. Studies on maltreated children have highlighted the long-term impact of the environment on social-cognitive development (Kim-Spoon, Rogosch, & Cicchetti, 2013; Rogosch, Cicchetti, Shields, & Toth, 1995). Various findings indicate that maltreated children have difficulties on false-belief understanding (Cicchetti, Rogosch, Maughan, Toth, & Bruce, 2003; Pears & Fisher, 2005) and on the early indicators of mentalizing ability such as joint attention and use of mental-state language (Beeghly & Cicchetti, 1994). Luke and Banerjee's meta-analysis (2013) also revealed that parental maltreatment had significant adverse effects on children's social and emotional understanding, and this effect was stronger for younger children (i.e., early and middle childhood). One of the proposed mechanisms for such relations is that abusive parenting during early neurobiological development contributes to neuropathological connections and inhibitory control skills (Pears, Fisher, Bruce, Kim, & Yoerger, 2010), which underlie deficits in ToM (Rogosch et al., 1995). Another explanation focuses on the low quality of parent–child communication in maltreatment contexts; these homes are characterized by a lack of parental consistency, empathy, and sensitivity, which all discourage children from discussing their feelings, desires, and thoughts, contributing to delays in ToM (Cicchetti et al., 2003).

Studies with deaf children have also emphasized the role of the environment in ToM development. Peterson and her colleagues' research shows that orally deaf children, late signers, and children with high-functioning autism all have delays in ToM development, whereas typically developing children and deaf children who are native signers do not (Peterson, 2002; Slaughter, Peterson, & Mackintosh, 2007). It is widely accepted that children's access to conversation, especially early conversations about abstract ideas and beliefs, provides the cognitive input that is necessary for ToM development (Peterson & Siegal, 1999, 2000).

Development of institution-reared children

Children's interactions with significant others in their microsystems (i.e., institutions and settings in which a child personally interacts) are critical for the child's development. Under normal circumstances, the typical context of development for children is home, and in this fundamental microsystem, the most significant interactions are those with parents and siblings (Dunn, 1983). But children do not always grow up in individual homes, and are not always reared by their parents or within the context of a family.

For various reasons, including parental death, chronic and severe psychiatric problems, mental retardation, imprisonment, abandonment due to severe poverty, homelessness, physical or sexual abuse, and prostitution, children can be taken into the protection of the state (Browne, 2005; Munoz-Hoyos et al., 2001). In many countries such as France, the UK (Browne, 2005), and the USA, children who cannot be cared for by their parents are placed in foster care or are adopted (Child Welfare Information Gateway, 2013). But there are still some countries where institutions provide a primary rearing context for vulnerable children, and Turkey is one of them. In Turkey, some children in institutions are abandoned when they are born; they are sometimes left by the mother or other family members at the institutions. These are sometimes babies who are born out of wedlock to underprivileged women. So, not all the children in the institutions are "orphans," but all have had some sort of traumatic experience.

Despite the differences in the nature and intensity of these traumatic experiences, all the children in institutions are from extremely poor families. This increases the likelihood that they were exposed to one or more of the prenatal or early-care risks like exposure to teratogens in the prenatal period, prenatal malnourishment, premature birth, or abandonment right after birth or at a young age (Miller, 2005).

Child-rearing institutions are typically deprived environments characterized by a high child–staff ratio, limited stimulation, and an unstable and restricted interaction with care providers (Hakimi-Manesh et al., 1984; The St. Petersburg–USA Orphanage Research Team, 2005). Peer relations are also interrupted because relocation between different institutions is common (Kaler & Freeman, 1994). Children generally live among large groups where they outnumber their caregivers and face several different caregivers every day. The turnover rate for caregivers working at institutions is also very high. One of the striking examples of discontinuity comes from three orphanages in St. Petersburg, Russia, where reports reveal that institutionalized children are exposed to about 50–100 caregivers by 2 years of age (The St. Petersburg–USA Orphanage Research Team, 2005). Such a high number of different caregivers makes it impossible to establish a consistent and meaningful interaction between caregivers and children. Many institutionalized children have very limited one-to-one interaction and very little communication with their care providers (Muhamedrahimov, 1999), which significantly restricts their opportunity to have conversations with the caregivers about abstract ideas, beliefs, or feelings.

Many, if not all, institutionalized children are children who were exposed to some form of maltreatment at an early stage of their lives (Miller, 2005). Although these children may get necessary nutrition in some cases, institutions are almost always characterized by a shortage of toys, especially educational toys and materials, thereby providing less enriched care for its residents.

Not surprisingly, research shows that children reared in institutions have notable difficulties in almost all domains (Juffer et al., 2011). They have more health problems, higher levels of anxiety and other psychiatric disorders (Zeanah et al., 2009), attachment disorder (Smyke, Dumitrescu, & Zeanah, 2002), as well as overfriendliness and attention-seeking behaviors (Chisholm, Carter, Ames, & Morison, 1995; Hodges & Tizard, 1989).

A delay in cognitive and social development plays a part in the academic difficulties these children face at school (Hodges & Tizard, 1989; Vorria, Rutter, Pickles, Wolkind, & Hobsbaum, 1998b). Deficits in executive function, inattention, hyperactivity, conduct problems, and delays in language skills are widely reported (Colvert et al., 2008; Rutter, Kreppner, O'Connor, & The English and Romanian Adoptees (ERA) Study Team, 2001; Smyke et al., 2002; Stevens et al., 2008). They experience difficulties in emotion understanding compared with never-institutionalized children (Camras, Perlman, Wismer Fries, & Pollak, 2006). However, sociocognitive understanding is far less investigated in institutionalized children compared to other developmental outcomes, such as intelligence, attention, self-regulation, and social behaviors such as externalizing and internalizing problems.

One exception was a study that examined ToM in children with an early institutionalization experience carried out by Tarullo, Bruce, and Gunnar (2007). They compared 6- and 7-year-old, post-institutionalized children with children reared by their biological parents in the USA. The children in the post-institutionalized group were born in one of nine different countries and internationally adopted; they had spent 12–36 months in institutional care and at the time the research was conducted had spent 3–6.5 years in the USA. Results of the Tarullo et al. study (2007) revealed that the post-institutionalized children showed significant delays in false-belief understanding (measured by one task) compared to the parent-reared American children. The results indicated that, "after controlling for verbal ability, post-institutionalized group membership was still related to delays in false-belief understanding" (Tarullo et al., 2007, p. 70). Tarullo et al. interpreted this finding as showing an association between institutional care and false-belief understanding development. The authors noted that none of the specific pre-adoption experiences "assessed – including prenatal exposure to alcohol and drugs, prenatal nourishment, preterm birth, physical abuse and neglect, social neglect, country of origin and age at adoption – were related to false belief understanding" (Tarullo et al., 2007, p. 71). Nevertheless, similar to all other studies in this field, the data on children's pre-adoption experience were based on retrospective reports of the adoptive parents who did not have sufficient knowledge of children's pre-adoption life. In many studies, researchers (Gunnar, van Dulmen, & the International Adoption Project Team, 2007; Hawk & McCall, 2011; Rutter et al., 2001) showed that the age of adoption and the duration of institutionalization are significantly related to children's developmental outcomes. This was not supported in the Tarullo et al. (2007) study.

In another study, Colvert et al. (2008) examined ToM in three groups of adopted children: Romanian adoptees in the UK with and without an experience of institutional care, and within-UK adoptees. These three groups showed significant variance in the time of adoptive placement, with the mean age ranging from 2.5 to 30.4 months. ToM was measured when the child was 11 years old, with one task (the Strange Stories Task). The results showed that the Romanian adoptees with an experience of institutional care displayed deficits in ToM compared with Romanian children adopted from their families and within-UK adoptees. The degree of ToM deficit was also larger for children who were adopted after 6 months of age. These findings were interpreted as an indication of the long-term adverse effects of profound early deprivation on ToM.

The literature in general reveals significant heterogeneity in the cognitive abilities (Colvert et al., 2008; Rutter, O'Connor, & The English and Romanian Adoptees Study Team, 2004) and social-emotional functioning of institution-reared children (Camras et al., 2006; Vorria, Rutter, Pickles, Wolkind, & Hobsbaum, 1998a). This heterogeneity might be due to various factors, including the level and duration of deprivation and the child's age at adoptive placement. It has been found that there are significant differences even in the interaction styles of caregivers. For example, American caregivers from family child-care homes were reported to be more responsive toward children, and they read more to children compared to caregivers working at Russian orphanages (The St. Petersburg–USA Orphanage Research Team, 2005). However, we believe it is worth noting that the findings in the literature of institutionalized children mostly pertain to *post-institutionalized* samples, which means that these children *do not live in the institution any longer* but have been adopted (Bauer, Hanson, Pierson, Davidson, & Pollak, 2009; Castle et al., 1999; Colvert et al., 2008; Hodges & Tizard, 1989; Rutter et al., 1999, 2001; Tarullo et al., 2007) or live with a foster family (e.g., Bos, Fox, Zeanah, & Nelson, 2009). There are only a few studies that present data on the development of children who are *still in institutional care* (Kaler & Freeman, 1994; Sloutsky, 1997; Vorria et al., 1998a, 1998b). These are mostly the institutions of the Eastern Bloc countries such as Romania, Ukraine, or Russia, and also Greece. However, these studies have not really focused on ToM, but rather on general cognitive abilities or IQ.

On an individual level, not much is known about why some institutionalized children continue to show delays, whereas others perform at the developmentally expected levels (Tarullo et al., 2007). In order to understand the causes of heterogeneity in developmental outcomes, early-care risk factors including child-care provider must be examined. For ToM specifically, it might also be useful to examine the main developmental precursors of social cognition such as language (de Rosnay & Hughes, 2006; Milligan, Astington, & Dack, 2007) and executive function (Devine & Hughes, 2014; Frye, Zelazo, & Burack, 1998; Moses & Tahiroglu, 2010; Razza & Blair, 2009). To investigate mental-state understanding in institutionalized children, we conducted two different studies in Turkey. In both studies, we compared home-reared children from different socioeconomic backgrounds with children who still lived in institutions, differing from the studies conducted with foster-care children or children who were adopted and had left the adverse rearing environments behind a considerable time ago.

Theory of mind in institution-reared children in Turkey

In our first study (Yağmurlu, Berument, & Celimli, 2005), institutionalized children living in a boarding home were compared to home-reared children coming from low- and middle-socioeconomic backgrounds. It was anticipated that if children who live in institutions are more at risk than those reared in low-socioeconomic status (SES) homes, then they would perform worse than children from low- and middle-SES homes. However, if it is the case that being among many peers facilitates the development of ToM, then children living at institutions should perform better than children raised in low- and middle-SES families. The Yağmurlu et al. study was conducted in one large boarding home in Ankara (the capital of Turkey), and included many children between the ages of 0 and 6 years. About 42 children resided on each floor, where two adults were present at a time. These children entered the institution when they were between 8 and 66 months old (mean = 43 months, sᴅ = 16), and the total time they spent living in the institution ranged from 7 to 66 months (mean = 24 months, sᴅ = 16). In both low-SES and middle-SES parent-reared samples, approximately 40 percent of the children had no siblings. And, in both samples, at least 60 percent of the children had at least four adults living in the household, with the family permanently. The average adult–child ratio for low-SES and middle-SES groups was 2.38 (sᴅ = 1.63) and 2.48 (sᴅ = 1.17), respectively.

The Turkish Peabody Picture Vocabulary Test (Katz, Demir, Onen, Uzlukaya, & Uludag, 1972) was used to measure receptive language, and Raven's Colored Progressive Matrices (Raven, 1938) was administered to measure non-verbal intelligence. In order to assess ToM, one deception task (Ruffman, Olson, Ash, & Keenan, 1993) and three false-belief tasks were used: the Changed Location false-belief task and Unexpected Contents task (see Appendix), plus the Misinformation story (Perner, Ruffman, & Leekam, 1994). Analyses of children belonging to the same age groups revealed that children raised in institutions were significantly different than those raised in low- and middle-SES families in terms of their developmental outcomes. Even though both low-SES and institution-reared groups were much the same on the language and non-verbal intelligence measures, institution-reared children scored lower on ToM compared to low-SES children. Children living at institutions also had lower language and ToM scores compared to the middle-SES group. This difference in ToM score was not likely due to

SES because, although the middle-SES sample performed better on the non-verbal intelligence and language measures compared to the low-SES sample, they did not differ on ToM.

The results of regression analysis further revealed that institution rearing predicted a lower level of ToM, even when differences in age, socioeconomic background, language, and non-verbal intelligence were accounted for. In addition, institutional rearing was more disadvantageous than low SES, and home-rearing differences due to SES (middle- vs. low-SES) did not predict the development of ToM.

These results show that institutionalized children are disadvantaged in the development of their ToM, but that SES is not the primary cause. Instead, what institutionalized children lack is adult contact, which, as summarized above, is important for ToM development. For this reason, we used regression to examine whether the adult–child ratio affected children's ToM. The results showed a significant increase in explained variance; adult–child ratio significantly predicted ToM over and above the child's age, SES, language and non-verbal intelligence for the institutionalized children ($\beta = 0.21$, $p = 0.03$), but not for the middle-SES parent-reared children ($\beta = -0.08$, NS). The predictive value of adult–child ratio was notable for the low-SES parent-reared children ($\beta = 0.30$, $p = 0.11$), but did not reach significance probably due to low sample size (Yağmurlu et al., 2005).

In sum, the Yağmurlu et al. (2005) study revealed that children raised at home performed better than those raised at institutions on ToM tasks, showing a context effect. Even after accounting for differences in child variables, living in institutions predicted lower level of ToM scores, while being raised in a middle-SES family did not individually predict ToM. This finding showed that institutions are more disadvantageous compared to low-SES family context; here the likely causal variable was the lack of contact with adults, and that differences in SES did not significantly predict ToM development.

In a more recent study (Yağmurlu, 2013), executive function was assessed to explain the heterogeneity in ToM development in institutionalized children. Many research findings show that institutional care is a risk factor for hyperactivity and inattention (O'Connor, Bredenkamp, Rutter, & the English and Romanian Adoption Study Team, 1999; Rutter et al., 2001; Stevens et al., 2008). In addition, the Cognitive Complexity Theory (Frye et al., 1998) and many research findings point to executive function, attention, and inhibitory control as important for ToM (Devine & Hughes, 2014).

In this study, we collected data from 102 3–6-year-old preschool children living in four different child-rearing institutions located in three different cities in Turkey. As the Ministry of Family and Social Policies established and operated all the institutions in Turkey, all four had identical regulations and similar furniture. Yet they were not exactly the same; there were some differences in building type (flats versus houses), facilities, and the child–staff ratio. The child–staff ratio in the Ankara institution was, for example, significantly higher (6.64) than the child–staff ratio in the two Istanbul institutions (4.35 and 4.39).

In this study, a comprehensive screening instrument was completed by the child's primary care provider in the institution. Ten children who were found to have developmental delay were not given the other tasks. None of the children in the sample had any chronic health problems. The Turkish Expressive and Receptive Language Test (Berument & Güven, 2010), which is the Turkish equivalent of the Peabody Picture Vocabulary Test, was used to assess receptive language. Executive function was measured by the day–night task (Gerstadt, Hong, & Diamond, 1994) and the peg-tapping task (Diamond & Taylor, 1996). To measure children's understanding of different mental states, the Theory of Mind Scale of Wellman and Liu (2004) was used (see Appendix). The results showed that age of placement and duration of institutionalization were not significantly related to any of the developmental outcomes of children assessed in this study (Yağmurlu, 2013), consistent with the results of Tarullo et al. (2007). But the child–caregiver ratio was significantly and negatively ($r = -0.21$, $p < 0.05$) associated with ToM after children's age was controlled. Regression analysis also revealed that children's age, receptive language, and the caregiver–child ratio were the three variables that significantly predicted the ToM score.

In the second year of the study, data were collected from 73 children, as some children were adopted within that time period and some were reunited with their families. In the remaining children, hierarchical regression analysis indicated that a lower child–caregiver ratio was associated with a higher ToM score one year later, even after the abilities associated with ToM such as language and executive function were taken into account. The path from caregiver–child ratio to ToM was not mediated by executive function or receptive language, but the direct path from adult–caregiver ratio to ToM was significant. One possibility is that caregivers who are responsible for fewer children have more chance to communicate with the child and use more mental-state discourse, causal discourse, feeling-state talk, etc., which has a positive influence on children's ToM development (de Rosnay & Hughes, 2006; Ruffman et al., 2002).

In the next step of the study (Yağmurlu, 2013), developmental outcomes of the parent-reared children ($n = 100$) were compared with those of the institution-reared children. When differences in age were controlled, parent-reared children had better ToM scores than institution-reared children. But the differences on executive function and language were not significant.

In summary, both studies that were conducted in Turkey (Yağmurlu, 2013; Yağmurlu et al., 2005) contributed to the limited literature on ToM development in deprived contexts, and pointed at the impeding influence of an institutional rearing. Although today none of the Turkish child-rearing institutions have those extremely impoverished and inhumane conditions observed in Romanian orphanages, they still have many aspects that are very disadvantageous for healthy development. Institutions lack stimulating materials such as books and educational toys; children do not have access to rich linguistic stimulation. In such a deprived environment, adult–child interaction might be even more important (Pollak et al., 2010). However, caregivers in these institutions have limited interaction with children, and when they do interact, it is usually to control, instruct, and forbid, all of which have been shown to be inversely related to the kind of perspective-taking discourse (Frampton, Perlman, & Jenkins, 2009) likely to facilitate a ToM.

In both studies conducted in Turkey (Yağmurlu, 2013; Yağmurlu et al., 2005), institutionalized children's ToM ability displayed a significant increase as the adult–child ratio increased. In Yağmurlu et al. (2005), the adult–child ratio was linked to ToM in the low-SES group but not the middle-SES group. It is possible that in adequate child-rearing contexts – that is, in families with at least a middle SES – the child–adult ratio may not be critical because the quality of interaction with the parent is typically higher. Having a high quality of interaction with one or both parents might be sufficient to provide the necessary stimulation to facilitate socio-cognitive understanding. Research has revealed that family background has a significant, positive influence on children's ToM (Hughes et al., 2005). This finding requires further investigation, but there is supporting evidence from another study that was conducted nationwide in Turkey. In a recent paper, Baydar et al. (2014) showed the positive contribution of extrafamilial support to young children's ($n = 1017$) receptive vocabulary under adverse conditions. It was found that, in families with the highest levels of risk, specifically in families with high economic distress and high maternal depression jointly present, support by the extended family and neighbors for caring for the child protected children's vocabulary development against these adverse conditions. At the same time, similar to Yağmurlu et al. (2005), getting support from the extended family and neighbors did not contribute to language development in middle or high SES.

The two studies conducted in Turkish child-rearing institutions suggested that the deficiency in mental-state understanding can be partly compensated for by adult–child interaction despite impoverished material stimulation. It appears that the adult–child ratio is most significant for children who live in disadvantaged environments. Using observational data may highlight the relative contribution of different stimulating agents in these contexts. However, this cannot be accomplished in studies conducted in institutions in Turkey, as using observational measures (via any form of audiotaping and video recording) is strictly forbidden.

Another limitation of research on institutionalized children is that children's personal information with regard to their pre-institution experiences is either not known or kept strictly confidential. To our knowledge, there are no studies that have adequate and accurate information about these children's pre-institutionalization and even pre-adoption experiences. Even so, some researchers argue that early, adverse circumstances in the institutions put children at risk for developmental problems above and beyond their pre-institution experiences. Overcoming these limitations would inform us better about specific influences of institutional rearing.

It is also noteworthy that institutionalized children do not seem to benefit from living with lots of children (e.g., Yağmurlu, 2013; Yağmurlu et al., 2005), suggesting that the positive influence of sibling interactions might be limited to normative contexts, where there is continual interaction with adults and where children who are in interaction do not typically have delayed development.

Interactions with children are helpful, but mainly when an adult is around to comment (e.g., on a sibling's desires, feelings, or other mental states). Findings on sibling relations, adult–child interaction, maltreatment, deafness, autism, and post-institutionalized children are all helpful in illuminating the factors contributing to children's developing ToM, yet this help is also limited. In particular, elucidating the mechanisms of development for children who grow in institutions has unique challenges; these challenges are partly due to restrictions imposed on the researcher (e.g., no video- or audiotaping, no pre-institution history) and partly due to the heterogeneity of these children's experiences. This means we can just "infer" the role of institutional rearing, with an erroneous presumption that children's pre-institutionalization experience is uniform.

Finally, it seems important to recognize that ToM ability might be particularly important for institution-reared children. These children display indiscriminate friendliness to adults (Chisholm et al., 1995; Hodges & Tizard, 1989), whereas understanding intentions and manipulation is protective against abuse. ToM is also significantly related with emotional difficulties, depression, social withdrawal, and externalizing behaviors (Inoue, Yamada, & Kanba, 2006; Werner, Cassidy, & Juliano, 2006), characteristics that are reported highly in institution-reared children. ToM is, of course, only one of the many factors that contribute to these undesirable outcomes. But it is one that we can potentially intervene in, and help improve, through different ways – via educating the care providers and one-to-one training sessions with children. To this end, the literature indicates that both preschool-aged (Appleton & Reddy, 1996; Hale & Tager-Flusberg, 2003; Lohmann & Tomasello, 2003; Slaughter & Gopnik, 1996) and school-aged children (Lecce, Bianco, Devine, Hughes, & Banerjee, 2014) can be trained in ways to improve their mental-state understanding and vocabulary (Ornaghi, Brockmeier, & Gavazzi, 2011).

While acknowledging all limitations of research in this unique sample, this review suggests that ToM is delayed in institution-reared children, and this delay is not always explained by the child's age at the time of institutionalization or the time spent in the institution. What matters more appears to be children's interactions with adults. The next step for researchers who work in this field might be to examine the specific features of caregiver–child interaction in institutions, and to conduct controlled intervention studies to improve ToM abilities of children at an early age.

Many studies that we conducted to examine ToM in Turkish children (Alaylı & Yağmurlu, 2015; Etel & Yağmurlu, in press) were inspired by the research of Candi Peterson, that we have followed with admiration. Her research has acted as an important guide not only for her fellows and students, but also for the researchers in the "majority world" – the non-Western societies. The research that we conduct in different parts of the world, with children speaking different languages, with different characteristics, being reared in a wide range of settings with different or similar socialization experiences will allow us to learn more about ToM and the role of environment in its development. For sure, this literature will always benefit immensely from Candi Peterson's meticulous work examining the effect of different aspects of the environment on children's ToM.

Author note

Prior to 2016, Bilge Selcuk's research was published under the author name Bilge Yağmurlu.

References

Alaylı, A., & Yağmurlu, B. (2015, March). *Sequential development of theory of mind and the role of social pretence in Turkish children with hearing impairment*. Poster presented at the 2015 Society for Research in Child Development Biennial Meeting (SRCD), Philadelphia, USA.

Appleton, M., & Reddy, V. (1996). Teaching three year-olds to pass false belief tests: A conversational approach. *Social Development, 5*, 275–291.

Baron-Cohen, S., Leslie, A. M., & Frith, U. (1985). Does the autistic child have a "theory of mind"? *Cognition, 21*, 37–46.

Bauer, P. M., Hanson, J. L., Pierson, R. K., Davidson, R. J., & Pollak, S. D. (2009). Cerebellar volume and cognitive functioning in children who experienced early deprivation. *Biological Psychiatry, 66*, 1100–1106.

Baydar, N., Küntay, A. C., Yağmurlu, B., Aydemir, N., Cankaya, D., Göksen, F., & Cemalcilar, Z. (2014). "It takes a village" to support the vocabulary development of children with multiple risk factors. *Developmental Psychology, 50*, 349–360.

Beckett, C., Maughan, B., Rutter, M., Castle, J., Colvert, E., Groothues, C., et al. (2006). Do the effects of early severe deprivation on cognition persist into early adolescence? Findings from the English and Romanian adoptees study. *Child Development, 77*, 696–711.

Beeghly, M., & Cicchetti, D. (1994). Child maltreatment, attachment, and the self system: Emergence of an internal state lexicon in toddlers at high social risk. *Development and Psychopathology, 6*, 5–30.

Berument, S. K., & Güven, A. G. (2010). *Turkish expressive and receptive language test: Receptive vocabulary subscale*. Ankara, Turkey: Turkish Psychological Association.

Bos, K. J., Fox, N., Zeanah, C. H., & Nelson, C. A., III. (2009). Effects of early psychosocial deprivation on the development of memory and executive function. *Frontiers in Behavioral Neuroscience, 3*, 1–7.

Browne, K. (2005). A European survey of the number and characteristics of children less than three years old in residential care at risk of harm. *Adoption and Fostering Journal, 4*, 23–33.

Camras, L. A., Perlman, S. B., Wismer Fries, A. B., & Pollak, S. D. (2006). Post-institutionalized Chinese and Eastern European children: Heterogeneity in the development of emotion understanding. *International Journal of Behavioral Development, 30*, 193–199.

Carpendale, J. I. M., & Lewis, C. (2004). Constructing an understanding of mind: The development of children's social understanding within social interaction. *Behavioral and Brain Sciences, 27*, 70–151.

Castle, J., Groothues, C., Bredenkamp, D., Beckett, C., O'Connor, T., & Rutter, M. (1999). Effects of qualities of early institutional care on cognitive attainment. *American Journal of Orthopsychiatry, 69*, 424–437.

Child Welfare Information Gateway. (2013). *Foster care statistics 2012*. Washington, DC: US Department of Health and Human Services, Children's Bureau. Retrieved from https://www.childwelfare.gov/pubs/factsheets/foster.pdf.

Chisholm, K., Carter, M. C., Ames, E. W., & Morison, S. J. (1995). Attachment security and indiscriminately friendly behavior in children adopted from Romanian orphanages. *Development and Psychopathology, 7*, 283–294.

Cicchetti, D. (1984). The emergence of developmental psychopathology. *Child Development*, *55*, 1–7.

Cicchetti, D. (2013). Developmental psychopathology. In P. Zelazo (Ed.), *Oxford handbook of developmental psychology* (Vol. 2, pp. 455–480). New York: Oxford University Press.

Cicchetti, D., & Ng, R. (2014). Emotional development in maltreated children. In K. H. Lagatutta (Ed.), *Children and emotion: New insights into developmental affective science* (Vol. 26, pp. 29–41). Basel: Karger.

Cicchetti, D., Rogosch, F. A., Maughan, A., Toth, S. L., & Bruce, J. (2003). False belief understanding in maltreated children. *Development and Psychopathology*, *15*, 1067–1091.

Colvert, E., Rutter, M., Kreppner, J., Beckett, C., Castle, J., Groothues, C., et al. (2008). Do theory of mind and executive function deficits underlie the adverse outcomes associated with profound early deprivation? Findings from the English and Romanian adoptees study. *Journal of Abnormal Child Psychology*, *36*, 1057–1068.

de Rosnay, M., & Hughes, C. (2006). Conversation and theory of mind: Do children talk their way to socio-cognitive understanding. *British Psychological Society*, *24*, 7–37.

Devine, R. T., & Hughes, C. (2014). Relations between false belief understanding and executive function in early childhood: A meta-analysis. *Child Development*, *85*, 1777–1794.

Diamond, A., & Taylor, C. (1996). Development of an aspect of executive control: Development of the abilities to remember what I said and to "do as I say, not as I do". *Developmental Psychobiology*, *29*, 315–334.

Dunn, J. (1983). Sibling relationships in early childhood. *Child Development*, *54*, 787–811.

Dunn, J., & Brophy, M. (2005). Communication, relationships, and individual differences in children's understanding of mind. In J. W. Astington & J. A. Baird (Eds.), *Why language matters for theory of mind* (pp. 50–69). New York: Oxford University Press.

Ensor, R., & Hughes, C. (2008). Content or connectedness? Mother–child talk and early social understanding. *Child Development*, *79*, 201–216.

Etel, E., & Yağmurlu, B. (in press). Social competence, theory of mind, and executive function in institution-reared Turkish children. *International Journal of Behavioral Development*. doi: 10.1177/0165025414556095.

Fonagy, P., Redfern, S., & Charman, T. (1997). The relationship between belief-desire reasoning and a projective measure of attachment security (SAT). *British Journal of Developmental Psychology*, *15*, 51–61.

Frampton, K. L., Perlman, M., & Jenkins, J. M. (2009). Caregivers' use of metacognitive language in child care centers: Prevalence and predictors. *Early Childhood Research Quarterly*, *24*, 248–262.

Frye, D., Zelazo, P. D., & Burack, J. A. (1998). I. Cognitive complexity and control: Theory of mind in typical and atypical development. *Current Directions in Psychological Science*, *7*, 116–121.

Gerstadt, C. L., Hong, Y. J., & Diamond, A. (1994). The relationship between cognition and action: Performance of children 3.5–7 years old on a Stroop-like day–night test. *Cognition*, *53*, 129–153.

Gunnar, M. R., van Dulmen, M. H., & the International Adoption Project Team (2007). Behavior problems in postinstitutionalized internationally adopted children. *Development and Psychopathology*, *19*, 129–148.

Hakimi-Manesh, Y., Mojdehi, H., & Tashakkori, A. (1984). Short communication: Effects of environmental enrichment on the mental and psychomotor development of orphanage children. *Journal of Child Psychology and Psychiatry and Allied Disciplines*, *25*, 643–650.

Hale, C. M., & Tager-Flusberg, H. (2003). The influence of language on theory of mind: A training study. *Developmental Science, 6,* 346–359.

Harris, P. L. (2005). Conversation, pretense, and theory of mind. In J. W. Astington & J. A. Baird (Eds.), *Why language matters for theory of mind* (pp. 70–83). New York: Oxford University Press.

Hawk, B. N., & McCall, R. B. (2011). Specific extreme behaviors of postinstitutionalized Russian adoptees. *Developmental Psychology, 47,* 732–738.

Hodges, J., & Tizard, B. (1989). Social and family relationships of ex-institutional adolescents. *Journal of Child Psychology and Psychiatry, 30,* 77–97.

Hughes, C., Jaffee, S. R., Happé, F., Taylor, A., Caspi, A., & Moffitt, T. E. (2005). Origins of individual differences in theory of mind: From nature to nurture? *Child Development, 76,* 356–370.

Inoue, Y., Yamada, K., & Kanba, S. (2006). Deficit in theory of mind is a risk for relapse of major depression. *Journal of Affective Disorders, 95,* 125–127.

Juffer, F., Palacios, J., LeMare, L., Sonuga-Barke, E., Tieman, W., Bakermans-Kranenburg, M. J., et al. (2011). Development of adopted children with histories of early adversity. *Monographs of the Society for Research of Child Development, 76,* 31–61.

Kaler, S. R., & Freeman, B. J. (1994). Analysis of environmental deprivation: Cognitive and social development in Romanian orphans. *Journal of Child Psychology and Psychiatry, 35,* 769–781.

Katz, J., Demir, N., Onen, F., Uzlukaya, A., & Uludag, A. (1972). *Turkce konusan cocuklar icin Peabody resim kelime testi resim dizisi [Peabody Picture-Vocabulary Test].* Ankara: Ankara Rehberlik ve Arastirma Merkezi.

Kim-Spoon, J., Rogosch, F. A., & Cicchetti, D. (2013). A longitudinal study of emotion regulation, emotion lability/negativity, and internalizing symptomatology in maltreated and nonmaltreated children. *Child Development, 84,* 297–312.

Kreppner, J. M., Rutter, M., Beckett, C., Castle, J., Colvert, E., Groothues, C., et al. (2007). Normality and impairment following profound early institutional deprivation: A longitudinal follow-up into early adolescence. *Developmental Psychology, 43,* 931–946.

Lawler, J. M., Hostinar, C. E., Mliner, S., & Gunnar, M. R. (2014). Disinhibited social engagement in postinstitutionalized children: Differentiating normal from atypical behavior. *Development and Psychopathology, 26,* 451–464.

Lecce, S., Bianco, F., Devine, R. T., Hughes, C., & Banerjee, R. (2014). Promoting theory of mind during middle childhood: A training program. *Journal of Experimental Child Psychology, 126,* 52–67.

Lohmann, H., & Tomasello, M. (2003). The role of language in the development of false belief understanding: A training study. *Child Development, 74,* 1130–1144.

Luke, N., & Banerjee, R. (2013). Differentiated associations between childhood maltreatment experiences and social understanding: A meta-analysis and systematic review. *Developmental Review, 33,* 1–28.

MacLean, K. (2003). The impact of institutionalization on child development. *Development and Psychopathology, 15,* 853–884.

McAlister, A. R., & Peterson, C. C. (2013). Siblings, theory of mind, and executive functioning in children aged 3–6 years: New longitudinal evidence. *Child Development, 84,* 1442–1458.

Miller, K. (2005). *The handbook of international adoption medicine: A guide for physicians, patients, and providers.* New York: Oxford University Press.

Milligan, K., Astington, J. W., & Dack, L. A. (2007). Language and theory of mind: Meta-analysis of the relation between language ability and false-belief understanding. *Child Development, 78,* 622–646.

Moses, L. J. & Tahiroglu, D. (2010). Clarifying the relation between executive function and children's theories of mind. In B. W. Sokol, U. Muller, J. I. M. Carpendale, A. R. Young, & G. Iarocci (Eds.), *Self and social regulation: Social interaction and the development of social understanding and executive functions* (pp. 218–233). New York: Oxford University Press.

Muhamedrahimov, R. J. (1999). New attitudes: Infant care facilities in St. Petersburg, Russia. In J. D. Osofsky, H. E. Fitzgerald (Eds.), *WAIMH handbook of infant mental health: Perspectives on infant mental health* (pp. 245–294). New York: Wiley.

Munoz-Hoyos, A., Augustin-Morales, M. C., Ruiz-Cosano, C., Molina-Carballo, A., Fernandez-Garcia, J. M., & Galdo-Munoz, G. (2001). Institutional childcare and the affective deficiency syndrome: Consequences on growth, nutrition and development. *Early Human Development, 65*, 145–152.

O'Connor, T. G., Bredenkamp, D., Rutter, M., & the English and Romanian Adoption Study Team. (1999). Attachment disturbances and disorders in children exposed to early severe deprivation. *Infant Mental Health Journal, 20*, 10–29.

Ornaghi, V., Brockmeier, J., & Gavazzi, I. G. (2011). The role of language games in children's understanding of mental states: A training study. *Journal of Cognition and Development, 12*, 239–259.

Pears, K. C., & Fisher, P. A. (2005). Emotion understanding and theory of mind among maltreated children in foster care: Evidence of deficits. *Development and Psychopathology, 17*, 47–65.

Pears, K. C., Fisher, P. A., Bruce, J., Kim, H. K., & Yoerger, K. (2010). Early elementary school adjustment of maltreated children in foster care: The roles of inhibitory control and caregiver involvement. *Child Development, 81*, 1550–1564.

Perner, J., Ruffman, T., & Leekam, S. (1994). Theory of mind is contagious: You catch it from your sibs. *Child Development, 65*, 1228–1238.

Peterson, C. C. (2002). Drawing insight from pictures: The development of concepts of false drawing and false belief in children with deafness, normal hearing, and autism. *Child Development, 73*, 1442–1459.

Peterson, C. C., Peterson, J. L., & Webb, J. (2000). Factors influencing the development of a theory of mind in blind children. *British Journal of Developmental Psychology, 18*, 431–447.

Peterson, C. C., & Siegal, M. (1999). Representing inner worlds: Theory of mind in autistic, deaf, and normal hearing children. *Psychological Science, 10*, 126–129.

Peterson, C. C., & Siegal, M. (2000). Insights into theory of mind from deafness and autism. *Mind and Language, 15*, 123–145.

Peterson, C. C., & Slaughter, V. (2003). Opening windows into the mind: Mothers' preferences for mental state explanations and children's theory of mind. *Cognitive Development, 18*, 399–429.

Peterson, C. C., Slaughter, V., Peterson, J., & Premack, D. (2013). Children with autism can track others' beliefs in a competitive game. *Developmental Science, 16*, 443–450.

Pollak, S. D., Nelson, C. A., Schlaak, M. F., Roeber, B. J., Wewerka, S. S., Wiik, K. L., et al. (2010). Neurodevelopmental effects of early deprivation in postinstitutionalized children. *Child Development, 81*, 224–236.

Premack, D., & Woodruff, G. (1978). Does the chimpanzee have a theory of mind? *Behavioral Brain Sciences, 1*, 515–526.

Randell, A. C., & Peterson, C. C. (2009). Affective qualities of sibling disputes, mothers' conflict attitudes, and children's theory of mind development. *Social Development, 18*, 857–874.

Raven, J. C. (1938). *Progressive matrices: A perceptual test of intelligence, individual form.* London: K. K. Lewis.

Razza, R. A., & Blair, C. (2009). Associations among false-belief understanding, executive function, and social competence: A longitudinal analysis. *Journal of Applied Developmental Psychology, 30*, 332–343.

Rogosch, F. A., Cicchetti, D., Shields, A., & Toth, S. (1995). Parenting dysfunction in child maltreatment. In M. H. Bornstein (Ed.), *Handbook of parenting* (Vol. 4, pp. 127–159). Hillsdale, NJ: Erlbaum.

Ruffman, T., Olson, D. R., Ash, T., & Keenan, T. (1993). The ABCs of deception: Do young children understand deception in the same way as adults? *Developmental Psychology, 29*, 74–87.

Ruffman, T., Perner, J., Naito, M., Parkin, L., & Clements, W. A. (1998). Older (but not younger) siblings facilitate false belief understanding. *Developmental Psychology, 34*, 161–174.

Ruffman, T., Perner, J., & Parkin, L. (1999). How parenting style affects false belief understanding. *Social Development, 8*, 395–411.

Ruffman, T., Slade, L., & Crowe, E. (2002). The relation between children's and mothers' mental state language and theory-of-mind understanding. *Child Development, 73*, 734–751.

Rutter, M. (1983) Cognitive deficits in the pathogenesis of autism. *Journal of Child Psychology and Psychiatry, 24*, 513–531.

Rutter, M., Andersen-Wood, L., Beckett, C., Bredenkamp, D., Castle, J., Groothues, C., et al. (1999). Quasi-autistic patterns following severe early global privation. *Journal of Child Psychology and Psychiatry, 40*, 537–549.

Rutter, M., Kreppner, J. M., O'Connor, T. G. & The English and Romanian Adoptees (ERA) Study Team (2001). Specificity and heterogeneity in children's responses to profound institutional privation. *British Journal of Psychiatry, 179*, 97–103.

Rutter, M., O'Connor, T. G., & The English and Romanian Adoptees Study Team (2004). Are there biological programming effects for psychological development? Findings from a study of Romanian adoptees. *Developmental Psychology, 40*, 81–94.

Shahaeian, A., Nielsen, M., Peterson, C. C., & Slaughter, V. (2014). Cultural and family influences on children's theory of mind development a comparison of Australian and Iranian school-age children. *Journal of Cross-Cultural Psychology, 45*, 555–568.

Slaughter, V., & Gopnik, A. (1996). Conceptual coherence in the child's theory of mind: Training children to understand belief. *Child Development, 67*, 2967–2988.

Slaughter, V., Peterson, C. C., & Mackintosh, E. (2007). Mind what mother says: Narrative input and theory of mind in typical children and those on the autism spectrum. *Child Development, 78*, 839–858.

Sloutsky, V. M. (1997). Institutional care and developmental outcomes of 6- and 7-year-old children: A contextualist perspective. *International Journal of Behavioral Development, 20*, 131–151.

Smyke, A. T., Dumitrescu, A., & Zeanah, C. H. (2002). Attachment disturbances in young children I: The continuum of caretaking casualty. *Journal of the American Academy of Child and Adolescent Psychiatry, 41*, 972–982.

St. Petersburg–USA Orphanage Research Team (The). (2005). Characteristics of children, caregivers, and orphanages for young children in St. Petersburg, Russian Federation. *Journal of Applied Developmental Psychology, 26*, 477–506.

Stellern, S., Esposito, E., Mliner, S., Pears, K., & Gunnar, M. (2014). Increased freezing and decreased positive affect in postinstitutionalized children. *Journal of Child Psychology and Psychiatry, 55*, 88–95.

Stevens, S. E., Sonuga-Barke, E. J., Kreppner, J. M., Beckett, C., Castle, J., Colvert, E., et al. (2008). Inattention/overactivity following early severe institutional deprivation:

Presentation and associations in early adolescence. *Journal of Abnormal Child Psychology, 36*, 385–398.

Symons, D. K., & Clark, S. E. (2000). A longitudinal study of mother–child relationships and theory of mind in the preschool period. *Social Development, 9*, 3–23.

Taumoepeau, M., & Ruffman, T. (2008). Stepping stones to others' minds: Maternal talk relates to child mental state language and emotion understanding at 15, 24, and 33 months. *Child Development, 79*, 284–302.

Tarullo, A. R., Bruce, J., & Gunnar, M. R. (2007). False belief and emotion understanding in post-institutionalized children. *Social Development, 16*, 57–78.

Vorria, P., Rutter, M., Pickles, A., Wolkind, S., & Hobsbaum, A. (1998a). A comparative study of Greek children in long-term residential group care and in two-parent families: I. Social, emotional, and behavioural differences. *Journal of Child Psychology and Psychiatry, 39*, 225–236.

Vorria, P., Rutter, M., Pickles, A., Wolkind, S., & Hobsbaum, A. (1998b). A comparative study of Greek children in long-term residential group care and in two-parent families: II. Possible mediating mechanisms. *Journal of Child Psychology and Psychiatry, 39*, 237–245.

Wellman, H. M., & Liu, D. (2004). Scaling of theory of mind tasks. *Child Development, 75*, 523–541.

Werner, R. S., Cassidy, K. W., & Juliano, M. (2006). The role of social-cognitive abilities in preschoolers' aggressive behaviour. *British Journal of Developmental Psychology, 24*, 775–799.

Yağmurlu, B. (2013, July). *ToM development in children from disadvantaged backgrounds.* Paper presented at the Australasian Human Development Association (AHDA) Biannual Conference, Brisbane, Australia.

Yağmurlu, B., Berument, S. K., & Celimli, S. (2005). The role of institution and home contexts in theory of mind development. *Journal of Applied Developmental Psychology, 26*, 521–537.

Zeanah, C. H., Egger, H. L., Smyke, A. T., Nelson, C. A., Fox, N. A., Marshall, P. J., & Guthrie, D. (2009). Institutional rearing and psychiatric disorders in Romanian preschool children. *American Journal of Psychiatry, 166*, 777–785.

7

THE EMPATHIC MIND IN CHILDREN WITH COMMUNICATION IMPAIRMENTS

The case of children who are deaf or hard of hearing (DHH); children with an autism spectrum disorder (ASD); and children with specific language impairments (SLI)

Carolien Rieffe, Evelien Dirks, Wendy van Vlerken and Guida Veiga

Being heard, being respected, being loved, belonging to a group, a family – these all reflect basic human needs which have devastating effects on a child's development when absent. Fortunately, children are born with a large set of skills which enable them to initiate, follow, and maintain meaningful, respectful, and loving relationships with people around them; to develop what we will call an "empathic mind." Skills to share interests with others, to recognize the emotions of others, to feel what the other person feels and to empathize with that person, to understand others' thoughts and desires, are all necessities for this empathic mind.

Albeit the capacity for these skills is supposedly innate, they do not develop automatically. Children are also born with innate capacities for language development, but only social experiences and social learning will indeed activate and develop these capacities to the extent that they can be applied meaningfully and adequately within a given social or cultural context. For some children, however, these social experiences are limited, distorted, or otherwise hampered.

Children who are deaf or hard of hearing (DHH), children with specific language impairments (SLI), or children with an autism spectrum disorder (ASD) all have communication impairments for one reason or another. For example, children who are DHH cannot fully overhear conversations between others; they cannot easily participate in discussions between their hearing siblings or peers; free-play situations for them are less easy to join since they are troubled by background noises. Consequently, children who are DHH miss out on full participation in many social situations and, therefore, have fewer opportunities for social learning.

How communication impairments in children can affect their social learning, and in turn their development of the empathic mind, will be the focus of this chapter. Examining special groups with communication impairments is not only worthwhile from a clinical perspective, but in fact can also reveal the extent to which normal development is affected by and relies on the ability and accessibility for social learning.

The empathic mind in children who are DHH

Some children are born deaf. Due to the neonatal hearing screening which has been implemented over the last decade in most Western countries, hearing loss in these children can now be detected within a few days of birth. Others develop deafness within their first few years of life, for example, after meningitis. Children who are DHH described in the studies within this chapter are all prelingually deaf (before their third year of life), lacking in other neurological problems, and as far as is known, have intelligence within the normal range (with an IQ > 80). These children hear less than their hearing peers, but theoretically, this should not necessarily prevent them from being able to fully participate in their social environment. The studies which Candida Peterson, for example, has done with native signers show no different outcomes on the classical false-belief tests compared to their hearing peers, indicating that these children can predict the actions of others based on their (false) beliefs equally well (Peterson & Siegal, 1999; Peterson, Wellman, & Liu, 2005).

Nevertheless, the story changes considerably when we examine children who are DHH and who grow up in a predominantly hearing social environment. This applies to most children who are DHH, since more than 95 percent of these children have hearing parents (Mitchell & Karchmer, 2004). Despite the fact that many hearing family members take classes in sign language and really try to master this well, it is too difficult to achieve the level of a native speaker (Knoors & Marschark, 2012). Therefore, children who have a profound hearing loss (> 90 dB HL) and who rely on sign language with their hearing family members miss out on many aspects of daily social interactions. Yet, this also applies to children with less severe hearing loss, who may rely on spoken language. Since the introduction of the neonatal hearing screening, in combination with the development of the cochlear implant (CI), more and more deaf infants and toddlers have received the implant at an increasingly younger age. These children hear more with their CI than without, but not to the level of their hearing peers. Also children with a CI are troubled by background noises, for example, and can participate less well in groups with hearing peers. The question is how this limited opportunity for social learning affects the development of capacities that are involved in an empathic mind in these DHH children.

Precursors of the empathic mind: intention understanding

An important initial step in developing insights into other people's minds is the appreciation of their intentions. In his book *Intentionality*, Searle (1983) argues that intentions drive our actions. Although intentions and desires both imply that our

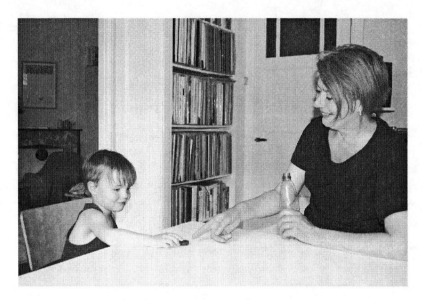

FIGURE 7.1 Experimenter points to request the lid of the bottle.

"world has to fit the mind" (p. 8), Searle argues that desires are met when they are fulfilled, whereas intentions are met when carried out. We measured intention understanding in three different ways in 72 young children with a CI (mean age 3 years and 1 month, range 12–60 months), and compared their performances to those of 69 hearing peers within the same age range.

First, based on Meltzoff's design (1995), children were presented with three tasks for intention understanding, which all involved a final goal that the experimenter failed to achieve, but which had no meaning for the child. For example, the experimenter tried (but failed) to put a string of beads into a cup. After three attempts, she gave the child the string and the cup and children received a score for success if they put the string in the cup.

Second, even before their first year of life, babies can already draw someone's attention to a topic of their interest, or follow the other person's gaze of attention. This so-called joint attention is also seen as an indicator for children's intention understanding (Tomasello, Carpenter, Call, Behne, & Moll, 2005). In our study, we used the "declarative comprehension task" (Colonnesi, Rieffe, Koops, & Perucchini, 2008), in which the experimenter looks in surprise to a stimulus behind the child, points there simultaneously, looks at the child, and looks and points again behind the child. Children received a score for success if they turned to see where the experimenter was looking.

Third, in the "imperative comprehension task" (Colonnesi et al., 2008), the experimenter points at an object which is closer to the child than to the experimenter on the table at which they are sitting (Figure 7.1). She looks at the child, and holds out her hand, nonverbally asking the child to hand her the object. Children received a score for success if they handed the experimenter the object.

Taken together, we found no differences between the CI and hearing children on all these three indices for intention understanding (Ketelaar, Rieffe, Wiefferink, & Frijns, 2012), thus young children with a CI seem to have an intention understanding that does not differ from their hearing peers. These findings are in contrast to DHH children without a CI, who engage less often in joint attention than hearing peers (Tasker, Nowakowski, & Schmidt, 2010).

Facial emotion recognition

How could we understand the minds of others, if we cannot read emotions from people's faces? Emotions not only reflect how someone feels affectively (positive or negative), but also show the level of activation. Think about anger and sadness, both emotions with a negative valence, but whereas one emotion indicates the person's intention to approach and solve the problem, the other emotion indicates withdrawal and helplessness. Being able to "read" others' emotions from their faces sets the scene for if and how to approach that person. Moreover, reading and reacting adaptively to the emotions of others help us to bond. A smile can signal, "I like you, I appreciate you," and it could also mean "I agree with what you just said or did." Not smiling back can give an awkward feeling to the initiator, and distort the feeling of togetherness and mutual understanding.

To examine children's capacity to read the emotions of others from facial expressions, we designed a nonverbal card-sorting task, in which children were shown examples of two categories. A card with a drawing of a flower, and a card with a drawing of a car were put in front of the child. Children were given cards with a flower or a car, which they were expected to place under the correct category. This posed no problem for CI and hearing children. Next, children were presented with cards showing drawings of faces with glasses or with hats. Again, sorting the same kinds of cards into the right category was no problem for both groups of children. However, when children then presented with cards showing happy or unhappy faces (Figure 7.2), children with CI (mean age 3 years) made more

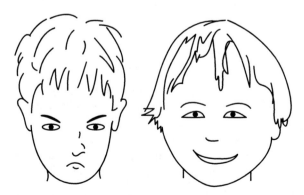

FIGURE 7.2   Faces with negative and positive emotion expressions for the card-sorting task.

mistakes sorting similar tasks into the correct category than their hearing peers (Wiefferink, Rieffe, Ketelaar, De Raeve, & Frijns, 2013). The task required no language, and the outcomes were unrelated to children's language proficiency.

The impaired performance of the children with CI on this task implies that, although the interpretation of faces can be done nonverbally, the social environment is a crucial source of information to learn this capacity. If you ever tried to read the faces of big cats, you will know that a lion's bared teeth certainly do not imply smiling or bonding. But the more subtle cues in big cats' facial expressions will be unknown to most of us humans, whereas the lions' cubs learn these signals implicitly through their daily social interactions. In other words, social learning is also critical in correctly interpreting facial expressions.

Nevertheless, other studies failed to find differences between DHH and hearing children when they are around 10 years of age (Hopyan-Misakyan, Gordon, Dennis, & Papsin, 2009), so DHH children seem to catch up on this capacity, at least on the basic emotions (anger, sadness, fear, happiness).

Affective empathy

In his book, *The Age of Empathy: Nature's lessons for a kinder society* (2009), the primatologist Frans De Waal makes a strong case for how empathy forms the basis to fight greed and feelings of indifference within the society in which we live. Only if we stop pursuing our own idiosyncratic goals, but rather focus on other people's feelings, needs, and rights for a while, will we be prepared to give up the idea of "survival of the fittest" and strive towards a society based on fairness. Empathy reflects the ability to feel for, acknowledge, and try to relieve emotional distress in others. It is the so-called "social glue," which helps to improve collaboration, strengthen group cohesion, and prevent us from harming one another (De Waal, 2009). Empathy starts with the innate capacity to mimic others, which we do automatically and can even be observed in neonates (McDonald & Messinger, 2011). By tensing the same facial muscles, it is assumed that we can feel what the other person feels, to a certain extent, of course, which is referred to as affective empathy (Baron-Cohen & Wheelwright, 2004). These feelings, in turn, should trigger supportive behaviors towards the person in distress (what we labeled prosocial motivation).

So, if the capacity for affective empathy is innate, we have no reason to assume that this would be delayed or impaired in children who are DHH. Alternatively, however, we could also argue that the innate capacity by itself is not sufficient. Possibly, social learning is also needed to put this capacity into practice. We have tested affective empathy in different ways in children with DHH.

First, we designed tasks in which the experimenter pretended to hurt herself, or she became angry with a pen which had failed to work. It was observed to what extent children would pay attention, mimic the emotion, and try to comfort or help the experimenter. Second, we designed a questionnaire where parents could indicate how often their child had shown certain behaviors which are associated with affective empathy over the last 4 weeks ("When another child cries, my child gets upset too," or "When another child is upset, my child tries to comfort him or her") (Rieffe, Ketelaar, & Wiefferink, 2010). Only with another newly designed self-report for empathy in older children (10 years and older) could we also ask children themselves about their feelings, instead of asking parents for their observations, which gives better information about their true affective states ("When my friend is upset, I also feel bad") (Netten et al., 2015).

Affective empathy was thus examined in two different age groups of children who are DHH, compared to a hearing control group. First, 61 children with CI (mean age 3 years and 3 months, range 14–79 months) were compared to 89 hearing peers of the same age (Ketelaar et al., 2013) on the observation tasks and parent report. Second, 122 teenagers who were DHH (mean age 11 years and 9 months, range 100–194 months) were compared to 162 hearing teenagers within the same age range on the observation tasks and self-report (Netten et al., 2015). Regardless of the method (observation, parent report, or self-report) or age group, the outcomes from these studies consistently demonstrate that children who are DHH and hearing children display equal levels of affective empathy. These outcomes indeed support the idea that some aspects of affective empathy are innate and independent of social learning.

Cognitive empathy: theory-of-mind understanding

Nevertheless, feeling what the other person feels is only half of the story. It helps if you feel sad, and someone puts an arm around you. But it helps even more if the other person also understands why you feel upset, a capacity which is referred to as cognitive empathy. Cognitive empathy is important especially when children become older and want to help their sad friend by giving him advice, or strategies to help him calm down ("Ah, you know he didn't mean it like that, let it go").

Cognitive empathy in young children is difficult to measure directly. From observations, it is impossible to deduce whether or not the child understands the causes of the other person's distress. However, cognitive empathy is intertwined with children's capacity for theory of mind, and most hearing children do appreciate and apply the protagonist's false beliefs in their prediction of the protagonist's behavior when they are around 4 years of age. Yet, many children who are DHH still fail these classical false-belief tasks, even when they are in their early teenage years (Kouwenberg, Rieffe, & Theunissen, 2011).

With the recent developments in the field of cochlear implantation, it was expected that the children who are implanted at a very young age would perform better on these theory-of-mind tasks than their predecessors who had been raised with a traditional hearing aid. Despite these positive predictions, children with a CI who did well on the precursor tasks (i.e., intention understanding, imperative and declarative pointing) still fell behind their hearing peers on the uncommon desire and false-belief tasks (Ketelaar et al., 2012), and this was also observed in other studies (Macaulay & Ford, 2006). These impaired outcomes for children who are DHH on theory-of-mind tasks suggest that they will also have problems with cognitive empathy.

Although it is impossible to measure cognitive empathy through observations, self-report provides a good alternative when children are around the age of 10 years and older. The newly designed self-report which was used to measure affective empathy also contained a scale for cognitive empathy (Netten et al., 2015). Items in this scale reflect the extent to which the teenagers themselves believe that they can usually understand the causes for distress in the people around them ("If a friend is sad, I understand mostly why"). The results on this scale confirm that also, in their teenage years, the DHH group falls behind on cognitive empathy (Netten et al., 2015). In other words, children who are DHH have more difficulties understanding the causes for distress in others compared to their hearing peers.

Note that these outcomes for cognitive empathy were positively related to children's language proficiency. Yet, when corrected for their language level, the hearing children still outperformed their DHH peers. This supports our view outlined at the start of this chapter that language skills alone are not sufficient for optimal social learning.

In sum, we find that younger and older children who are DHH feel touched by another person's emotion. Yet, their theory-of-mind scores, and their results on other indices, indicate that they have difficulties understanding the causes for those emotions. The key question is if and how this affects their willingness to support or console their friend who is upset. Do we need both affective and cognitive empathy to support the person in distress, or is affective empathy alone sufficient? Unfortunately, both the study on the young children with CI by Ketelaar and colleagues, and the study on teenagers who are DHH by Netten and colleagues, show that children who are DHH show less prosocial motivation and are less inclined to help the person who might need their support. Possibly, equal levels of affective empathy combined with a failure to understand the causes well might even result in frustration or negative overarousal by the onlooker who has no idea what to do or how to react. This assumption is supported by a study in which children who are DHH with lower scores on a theory-of-mind task also report more symptoms of depression (Kouwenberg et al., 2011).

The empathic mind in children with ASD

For children with ASD, social and communication impairments are two of the three main pillars upon which their diagnosis rests (*Diagnostic and Statistical Manual of Mental Disorders*, 5th edition: APA, 2013). Although many children with ASD do want to have friends, they have difficulties initiating and maintaining social relationships. For example, during play situations, children with ASD more often play alongside each other, share less positive affect, and are less interactive when compared to their typically developing (TD) peers (Bauminger et al., 2008). Despite children with ASD being less accepted by their peers, they do not report more feelings of loneliness (Chamberlain, Kasari, & Rotheram-Fuller, 2007; Howard,

Cohn, & Orsmond, 2006). Possibly, many children with ASD do not necessarily feel the urge, like TD children, to share emotions and intimacy with their friends, but merely want to share activities. The combination of social and communication impairments with fewer, or qualitatively different, social experiences will deprive children with ASD even further from full social participation, with again fewer opportunities for social learning as a result. The question is how this affects the development of the empathic mind in this particular group with ASD.

Precursors of the empathic mind

Joint attention is a widely studied topic in young children with ASD. Various studies show that children with ASD have more difficulties in establishing joint attention than TD children (e.g., Dawson et al., 2004). The children with ASD in our study (4 years and 7 months, range 21–72 months) also performed less well on the declarative comprehension pointing task than the children in a TD control group (Broekhof et al., 2015). When we examined the videos taken during our test sessions, it became apparent that many children with ASD less often made eye contact with the experimenter, looked at her finger, but not where she was pointing to. Some children looked around, but stopped when they saw the camera.

In contrast, during tasks in which children were supposed to focus on objects instead of the experimenter (intention understanding and imperative comprehension), children with ASD had no problem completing the failed task by the experimenter or handing her the bottle lid (Broekhof et al., 2015). So it seems that the social component of the joint attention forms an obstacle for children with ASD, which suggests that the children lack the social motivation, but not the social understanding *per se*.

Facial emotion recognition

The read the mind in the eyes task has been very popular for examining emotion recognition in individuals with ASD. In this task, a series of pictures are shown which only portray the part of the face around the eyes. The participant is asked to select the matching emotion word from a set of four words which are offered with each photograph (Baron-Cohen, Wheelwright, Hill, Raste, & Plumb, 2001). Children with ASD fall behind their TD peers on this task (Uljarevic & Hamilton, 2013).

Other studies have also shown consistent impairments in facial emotion recognition in children with ASD compared to their TD peers (Begeer, Koot, Rieffe, Meerum Terwogt, & Stegge, 2008). Preliminary outcomes from our own study show that young children with ASD ($n = 69$, mean age 4 years and 7 months, range 2.5–5 years) perform less well than their TD peers ($n = 125$) on the card-sorting task for emotion recognition, which we have described earlier in this chapter (Rieffe, Li, Kok, Stockmann, & Van Zijp, in preparation).

Affective empathy

Are children with ASD less empathic, as has been frequently suggested in the clinical literature? Are they unable to feel for another person? It had been suggested that children with ASD have indeed a neurological deficit in their mirror neuron system, prohibiting them from mimicking, which forms the basis for affective empathy (Williams, Whiten, Suddendorf, & Perrett, 2001). Alternatively, Adam Smith (2009) proposed that children with ASD have difficulties regulating their own emotional arousal. This overarousal would also affect these children with ASD when they witness emotions and thus are aroused by the emotions of people around them, as is the case with affective empathy. In our study, which included 67 teenagers with ASD and 66 TD children (mean age 11 years and 6 months, range 109–176 months), we measured affective empathy using the same previously mentioned self-reports for empathy (Netten et al., 2015) and found no differences in the level of affective empathy between both groups (Pouw, Rieffe, Oosterveld, Huskens, & Stockmann, 2013). Similar results appeared in a sample with 62 younger children with ASD and 75 TD children (mean age 4 years and 7 months, range 2–6 years). Parents and teachers also reported similar levels of affective empathy for both groups of children (Van Zijp, Rieffe, Ketelaar, Kok, & Stockmann, 2011). These results have been confirmed in other studies in both groups of children, also based on self-, parent, and teacher reports (Deschamps, Been, & Matthys, 2014; Schwenck et al., 2012).

Importantly, higher affective empathy in the TD group was related to lower reactive aggression, as one would expect. In contrast, for the adolescents with ASD, higher affective empathy was related to higher levels of aggression. This supports the overarousal hypothesis of Smith (2009), suggesting that children with ASD might try to avoid becoming aroused by the distress of someone else, since they will have difficulties dealing appropriately with that arousal adaptively and socially.

Cognitive empathy: theory of mind understanding

The same teenagers with ASD, who had filled out the self-report scale for affective empathy, also reported how much they think they understand the causes for the emotions of others. On this self-report scale for cognitive empathy, the teenagers with ASD scored lower than their TD peers. Yet, to test their false-belief understanding, the classical false-belief task would be too childish. Instead, we showed them two clips of scenes with Mr. Bean, which they all loved to watch. In these clips Mr. Bean created false beliefs in another story character. Afterwards, we asked children the classical false-belief questions. Again, the teenagers with ASD scored lower than the TD sample (Pouw et al., 2013). These outcomes only confirm the wealth of other studies showing the difficulties that children and adolescents with ASD have to overcome their own knowledge about reality, but instead reason from another person's perspective and desires.

In sum, the pattern in the ASD children is highly comparable to the pattern in the DHH children, but the only difference is the lower score on the imperative comprehension task, which seems to direct towards a lack of interest in the other mind. Therefore, it is unclear if social motivation adds to the problem for this group, partly explaining their impaired theory-of-mind results. Alternatively, a lack of social motivation could also originate from overarousal when being confronted with other people's minds and emotions, as the positive relationship between affective empathy and aggression for the ASD children suggests.

The empathic mind in children with SLI

An SLI applies when children are severely impaired (1.5 sp below the mean) on either language production or language comprehension, or both (Gerrtis & Van Niel, 2012), and when a neurological, intellectual, or physical cause cannot explain this impairment (Bishop, 1997). Especially with an impairment in language comprehension but in the absence of any other impairment, it is easy to overestimate their social participation, and to underestimate the special needs of these children.

Many conversations will appear to be too fast for children with SLI, or will be too difficult to comprehend. Missing out only one single word in a sentence can change its whole content. And by the time children with SLI have formulated the words they want to say, the conversation may have already moved on. Also play situations with their peers, an important context for social learning, will be more challenging. Children with SLI might not fully understand what is happening. For example, they might not understand when rules are spontaneously changed, as children frequently do change them during free play.

Several studies show that children with SLI do less well than their TD peers on different social tasks, such as resolving conflicts (Stevens & Bliss, 1995), negotiating (Brinton, Fujiki, & McKee, 1998), joining in with ongoing interactions (Liiva & Cleave, 2005), or participating in group decisions (Fujiki, Brinton, Robinson, & Watson, 1997). Moreover, children with SLI show more solitary play and withdrawn behaviors than their TD peers (Fujiki, Brinton, Isaacson, & Summers, 2001), which further limits their possibilities for social interactions and social learning. The question is, again, what impact this might have on the development of their empathic mind. To date, not many studies are available on this specific group, but the limited studies that we could find, in combination with our own preliminary outcomes, are presented here.

Precursors of the empathic mind

When tested on their intention understanding, the 90 children with SLI who had participated in our study (mean age 3 years and 6 months, range 28–57 months) showed an identical pattern as we saw in children with ASD: they had no problem completing the failed tasks by the experimenter, nor in giving the experimenter the bottle lid upon her request, but on the declarative comprehension tasks they performed less well than a TD control group ($n = 208$) (Van Der Zee, Wiefferink, Van Den Bedem, & Rieffe, in preparation). As we saw in the ASD children, intention understanding seems intact when children with SLI can focus on objects, but not when they need to follow the gaze of someone else.

Facial emotion recognition

The same sample was also tested on their capacity to recognize facial emotion expressions. As we saw in the children with a CI, and the children with ASD, the children with SLI also more often failed to correctly sort the cards with happy or sad/angry faces compared to TD children (Rieffe & Wiefferink, in revision). To our knowledge, only few other studies have examined facial emotion recognition in children with SLI. For example, children with SLI were asked to label the basic emotions from facial expressions, and did so as well as their TD peers (Delaunay-El Allam, Guidetti, Chaix, & Reilly, 2011). Yet, these children were around 6 years old, thus older than in our sample. Possibly, children with SLI just need more time in order to catch up with their TD peers, as we also saw in the DHH children.

Theory-of-mind understanding

To our knowledge, there are no studies yet that shed light on the capacity for affective and cognitive empathy in children with SLI. There are, however, some studies on their theory-of-mind functioning, and these find that 5-year-old children with SLI have difficulties with different theory-of-mind tasks (Andrés-Roqueta, Adrian, Clemente, & Katsos, 2013). In our study, 90 children with SLI around the age of 4 showed impairments compared to their TD peers on both false beliefs and diverse desires tasks. This trend was still evident in a sample consisting of 45 teenagers with SLI who watched the clips of Mr. Bean, which also were used in the studies with DHH and ASD teenagers (Van Der Zee et al., in preparation).

In sum, children with SLI do show the same impairments compared to the other two groups with communication impairments (DHH and ASD) in their "empathic mind."

Conclusions: the importance of social participation

What can we now say about the empathic mind in children with communication impairments? The picture which emerges quite clearly shows that all three groups of children (DHH, ASD, and SLI) have difficulties recognizing emotions in faces, and in the more advanced theory-of-mind tasks. Intention understanding poses no problem for any of the groups, nor does affective empathy. This suggests that these two aspects of the empathic mind might be innate capacities which are independent of social learning. Only sharing attention differentiated between the three groups. Whereas sharing attention posed no problem for children who are DHH, children with ASD and children with SLI performed less well when the task concerned purely sharing attention in focus.

Based on these outcomes, it becomes obvious that language is not the key factor for the impairments in the development of an empathic mind. Various tasks were unrelated to children's language proficiency (e.g., facial recognition), whereas other tasks were related (e.g., cognitive empathy). Nevertheless, when controlled for language levels, the impairments still remained. This emphasizes that language in itself is important, but not sufficient. Background noises, interactions that go too fast, implicit rules, or abstract concepts might be too difficult for many children with communication impairments to fully understand what is going on. Instead, a true understanding of other people's minds and emotions depends on social participation, being able to overhear others, step in when you want to, and learn about other people's motives and strategies. Thus, full access to a social world is an important factor which enhances social learning. A lack of these experiences disadvantages children, with serious consequences for their development of an empathic mind.

Although we have now collected longitudinal data on all tasks which were administered in our own studies for the younger samples (1–6 years old), and the teenage samples (10–15 years old), these data are not yet fully analyzed. In the future, we hope to be able to say more about the developmental trajectories of these impairments, because it seems that, for example, children with SLI or DHH might need more time, but catch up eventually. Nevertheless, a late start might still hamper children's social and emotional development. The picture described in this chapter can easily evolve into a vicious circle: fewer opportunities for full social participation negatively affect the development of the empathic mind, and is a risk factor for children with communicative impairments. In turn, deficits in the empathic mind can hinder children entering social situations with peers, decreasing their social experiences even further.

For example, children who are DHH initiate interactions as often as their hearing peers, but are less successful. Instead of joining an ongoing play activity, by making a comment or doing something related with the activity, as TD children often do, DHH children more often wait or disturb the play situation (Brown, Remine, Prescott, & Rickards, 2000; Duncan, 2001). Therefore, it is important to better understand the effect of the social environment and the importance of access to it on children's social and emotional development, in order to break this vicious circle and give all children the opportunity for optimal development.

Acknowledgments

This research was supported by the Innovational Research Incentives Scheme (VIDI), The Netherlands Organisation for Scientific Research (NWO) (grant number 452-07-004) to Carolien Rieffe; the Care for the Young: Innovation and Development program by Zon-Mw (grant number 80-82430-98-8025), and Fonds NutsOhra (grant number 0903-055). The authors would like to thank all participating children, parents and schools, and give thanks to (in alphabetical order) Annette Van Zijp, Anouk Netten, Evelien Brockhof, Karin Wiefferink, Kim Davitt, Lizet Ketelaar, Lucinda Pouw, Maartje Kouwenberg, Neeltje Van

Den Bedem, Rosanne Van Der Zee, Sigrid Kok, and Suzanne Van Der Groep, for their help in the production and development of this chapter.

References

Andrés-Roqueta, C., Adrian, J. E., Clemente, R. A., & Katsos, N. (2013). Which are the best predictors of theory of mind delay in children with specific language impairment? *International Journal of Language & Communication Disorders, 48*(6), 726–737. doi: 10.1111/1460-6984.12045.

APA. (2013). *Diagnostic and Statistical Manual of Mental Disorders* (5th edn). Arlington, VA: American Psychiatric Publishing.

Baron-Cohen, S., & Wheelwright, S. (2004). The empathy quotient: an investigation of adults with Asperger syndrome or high functioning autism, and normal sex differences. *Journal of Autism and Developmental Disorders, 34*(2), 163–175. doi: 10.1023/B:J add.0000022607.19833.00.

Baron-Cohen, S., Wheelwright, S., Hill, J., Raste, Y., & Plumb, I. (2001). The "Reading the Mind in the Eyes" Test revised version: a study with normal adults, and adults with Asperger syndrome or high-functioning autism. *Journal of Child Psychology and Psychiatry, 42*(2), 241–251. doi: 10.1111/1469-7610.00715.

Bauminger, N., Solomon, M., Aviezer, A., Heung, K., Brown, J., & Rogers, S. J. (2008). Friendship in high-functioning children with autism spectrum disorder: mixed and non-mixed dyads. *Journal of Autism and Developmental Disorders, 38*(7), 1211–1229. doi: 10.1007/s10803-007-0501-2.

Begeer, S., Koot, H. M., Rieffe, C., Meerum Terwogt, M., & Stegge, H. (2008). Emotional competence in children with autism: diagnostic criteria and empirical evidence. *Developmental Review, 28*(3), 342–369. doi: 10.1016/j.dr.2007.09.001.

Bishop, D. V. M. (1997). Pre- and perinatal hazards and family background in children with specific language impairments: a study of twins. *Brain and Language, 56*(1), 1–26. doi: 10.1006/brln.1997.1729.

Brinton, B., Fujiki, M., & McKee, L. (1998). Negotiation skills of children with specific language impairment. *Journal of Speech, Language, and Hearing Research, 41*(4), 927–940. doi: 10.1044/jslhr.4104.927.

Broekhof, E., Ketelaar, L., Stockmann, L., Van Zijp, A., Bos, M. G. N., & Rieffe, C. (2015). The understanding of intentions, desires and beliefs in young children with autism spectrum disorder. *Journal of Autism and Developmental Disorders, 45*(7), 2035–2045. doi: 10.1007/s10803-015-2363-3.

Brown, P. M., Remine, M. D., Prescott, S. J., & Rickards, F. W. (2000). Social interactions of preschoolers with and without impaired hearing in integrated kindergarten. *Journal of Early Intervention, 23*(3), 200–211. doi: 10.1177/105381510002300301.

Chamberlain, B., Kasari, C., & Rotheram-Fuller, E. (2007). Involvement or isolation? The social networks of children with autism in regular classrooms. *Journal of Autism and Developmental Disorders, 37*(2), 230–242. doi: 10.1007/s10803-006-0164-4.

Colonnesi, C., Rieffe, C., Koops, W., & Perucchini, P. (2008). Precursors of a theory of mind: a longitudinal study. *British Journal of Developmental Psychology, 26*(4), 561–577. doi: 10.1348/026151008X285660.

Dawson, G., Toth, K., Abbott, R., Osterling, J., Munson, J., Estes, A., & Liaw, J. (2004). Early social attention impairments in autism: social orienting, joint attention, and attention to distress. *Developmental Psychology, 40*(2), 271–283. doi: 10.1037/0012-1649.40.2.271.

De Waal, F. B. M. (2009). *The age of empathy: Nature's lessons for a kinder society.* New York: Harmony Books.

Delaunay-El Allam, M., Guidetti, M., Chaix, Y., & Reilly, J. (2011). Facial emotion labeling in language impaired children. *Applied Psycholinguistics, 32*(4), 781–798. doi: 10.1017/S0142716411000063.

Deschamps, P. K., Been, M., & Matthys, W. (2014). Empathy and empathy induced prosocial behavior in 6- and 7-year-olds with autism spectrum disorder. *Journal of Autism and Developmental Disorders, 44*(7), 1749–1758. doi: 10.1007/s10803-014-2048-3.

Duncan, J. (1999). Conversational skills of children with hearing loss and children with normal hearing in an integrated setting. *Volta Review, 101*(4), 193–212.

Fujiki, M., Brinton, B., Isaacson, T., & Summers, C. (2001). Social behaviors of children with language impairment on the playground: a pilot study. *Language, Speech, and Hearing Services in Schools, 32*(2), 101–113. doi: 10.1044/0161-1461(2001/008).

Fujiki, M., Brinton, B., Robinson, L. A., & Watson, V. J. (1997). The ability of children with specific language impairment to participate in a group decision task. *Communication Disorders Quarterly, 18*(2), 1–10. doi: 10.1177/152574019701800201.

Gerrtis, E., & Van Niel, E. (2012). Taalachterstand of Taalontwikkelingsstoornis? *Logopedie, 84*(11), 6–10.

Hopyan-Misakyan, T. M., Gordon, K. A., Dennis, M., & Papsin, B. C. (2009). Recognition of affective speech prosody and facial affect in deaf children with unilateral right cochlear implants. *Child Neuropsychology, 15*(2), 136–146. doi: 10.1080/09297040802403682.

Howard, B., Cohn, E., & Orsmond, G. I. (2006). Understanding and negotiating friendships: perspectives from an adolescent with Asperger syndrome. *Autism, 10*(6), 619–627. doi: 10.1177/1362361306068508.

Ketelaar, L., Rieffe, C., Wiefferink, C. H., & Frijns, J. H. M. (2012). Does hearing lead to understanding? Theory of mind in toddlers and preschoolers with cochlear implants. *Journal of Pediatric Psychology, 37*(9), 1041–1050. doi: 10.1093/jpepsy/jss086.

Ketelaar, L., Rieffe, C., Wiefferink, C. H., & Frijns, J. H. M. (2013). Social competence and empathy in young children with cochlear implants and with normal hearing. *Laryngoscope, 123*(2), 518–523. doi: 10.1002/lary.23544.

Knoors, H., & Marschark, M. (2012). Language planning for the 21st century: revisiting bilingual language policy for deaf children. *Journal of Deaf Studies and Deaf Education, 17*(3), 291–305. doi: 10.1093/deafed/ens018.

Kouwenberg, M., Rieffe, C., & Theunissen, S. C. P. M. (2011). Intrapersonal and interpersonal factors related to self-reported symptoms of depression in DHH youth. *International Journal on Mental Health and Deafness, 1*(1), 46–57.

Liiva, C. A., & Cleave, P. L. (2005). Roles of initiation and responsiveness in access and participation for children with specific language impairment. *Journal of Speech, Language, and Hearing Research, 48*(4), 868–883. doi: 10.1044/1092-4388(2005/060).

Macaulay, C. E., & Ford, R. M. (2006). Language and theory-of-mind development in prelingually deafened children with cochlear implants: a preliminary investigation. *Cochlear Implants International, 7*(1), 1–14. doi: 10.1002/cii.22.

McDonald, N. M., & Messinger, D. S. (2011). The development of empathy: how, when, and why. In A. Acerbi, J. A. Lombo, & J. J. Sanguineti (Eds.), *Free will, emotions, and moral actions: Philosophy and neuroscience in dialogue*. London: IF-Press.

Meltzoff, A. N. (1995). Understanding the intentions of others: re-enactment of intended acts by 18-month-old children. *Developmental Psychology, 31*(5), 838–850. doi: 10.1037/0012-1649.31.5.838.

Mitchell, R. E., & Karchmer, M. A. (2004). Chasing the mythical ten percent: parental hearing status of deaf and hard of hearing students in the United States. *Sign Language Studies, 4*(2), 138–163. doi: 10.1353/sls.2004.0005.

Netten, A. P., Rieffe, C., Theunissen, S. C. P. M., Soede, W., Dirks, E., Briaire, J. J., & Frijns, J. H. M. (2015). Low empathy in deaf or hard of hearing (pre)adolescents compared to normal hearing controls. *PLoS ONE, 10*(e0124102). doi: 10.1371/journal.pone.0124102.

Peterson, C. C., & Siegal, M. (1999). Representing inner worlds: theory of mind in autistic, deaf, and normal hearing children. *Psychological Science, 10*(2), 126–129. doi: 10.1111/1467-9280.00119.

Peterson, C. C., Wellman, H. M., & Liu, D. (2005). Steps in theory-of-mind development for children with deafness or autism. *Child Development, 76*(2), 502–517. doi: 10.1111/j.1467-8624.2005.00859.x.

Pouw, L. B. C., Rieffe, C., Oosterveld, P., Huskens, B., & Stockmann, L. (2013). Reactive/proactive aggression and affective/cognitive empathy in children with ASD. *Research in Developmental Disabilities, 34*(4), 1256–1266. doi: 10.1016/j.ridd.2012.12.022.

Rieffe, C., Ketelaar, L., & Wiefferink, C. H. (2010). Assessing empathy in young children: construction and validation of an Empathy Questionnaire (EmQue). *Personality and Individual Differences, 49*(5), 362–367. doi: 10.1016/j.paid.2010.03.046.

Rieffe, C., Li, B., Kok, S., Stockmann, L., & Van Zijp, A. (in press). Reading faces; emotion recognition in toddlers and preschool children with an autism spectrum disorder.

Rieffe, C. & Wiefferink, C. (in press). Happy faces, sad faces; Emotion understanding in toddlers and preschoolers with language impairments.

Schwenck, C., Mergenthaler, J., Keller, K., Zech, J., Salehi, S., Taurines, R., et al. (2012). Empathy in children with autism and conduct disorder: group-specific profiles and developmental aspects. *Journal of Child Psychology and Psychiatry, 53*(6), 651–659. doi: 10.1111/j.1469-7610.2011.02499.x.

Searle, J. R. (1983). *Intentionality*. Cambridge: Cambridge University Press.

Smith, A. (2009). Emotional empathy in autism spectrum conditions: weak, intact, or heightened? *Journal of Autism and Developmental Disorders, 39*(12), 1747–1748. doi: 10.1007/s10803-009-0799-z.

Stevens, L. J., & Bliss, L. S. (1995). Conflict resolution abilities of children with specific language impairment and children with normal language. *Journal of Speech, Language, and Hearing Research, 38*(3), 599–611. doi: 10.1044/jshr.3803.599.

Tasker, S. L., Nowakowski, M. E., & Schmidt, L. A. (2010). Joint attention and social competence in deaf children with cochlear implants. *Journal of Developmental and Physical Disabilities, 22*(5), 509–532. doi: 10.1007/s10882-010-9189-x.

Tomasello, M., Carpenter, M., Call, J., Behne, T., & Moll, H. (2005). Understanding and sharing intentions: the origins of cultural cognition. *Journal of Behavioral and Brain Sciences, 28*(5), 675–691; discussion 691-735. doi: 10.1017/s0140525x05000129.

Uljarevic, M., & Hamilton, A. (2013). Recognition of emotions in autism: a formal meta-analysis. *Journal of Autism and Developmental Disorders, 43*(7), 1517–1526. doi: 10.1007/s10803-012-1695-5.

Van Der Zee, R., Wiefferink, C. H., Van Den Bedem, N., & Rieffe, C. (in press). Theory of mind in children with specific language impairments.

Van Zijp, A., Rieffe, C., Ketelaar, L., Kok, S., & Stockmann, L. (2011). Gedeelde smart? Empathie bij jonge kinderen met autisme. *Wetenschappelijk Tijdschrift Autisme, 10*, 65–74.

Wiefferink, C. H., Rieffe, C., Ketelaar, L., De Raeve, L., & Frijns, J. H. M. (2013). Emotion understanding in deaf children with a cochlear implant. *Journal of Deaf Studies and Deaf Education, 18*(2), 175–186. doi: 10.1093/deafed/ens042.

Williams, J. H., Whiten, A., Suddendorf, T., & Perrett, D. I. (2001). Imitation, mirror neurons and autism. *Neuroscience and Biobehavioral Reviews, 25*(4), 287–295. doi: 10.1016/S0149-7634(01)00014-8.

8

ENVIRONMENT AND LANGUAGE EXPERIENCE IN DEAF CHILDREN'S THEORY OF MIND DEVELOPMENT

Gary Morgan, Marek Meristo and Erland Hjelmquist

We focus in this chapter on the human social cognitive ability to connect with each other at the level of different inner and unobservable mental states such as knowledge and beliefs; a development encapsulated in the term *theory of mind* (ToM). The development of children's ToM has been a major research topic for the last 30 years and recently attention has turned to the environmental enablers of social cognition found in early parent–child interaction.

Identifying when children start to understand others

The question of how nature and nurture influence ToM development resembles, and is closely related to, the long-standing debate in research on language acquisition. While there are clear biological factors inherent in child language development (e.g. a bias for neonates to do analyses of statistical frequency of phonemes; see Saffran, Aslin, & Newport, 1996) there is also a strong cultural influence. All children need linguistic communication and interaction with adults to develop native language skills, although the timing and extent of such input are still controversial. Research on hearing bilingual infants is instructive in this respect. For example, in a recent longitudinal study of language acquisition, Garcia-Sierra et al. (2011) found that bilingual children were perceptually open to phonetic contrasts longer than monolingual infants, a clear effect of communicative experiences on early language learning. Similarly, research is divided on the extent of biological and cultural influence on the development of children's ToM (Heyes & Frith, 2014).

In this chapter we take advantage of recent research with deaf infants and toddlers to argue for the importance of very early language environments in the emergence of understanding others' behaviour in terms of their mental states. An interesting finding from research on children born deaf is that, while deaf children with deaf parents pass standard ToM tasks at age-appropriate stages, deaf children of hearing parents have major delays in this aspect of social cognition. While the early literature focused on delays in language development as an explanation, more recent research has looked at early environmental differences deaf children of hearing parents experience, especially disturbances in joint attention and impoverished interaction in conversations, as a cause of subsequent ToM deficits.

To explain the reasons for this shift in focus, we first describe a number of studies that have looked at ToM abilities both as an explicit verbal capacity and as an implicit non-verbal capacity in deaf and hearing children. We then explore the impact of variations in early environments between deaf and hearing children, which include differences in the establishment of joint attention, the content of conversations and the connectedness of early interaction, and we examine possible consequences of these environmental factors on social cognition. We conclude the chapter by examining some potential future directions, and describe aspects of current research that could be applied to intervention work.

Developing a theory of mind: implicit and explicit knowledge of others' minds

While the original article by Premack and Woodruff (1978) encompassed a wide range of mental-state concepts – understanding emotions, motivational states and intentions – most subsequent work on ToM has focused on the concept of false belief. As such, ToM has become synonymous with a person's ability to predict what an actor is likely to do, based on what he or she believes or expects. There are differing theoretical views on how best to characterize children's development of ToM abilities and the role of language in this unfolding. Much research argues that ToM is dependent on access to linguistic features in terms of structure or content, or both. A strong linguistic hypothesis was put forward by de Villiers and Pyers (2002), who argued that before children could conceptualize false beliefs, they need to have developed an understanding of the syntax necessary to embed one clause in another (termed sentence complements) in non-mentalistic contexts; for example, Sally said that *the marble was in the basket*. Their argument was that, by first mastering the syntax of complementation linguistically, children would be able to manipulate the two clauses in an internal meta-representation of mental attitudes (de Villiers & Pyers, 2002).

Other researchers have argued that, rather than syntax, it is lexical development that enables children to think about mental states more explicitly (see Milligan, Astington, & Dack, 2007, for a discussion). This research highlights the acquisition of vocabulary linked to mental-state verbs – "to think", "to know", "to not know", and so on. Finally, still other researchers have instead claimed that the key to understanding the role of language in children's ToM development is to look not at their acquisition of formal properties (verb semantics, syntax, etc.) but instead their experience of language and communication in conversation (Peterson

& Siegal, 1995). This final framework focuses on how children come to develop the pragmatic skills necessary to understand conversations and interaction between themselves and others, and this interaction is thought to be the enabling condition for ToM development.

However, up until recently these different lines of investigation have focused almost exclusively on how language enables ToM in passing *explicit* versions of the standard false-belief task, e.g. the Sally–Anne task (see Appendix). Based on their research with typical children using this task, Wimmer and Perner (1983) argued that the ability to appreciate another person's false belief went through a change from 4 to 6 years of age. While younger children answer that Sally will look for her shoes where they actually are, older children answer correctly that she will look for them in the original location where she *believes* them to be.

The age at which children begin to solve this type of false-belief problem has been debated for many years. Some researchers argue that it begins at 4 years of age (Wimmer & Perner, 1983; Baron-Cohen, Leslie, & Frith, 1985), while others have brought this down to the second half of the first year of life (Kovács, Téglás, & Endress, 2010; Onishi & Baillargeon, 2005; Southgate & Vernetti, 2014). On the basis of these more recent results, some cognitive scientists argue for a specific innate *social sense* that develops very early with little external input. The *social sense* view has been supported by studies employing infants' implicit, or spontaneous non-verbal behaviours such as pointing gestures, helping, and preferential looking (Buttelmann, Carpenter, & Tomasello, 2009; Southgate, Chevallier, & Csibra, 2010). Against the backdrop of such apparently early demonstrations of understanding mind, it has been argued that explicit verbal responses required in Sally–Anne-type tasks make additional demands on children's limited executive functioning skills, which are dramatically reduced in non-verbal paradigms.

An example of such a non-verbal paradigm is a test situation in which an agent who has not seen the displacement of an object holds a false belief about its location (e.g. Onishi & Baillargeon, 2005). However, infants' responses are not verbal but measured by their preferential or anticipatory looking. Such looking patterns indicate an accurate expectation about the actor's search behaviour. Infant looking times are notoriously difficult to interpret and such studies have met with criticism (see Perner & Ruffman, 2005). Yet, there are now looking time data from several studies employing various tasks and dependent measures which are consistent with the view that infants are able to attribute beliefs and belief-like states spontaneously to ignorant agents (Baillargeon, Scott, & He, 2010; Buttelmann et al., 2009; Senju, Southgate, Snape, Leonard, & Csibra, 2011; Southgate et al., 2010).

Returning to deafness in both verbal elicited-response and non-verbal spontaneous-response measures of ToM, deaf children of hearing parents with normal non-verbal IQ have been shown to have difficulties. At the same time, deaf children of deaf parents who use sign language when communicating with their children at home perform well on traditional explicit verbal ToM measures; their performance is in fact comparable to the level of hearing children (Schick, de Villiers, de Villiers, & Hoffmeister, 2007; Woolfe, Want, & Siegal, 2002). Because deaf children of hearing parents typically have both signed and spoken language delay, the common explanation for ToM difficulties has been based in a disruption in the typical development of linguistic skills or communicative interaction. The results of many empirical studies with deaf children of hearing parents document that the developmental trajectory of performance on explicit verbal ToM is highly variable, often delayed and very dependent on the communicative experiences of the child (Meristo et al., 2007). In fact, deaf children from hearing homes often have difficulties with ToM which can persist up to teenage years and, in some cases, even among deaf adults (Pyers & Senghas, 2009). One reasonable explanation for this discrepancy between the two groups of deaf children might be that deaf children from hearing homes also have a delayed language development and might have difficulties in following the storyline or formulating an answer in the explicit kind of highly verbal tasks.

In our recent work (Meristo et al., 2012), we have therefore asked whether deaf infants from hearing homes who do not have access to daily fluent verbal interactions with their family members show a similar pattern of performance in various mentalizing tasks; that is, do they demonstrate an implicit, possibly innate, experience-independent social sense, such as that suggested by Kovács et al. (2010), Surian, Caldi, and Sperber (2007), and Onishi and Baillargeon (2005)?

To address this question, Meristo et al. (2012) examined whether deaf infants from hearing homes show similar anticipatory looking to hearing infants when the measures are simplified, administered on an eye tracker and do not require verbal comprehension or responses to questions. Alternatively, anticipatory looking behaviours that are consistent with false-belief understanding may in fact be enabled through early joint interactions. If such early ToM behaviour emerges as a function of social interaction, there would be reason to expect that deaf children from hearing homes should show impairments in spontaneous-response ToM tasks. Thus, deaf children with varying linguistic experiences can illuminate in a novel way our understanding of the environmental preconditions of ToM in terms of perceptual, linguistic and cooperative affordances.

Our findings showed that deaf 2-year-old children of hearing parents had difficulties with ToM using these implicit measures, unlike their age-matched hearing peers. It seems that deafness blocks the ability to use the innate social sense that has been argued for in previous implicit studies of ToM. Such findings suggest that there must be an environmental element involved in enabling early false-belief understanding. This work with deaf children, coupled with other studies on environmental enablers of social cognition, has moved the focus of attention from the developmental origins of ToM to the interactions children take part in during the first 2 years of life. Deaf children of hearing parents fail implicit measures of false belief at 2 years while their hearing peers pass these tasks, despite both groups having quite limited formal language skills (syntax and abstract vocabulary knowledge). This pattern of results suggests that the enablers of ToM might be more linked with differing environments, and in particular different patterns of adult–child communication differences.

As mentioned previously, the first studies of implicit mentalizing, such as that of Onishi and Baillargeon (2005), were met with criticism and also alternative interpretations of the empirical results. Perner and Ruffman (2005) suggested, for example, that the infant only needed to rely on neuronal learning, behavioural regularities and perceptual information, without imputing a mediating mind to the protagonists observed. This kind of criticism was recently revived by Heyes (2014), who concluded that the empirical results interpreted as infant mindreading could be explained more simply by retroactive memory effects and low-level perceptual novelty, reflecting domain-general processes. That criticism also referred to the studies of deaf infants of hearing parents (Meristo et al., 2012). The group of deaf infants becomes interesting as a possibility for delineating the genesis of mentalizing.

If one adopts the perspective presented by Heyes (2014), it is difficult to see why deaf children of hearing parents should not have attained the same kind of memory/perceptual mechanisms that same-age hearing children have, if looked at in the perspective of Heyes's (2014) framework. Especially if one assumes a domain-general mechanism explaining infants' behaviour, it seems that a minimum, but crucial, conversational influence in early environments is necessary to account for the fact that 24-month-old hearing infants, but not same-aged deaf infants of hearing parents, at least behave as if (according to Heyes, 2014) they imputed a mind to the protagonists observed (Meristo et al., 2012). In a non-mentalizing framework, one would have to assume some domain-general deficit among that group of deaf children. This could be the case, but there is little, if any, evidence speaking in favour of this possibility. Alternatively, as Heyes (2014) claims, it could be that the looking pattern of deaf infants is due to the fact that they were less distracted than hearing infants of the same age (supplementary material, p. 7). So far this claim is unfounded, and it seems more parsimonious to assume that typically developing infants no later than around 2 years of age do ascribe mental states to observed agents, and that they interpret these agents as guided by their mental states. Hearing children of this age have continuously, from birth, benefitted from an environment replete with conversational experiences.

Our conclusion is that a number of studies are best interpreted as showing that implicit mindreading can be present without explicit mindreading skills. This fits nicely with another branch of research on ToM and the empirical data showing considerable variability in the age when verbally elicited or explicit mindreading emerges (Heyes & Frith, 2014). However, the more precise relation between the two types of mindreading remains unsettled: it is not clear if they rely on two different systems in a neurocognitive sense, if it is one system with different developmental preconditions or if implicit mindreading reflects a general neurocognitive mechanism with only explicit mindreading relying on a specific neurocognitive mechanism (Heyes & Frith, 2014).

The relationship between implicit and explicit mentalizing has been discussed in the literature in the context of other atypical developmental conditions. Adults with high-functioning autism spectrum disorder (ASD) can be proficient at explicit response tasks, but lack the ability to cope with implicit tasks (Senju, Southgate, White, & Frith, 2009). Consequently, implicit non-verbal belief attribution does not seem to be a necessary precursor for the later-developing explicit understanding of other minds (Frith & Frith, 2008; Senju et al., 2009). Therefore we have empirical evidence that infants during the latter half of the first year implicitly interpret events, including agents, in terms of mental states, and at this age they do not pass traditional explicit ToM tasks, perhaps because these rely on verbal language skills. The findings of Senju et al. (2009) clearly show that coping with verbally loaded tasks is crucially facilitated by typical verbal skills, which should be no surprise. In this sense, implicit and explicit mentalizing are decoupled, but in an atypical way among persons with ASD. At the same time, the results from ASD show how effective and compelling language is as a tool for reasoning, and for learning to reason about other minds, despite a "reluctant" social mind.

From our point of view, implicit ToM in the sense of Heyes and Frith (2014) is compatible with social cognition being open to an influence of environmental experience in conversational settings. We suggest that deaf parents foster implicit mindreading skills in interaction with their children in ways that hearing parents of deaf children do much less. The same should be expected for explicit ToM, where more verbal instruction to deaf children is needed than could be provided by hearing parents. Studies of deaf children shed new light on the conditions of the emerging implicit and non-verbal belief attribution skills by suggesting that these skills are fostered and learnt through conversational input from caregivers during the first 2 years of life (Meristo et al., 2012; Morgan et al., 2014). We reiterate from Meristo et al. (2012) that the preferred explanation of the delayed ToM among deaf children of hearing parents is: "the very reduced early experience of conversation and its role as a vehicle for mind-coordination" (p. 58). We now turn to a discussion of what this early experience of conversation may entail.

Environmental enablers of theory of mind: early interaction

Infants during their first year of life have already been involved in countless interactions with their parents. Language in these contexts is a prominent vehicle for gaining the attention of the infant, for monitoring and commenting on the infant´s actions, and for guiding the attention of the infant to outer and inner experiences (Meins, Fernyhough, Arnott, Leekam, & de Rosnay, 2013; Meins, Fernyhough, Johnson, & Lidstone, 2006). In studies of hearing children by Meins and her colleagues, parents' references to mental states of the infant at 6 months of age were predictive of ToM at 4 years of age. A methodological issue is, of course, the common genetic affordances of children and parents. Strictly speaking, the common genetic variation might explain the correlation between parental talk and children's ToM, with little environmental influence. On the other hand, the rich experience of talk, and mental-state talk in particular, might explain the presence of very early non-verbal belief attribution. Presently, the empirical evidence strongly favours the latter alternative. Hughes et al. (2005), in a longitudinal study, showed that individual differences in explicit ToM were explained mainly by environmental factors. This finding is also concordant with the accumulating evidence for considerable cultural variation in explicit-response ToM development (Mayer & Träuble, 2015; Vinden, 2001).

Related to the importance of very early communicative experiences, there is evidence of the perceptual attraction to characteristics of sign language during the first year of life, though only among hearing children (Krentz & Corina, 2008). This study showed that hearing 6-month-old infants, the age at which Meins et al. (2006) studied parents' references to infants' mental states, were more sensitive to sign language information compared to complex pantomimes. This finding mirrors hearing infants' sensitivity to speech stimuli compared to complex non-speech sounds. Such findings speaks strongly in favour of deaf children of deaf parents processing sign language in the same perceptual and categorical way as hearing infants process spoken language.

Although there is no known direct link between the perceptual level of language and ToM, the findings by Krentz and Corina (2008) underline the importance of early access to conversational experience, whether spoken or signed, for stabilizing the building blocks of linguistic communication. Such an interpretation seems especially compelling given that hearing 10-month-olds do not show any specific sensitivity to sign language information (Krentz & Corina, 2008), paralleling the loss of sensitivity to spoken linguistic contrasts within the same age group. It seems very likely, therefore, that deaf children need sign language experiences from conversational contexts in the same way that hearing children need spoken conversational experience, in order to benefit from the informational potential inherent in linguistic communication (Kuhl, Tsao, & Liu, 2003).

Deaf children also offer natural variation in terms of access to adult linguistic communication, since deaf children born to hearing parents (about 90 per cent of all deaf children), from the very beginning, will not be enculturated into, and via, a common language. Until the point later in development when cochlear implants and intensive speech and language therapy begin to provide deaf children with functional spoken language skills, they will not be immersed in accessible linguistic communication directed at them, notwithstanding that in several societies, as soon as deafness is discovered, parents are offered classes in a sign language. Signing with your baby is currently a very fashionable pastime for hearing parents with hearing infants; paradoxically, however, the increasing use of cochlear implants at early ages reduces deaf infants' parents' interest in learning sign language. Irrespective of these considerations, during their first year, deaf children generally have very restricted access to a common mother tongue. However, this is not the case for all deaf children. As already indicated, deaf children of deaf parents have age-appropriate explicit ToM development and we know, as is discussed in the following section, a lot about how early interaction in deaf families enables this.

Interaction environments in deaf and hearing parents of deaf children – what they do differently

Early studies of the interaction style of hearing mothers of deaf children compared to hearing mothers of hearing children described the former group as demonstrating a more directive style that resulted in less participation and initiation from children. Consequently, children were less able to interpret their mothers' intentions (Jamieson, 1995; Lederberg & Mobley, 1990; Meadow-Orlans & Steinberg, 1993; Spencer, Bodner-Johnson, & Gutfreund, 1992; Wedell-Monnig & Lumley, 1980). Early research also making reference to mothers' anxiety and feelings of incompetence relating to how to interact with a deaf child has been put forward as possible causes for interruptions in maternal responsiveness (Meadow-Orlans & Spencer, 1996). At the time parents are getting used to a new infant, the hearing parent of a deaf infant is dealing with the stress and anxiety that can accompany a diagnosis of hearing impairment, making important decisions about amplification or implantation, and often having to learn a new (sign) language at a time when language input is key (Koester & Meadow-Orlans, 1990). It is undoubtedly the case that early communication between a hearing parent and a deaf child is challenging. Hearing parents are accustomed to communication via hearing and need time to adapt to the visual/tactile communication mode that is more appropriate for their deaf infant.

In contrast, deaf mothers of deaf children are reported in several studies to be more responsive to their children's changes in attention marked by small shifts in eye gaze. Hearing mothers were more likely to miss these subtle signals or misinterpret them as inattention from the deaf child (Swisher, 1992). For the deaf mother, her child making eye contact is interpreted as a request and looking away is a new-topic initiation or an opportunity for her child to scan the environment before returning her gaze (Gale & Schick, 2009; Kyle, Woll, & Ackerman, 1989; Loots, Devisé, & Jacquet, 2005). Spencer et al. (1992) reported that deaf mothers were much more likely to wait for their child to look back at them before responding than hearing mothers of deaf children (70 per cent of the time compared to only 16 per cent of the time by hearing mothers).

Several studies of deaf children of hearing parents have reported delays in establishing and using joint attention with their parents. In contrast, when deaf children are immersed in an environment with sufficient visual communication with deaf parents, they develop joint attention skills at the same age and follow the same stages as hearing children (Harris, Clibbens, Chasin, & Tibbitts, 1989; Lieberman, Hatrak, & Mayberry, 2014; Tasker, Nowakowski, & Schmidt, 2010). Meadow-Orlans and Spencer (1996) and Spencer (2000) reported that deaf parents–deaf child dyads spend just as much time in coordinated joint attention as hearing parents–hearing child pairs at 18 months. By contrast, the hearing parent–deaf child dyads spend a reduced total amount of time in joint attention at this same age (Gale & Schick, 2009; Spencer, 2000; Spencer & Waxman, 1995).

Linked to the idea that early conversations play a role in the development of ToM skills is work on the importance of the input to young children from their caregivers containing certain mental-state words and conversation styles. Taumoepeau and Ruffman (2006) showed that maternal mental-state talk to hearing 15-month-olds correlated with later mental-state language and emotion understanding at 24 months of age. Furthermore, mothers' reference to others' thoughts and knowledge at 24 months was the strongest predictor of children's mental-state language at 33 months.

In keeping with the key findings presented by Taumoepeau and Ruffman (2006), Morgan et al. (2014) carried out an analysis of conversational experiences of deaf and hearing children aged 17–35 months with hearing parents in two languages, English and Swedish. The majority of the children tested by Morgan et al. (2014) knew spoken and signed language, although language levels varied greatly between children. In the English sample, all deaf children had hearing parents who had minimal familiarity with British Sign Language (BSL). The children's language scores were assessed using the BSL and English MacArthur Bates Communicative Development Inventory (Herman, Woolfe, Roy, & Woll, 2010). Language scores in BSL ranged from 20 to 481 signs in comprehension and from 8 to 372 signs in production. Participants' English scores ranged from 4 to 393 words in comprehension and from 3 to 316 words in production. This massive individual variation was also reported for similar-age children by Woll (2013). The procedure was the same for the English and Swedish sample. Morgan et al. (2014) asked parents to describe pictures that elicit mental- and emotional-state language to their children following the Taumoepeau and Ruffman (2006) methodology.

Results showed that the input to the deaf children from their hearing caregivers differed greatly in terms of mental-state labels when compared with hearing mothers talking to their hearing same-age children. Parents of hearing children referred to cognitions (i.e., using words like "think", "know" or "remember") significantly more often than did mothers of deaf children. There were no differences between groups in references to desires or emotions. For turn taking we found that the hearing parent–child dyads produced significantly more utterances semantically related to the interlocutor's previous turn than did the hearing parent–deaf child dyads – so-called *connected turns*. Parents with a deaf child thus have a difficulty maintaining a conversation and are less likely to relate to the child's immediately preceding conversational turn. Generally speaking, the results held for both language samples in two different cultures, and are compatible with the hypothesis that the lack of a common language for directing attention and sharing experiences has consequences for the quality of dialogues and the development of mentalizing.

An interesting finding came from an analysis of a subgroup of the parents with deaf children who had sets of twins (one deaf and one hearing). Three sets of such parents talked very differently to their two children depending on the hearing status of each child. When they described pictures to hearing offspring they used appropriate levels of mental-state language (as compared with data reported in Taumoepeau & Ruffman, 2006), but they drastically reduced this input when describing pictures to their deaf children, instead using descriptions of colours, sizes and labelling (Morgan, unpublished data). This suggests that conversations are more parent-led when a deaf child takes part. Morgan et al. (2014) also examined the child vocabulary data as a variable in a correlation analysis and found no consistent patterns. Thus language itself as measured by the vocabulary size was not predicting how rich in mental-state language these deaf children's interaction was with their parents. There are other things in language, especially pragmatics, that facilitate how interaction develops in deaf children. This difference between good vocabulary and poor pragmatics was also reported in an Italian study of children with CI at 24 months (Rinaldi, Baruffaldi, Burdo, & Caselli, 2013).

In summary, deaf children of hearing parents show a consistently delayed development of ToM compared to hearing children of hearing parents and deaf children of deaf parents. Nevertheless, deaf children of hearing parents follow the same progression from simple to more complex mental-state understanding as hearing children, but this progression is considerably delayed (Peterson, Wellman, & Slaughter, 2012). Such protracted development is in line with degraded conversational and linguistic input.

Suggestions from the research for future intervention practices for families with deaf children

The findings from Morgan et al. (2014) have consequences for how we think about early language intervention with young deaf children and their hearing caregivers. For example, the results emphasize that the quality of the environment is an enabler of social cognitive skills, but that this enabler need not be a massive part of the interaction. In the hearing parent–child dyads, only 2–5 per cent of verbal interactions concerned references to cognitive and mental states, yet this will be sufficient to enable age-appropriate ToM development. This point highlights how important early intervention in nursery schools and other settings is for deaf children, but it also suggests that training does not have to entail a large amount of adaptation. While the implementation of early communication training packages is complex, from a review of the evidence on ToM development in deaf children we would recommend that interventions should be based on what is known about the interactive styles of deaf parents with deaf children (see Spencer et al., 1992). Based on the available evidence for ToM in deaf children with hearing parents, our guidance to parents would be to focus on developing communication strategies that work for a deaf child based on visual and tactile cues, and to learn to use a sign language from as early as possible. Such an approach is behind the creation of the UK's National Deaf Children's Society Family Sign Language Curriculum (www.familysignlanguage.org.uk). Of course, our stance does not mean that speech input should not be used with young deaf children. Clearly, a deaf child should be exposed to the richest input possible in terms of spoken language, but this should definitely not preclude natural gesture and exposure to a signed language from as fluent an adult user as possible. These early communicative practices in an accessible language can of course change over time, with the expectation that many deaf children of hearing parents will go on to develop spoken language skills to their full potential (see Perez, Valsameda, & Morgan, 2015). We would not recommend approaches which either force deaf children to avoid visual communication strategies (including gestures, signs and lip reading) or which advise parents to "wait and see" if their deaf child develops spoken language before deciding to sign. As it stands, the evidence suggests that any delays in establishing and taking part in communication or access to social interaction via an accessible language code will have consequences for ToM that can be both problematic and long lasting.

Acknowledgments

Gary Morgan's work was supported by the Economic and Social Research Council of Great Britain (Grant 620-28-600 Deafness, Cognition and Language Research Centre).

The writing of this chapter was assisted by funds from the Swedish Research Council for Health, Working Life and Welfare, and the Jerring Foundation to Marek Meristo; and from the Swedish Research Council for Health, Working Life and Welfare, and the Stena A Olsson Foundation for Research and Culture to Erland Hjelmquist.

Address for correspondence: Gary Morgan, City, University of London – Language and Communication Science, Northampton Square, London EC1V0HB, United Kingdom. e-mail: G.Morgan@city.ac.uk

References

Baillargeon, R., Scott, R. M., & He, Z. (2010). False-belief understanding in infants. *Trends in Cognitive Sciences*, *14*, 110–118.

Baron-Cohen, S., Leslie, A. M., & Frith, U. (1985). Does the autistic child have a "theory of mind"? *Cognition*, *21*(1), 37–46.

Buttelmann, D., Carpenter, M., & Tomasello, M. (2009). Eighteen-month-old infants show false belief understanding in an active helping paradigm. *Cognition, 112* (2), 337–342.

de Villiers, J. & Pyers, J. (2002). Complements to cognition: a longitudinal study of the relationship between complex syntax and false-belief-understanding. *Cognitive Development, 17,* 1037–1060.

Frith, C. D., & Frith, U. (2008). Implicit and explicit processes in social cognition. *Neuron, 60*(3), 503–510.

Gale, E., & Schick, B. (2009). Symbol-infused joint attention and language use in mothers with deaf and hearing toddlers. *American Annals of the Deaf, 153*, 484–503.

Garcia-Sierra, A., Rivera-Gaxiola, M., Percaccio, C. R., Conboy, B. T., Romo, H., Klarman, L., Ortiz, S., & Kuhl, P. K. (2011). Bilingual language learning: an ERP study relating early brain responses to speech, language input, and later word production. *Journal of Phonetics, 39*, 546–557.

Harris, M., Clibbens, J., Chasin, J., & Tibbitts, R. (1989). The social context of early sign language development. *First Language, 9*, 81–97.

Herman, R., Woolfe, T., Roy, P., & Woll, B. (2010). Early vocabulary development in deaf native signers: a British Sign Language adaptation of the communicative development inventories. *Journal of Child Psychology and Psychiatry, 51*, 322–331.

Heyes, C. M. (2014). False belief in infancy: a fresh look. *Developmental Science, 17*, 647–659.

Heyes, C. M., & Frith, C. (2014). The cultural evolution of mind reading. *Science, 344*, doi: 10.1126/science.1243091.

Hughes, C., Jaffee, S. R., Happe, F., Taylor, A., Caspi, A., & Moffitt, T. E. (2005). Origins of individual differences in theory of mind: from nature to nurture? *Child Development, 76*, 356–370.

Jamieson, J. (1995). Visible thought: deaf children´s use of signed and spoken private speech. *Sign Language Studies, 86*, 63–80.

Koester, L., & Meadow-Orlans, K. (1990). Parenting a deaf child: stress, strength and support. In D. F. Moores & K. Meadow-Orlans (Eds.), *Educational and Developmental Aspects of Deafness*. Washington, DC: Gallaudet University Press.

Kovács, Á. M., Téglás, E., & Endress, A. D. (2010). The social sense: susceptibility to others' beliefs in human infants and adults. *Science, 330*(6012), 1830–1834.

Krentz, U., & Corina, D. (2008). Infant perception of American Sign Language and nonlinguistic biological motion: the language instinct is not speech specific. *Developmental Science, 11*(1), 1–9.

Kuhl, P. K., Tsao, F., & Liu, H. (2003). Foreign-language experience in infancy: effects of short-term exposure and social interaction on phonetic learning. *Proceedings of the National Academy of Sciences of the United States of America, 100*, 9096–9101.

Kyle, J. G., Woll, B., & Ackerman, J. A. (1989). *Gesture to sign and speech*. Bristol: Centre for Deaf Studies.

Lederberg, A., & Mobley, G. (1990). The effect of hearing impairment on the quality of attachment and mother–toddler interaction. *Child Development, 61*, 1596–1604.

Lieberman, A. M., Hatrak, M., & Mayberry, R. (2014). Learning to look for language: development of joint attention in young deaf children. *Language Learning and Development, 10*, 19–35.

Loots, G., Devisé, I., & Jacquet, W. (2005). The impact of visual communication on the intersubjective development of early parent-child interaction with 18- to 24-month-old deaf toddlers. *Journal of Deaf Studies and Deaf Education, 10*, 357–375.

Mayer, A., & Träuble, B. (2015). The weird world of cross-cultural false belief research and why true belief tasks might be of help: a study among Samoan children based on commands. *Journal of Cognition and Development, 16*, 650–665.

Meadow-Orlans, K., & Spencer, P. (1996). Maternal sensitivity and the visual attentiveness of children who are deaf. *Infant Child Development 5*, 213–223.

Meadow-Orlans, K., & Steinberg, A. (1993). Effects of infant hearing loss and maternal support on mother–infant interactions at 18 months. *Journal of Applied Developmental Psychology, 14*, 407–426.

Meins, E., Fernyhough, C., Arnott, B., Leekam, S., & de Rosnay, M. (2013). Mind-mindedness and theory of mind: mediating roles of language and perspectival symbolic play. *Child Development, 84*(5), 1777–1790.

Meins, E., Fernyhough, C., Johnson, F., & Lidstone, J. (2006). Mind-mindedness in children: individual differences in internal-state talk in middle childhood. *British Journal of Developmental Psychology, 24*, 181–196.

Meristo, M., Falkman, K. W., Hjelmquist, E., Tedoldi, M., Surian, L., & Siegal, M. (2007). Language access and theory of mind reasoning: evidence from deaf children in bilingual and oralist environments. *Developmental Psychology, 43*, 1156–1169.

Meristo, M., Morgan, G., Geraci, A., Iozzi, L., Hjelmquist, E., Surian, L., & Siegal, M. (2012). Belief attribution in deaf and hearing infants. *Developmental Science, 15*, 633–640.

Milligan, K., Astington, J. W., & Dack, L. A. (2007). Language and theory of mind: meta-analysis of the relation between language ability and false-belief understanding. *Child Development, 78*, 622–646.

Morgan, G., Meristo, M., Mann, W., Hjelmquist, E., Surian, L., & Siegal, M. (2014). Mental state language and quality of conversational experience in deaf and hearing children. *Cognitive Development, 29*, 41–49.

Onishi, K., & Baillargeon, R. (2005). Do 15 month old infants understand false beliefs? *Science, 308*, 255–258.

Perez, M., Valsameda, M., & Morgan, G. (2015). Bilingual sign education in Madrid, Spain. In G. Tang, H. Knoors, & M. Marschark (Eds.), *Bilingualism and Bilingual Deaf Education*. New York: Oxford University Press.

Perner, J., & Ruffman, T. (2005). Infants insight into the mind: how deep? *Science, 308*, 214–216.

Peterson, C. C., & Siegal, M. (1995). Deafness, conversation and theory of mind. *Journal of Child Psychology and Psychiatry, 36*(3), 459–474.

Peterson, C. C., Wellman, H. M., & Slaughter, V. (2012). The mind behind the message: advancing theory of mind scales for typically developing children, and those with deafness, autism, or Asperger syndrome. *Child Development, 83*, 469–485.

Premack, D., & Woodruff, G. (1978). Does the chimpanzee have a theory of mind? *Behavioral and Brain Sciences, 4*, 515–526.

Pyers, J., & Senghas, A. (2009). Language promotes false-belief understanding: evidence from a new sign language. *Psychological Science, 20*(7), 805–812.

Rinaldi, P., Baruffaldi, F., Burdo, S., & Caselli M. C. (2013). Linguistic and pragmatic skills in toddlers with cochlear implant. *International Journal of Language and Communication Disorders, 48*, 715–725.

Saffran, J. R., Aslin, R. N., & Newport, E. L. (1996). Statistical learning by 8-month-old infants. *Science, 274*, 1926–1928.

Schick, B., de Villiers, P., de Villiers, J., & Hoffmeister, R. (2007). Language and theory of mind: a study of deaf children. *Child Development, 78*, 376–396.

Senju, A., Southgate, V., Snape, C., Leonard, M., & Csibra, G. (2011). Do 18-month-olds really attribute mental states to others? A critical test. *Psychological Science, 22*, 878–880.

Senju, A., Southgate, V., White, S., & Frith, U. (2009). Mindblind eyes: an absence of spontaneous theory of mind in Asperger syndrome. *Science, 325*(5942), 883–885.

Southgate, V., Chevallier, C., & Csibra, G. (2010). Seventeen-month-olds appeal to false beliefs to interpret others' referential communication. *Developmental Science, 16*, 907–912.

Southgate, V., & Vernetti, A. (2014). Belief-based action prediction in preverbal infants. *Cognition, 130*, 1–10.

Spencer, P. (2000). Looking without listening: is audition a prerequisite for normal development of visual attention during infancy? *Journal of Deaf Studies and Deaf Education, 5*, 291–302.

Spencer, P., Bodner-Johnson, B., & Gutfreund, M. (1992). Interacting with infants with a hearing loss: what can we learn from mothers who are deaf? *Journal of Early Intervention, 16*, 64–78.

Spencer, P., & Waxman, S. (1995). Joint attention and maternal attention strategies: 9, 12, and 18 months. In *Maternal responsiveness and child competency in deaf and hearing children*. Final report, grant H023C10077. Washington, DC: U.S. Department of Education.

Surian, L., Caldi, S., & Sperber, D. (2007). Attribution of beliefs by 13-month-old infants. *Psychological Science*, *18*(7), 580–586.

Swisher, V. (1992). The role of parents in developing visual turn-taking in their young deaf children. *American Annals of the Deaf*, *137*, 92–100.

Tasker, S. L., Nowakowski, M. E., & Schmidt, L. A. (2010). Joint attention and social competence in profoundly deaf children with cochlear implants. *Journal of Developmental and Physical Disabilities*, *22*, 509–532.

Taumoepeau, M., & Ruffman, T. (2006). Mother and infant talk about mental states relates to desire language and emotion understanding. *Child Development*, *77*, 465–481.

Vinden, P. G. (2001). Parenting attitudes and children's understanding of mind. a comparison of Korean American and Anglo-American families. *Cognitive Development*, *16*(3), 793–809.

Wedell-Monnig, J., & Lumley, J. (1980). Child deafness and mother–child interaction. *Child Development*, *51*, 766–774.

Wimmer, H., & Perner, J. (1983). Beliefs about beliefs: representation and constraining function of wrong beliefs in young children's understanding of deception. *Cognition*, *13*, 103–128.

Woll, B. (2013). Sign language and spoken language development in young children: measuring vocabulary by means of the CDI. In L. Meurant, A. Sinte, M. van Heereweghe, & M. Vermeerbergen (Eds.), *Sign language research, uses and practices: Crossing views on theoretical and Applied Sign Language linguistics*. Berlin: deGruyter Mouton & Ishara Press.

Woolfe, T., Want, S., & Siegal, M. (2002). Signposts to development: theory of mind in deaf children. *Child Development*, *73*, 768–778.

9

MINDREADING AS A TRANSACTIONAL PROCESS

Insights from autism

Peter Mitchell

If we make advances in understanding how autism affects development, then this knowledge will be of tremendous value when designing programmes of intervention to promote socialisation and cognition. Over the past decades, researchers have strived to explain the cognitive basis of autism and three theories stand out: the theory-of-mind hypothesis, the theory of executive dysfunction and the theory of weak central coherence (Rajendran & Mitchell, 2007). The champions of these various theories are united in the quest to identify the core cognitive impairment. Take, for example, the theory-of-mind hypothesis: the authors of this account believe that autism is explained as a basic cognitive deficit in mentalising – an inability to calculate what another person is thinking (Baron-Cohen, 1995). Such inability reputedly creates a barrier to predicting and explaining how another person will behave; and it also presents an obstacle to understanding how another person feels. This central deficit supposedly explains the features of autism, with the implication that if we could remedy the impaired theory of mind, then perhaps autism would be cured (e.g. Hadwin, Baron-Cohen, Howlin, & Hill, 1996). The other theories similarly seek to explain autism as a core cognitive deficit (but of a different kind).

In short, the theory-of-mind hypothesis purports to offer a *causal explanation* for autism. Suppose, however, that an underdeveloped ability to mentalise is not the cause but a *consequence* of autism. This possibility comes into focus when we remind ourselves that autism is a developmental disorder. Is it possible that growing up with autism denies one the kinds of social experiences that are critical for developing interpersonal skills and psychological understanding? Is it possible that the condition of autism creates an obstacle to the social experiences that are vital for developing the level of expertise necessary for engaging effectively with the social world? The purpose of this chapter is to articulate such a speculation.

Having introduced the principal question, it is timely to summarise how this chapter approaches the problem. To begin, there is a brief review of evidence relating to the putative lack of mentalising abilities in people with autism. One benefit of being able to mentalise is that we are able to guess what happened in the world by interpreting another person's reaction; effectively, we are able to use the person's reaction as a kind of lens on to a part of the world that we can't see directly. Recent research is summarised, showing that people with autism sometimes have difficulty making these kinds of inferences. The middle of the chapter addresses the central question of whether or not people with autism are effective in following the gaze of another person, drawing upon evidence from eye movement recording as well as behavioural data. The findings seem to suggest that people with autism do spend as much time looking at eyes as comparison participants and they perform just as well in following gaze. The critical difference is that people with autism appear to be slow in reacting to interpersonal signals. Such slowness could have far-reaching negative consequences for development in socialisation, which is a key speculation articulated towards the end of this chapter.

Mentalising in autism – summary of background research

About 30 years ago researchers set out to determine whether or not children with autism have a theory of mind by presenting a test of false belief (Baron-Cohen, Leslie, & Frith, 1985). As many as 80 per cent of the sample failed to show any signs that they understood that another person held a simple factual belief that was different than their own. Poor performance could not be explained by low mental age, because the children were screened for general intellectual ability: even many of those with a mental age above 4 years, the age at which typically developing children pass the test, showed no sign of understanding that others can be in a state of false belief. And neither could poor performance be explained by developmental delay: a control group of children with learning disability but without autism matched for chronological and mental age had much greater success in acknowledging states of false belief.

How can we explain the finding that as many as 20 per cent of the sample with autism successfully acknowledged states of false belief? We might wonder if correct performance is unstable or whether these children had been incorrectly diagnosed – both of those explanations are incorrect (Rajendran & Mitchell, 2007). In that case, perhaps a simple test of false belief is not the ideal task for identifying limitations in mentalising and, in view of this possibility, Baron-Cohen (1989) presented a more complicated test. In this, participants are asked to calculate what A thinks B thinks about a state in the world. In this task, B's belief is embedded within A's, thus placing considerable demands on the working memory of any participant who is asked to solve the problem. Baron-Cohen discovered that most children with autism who passed a simple test of false belief were unable to solve this more complicated and challenging puzzle, while typically developing children of similar mental age succeeded. Baron-Cohen concluded that children with autism really do have impairment in mentalising and, if this is not detected by a simple test of false belief, then at least it will be detected by a more complicated task.

This conclusion turned out to be incorrect: Bowler (1992) demonstrated that many high-functioning adults with autism are able to pass an embedded test of belief. We now know that people with autism are developmentally delayed, relative to their mental age, in giving correct judgments in simple and in more complicated tests of belief (Happé, 1995). We certainly cannot say, then, that failing a simple or a complicated test of belief is a defining feature of autism.

Baron-Cohen responded by substantially changing the theory-of-mind hypothesis to shift emphasis away from the cognitive architecture required to make judgements of belief to speculations about abnormalities in face processing (Baron-Cohen & Ring, 1994). Specifically, it was suggested that perhaps people with autism have a primary impairment in interpreting psychological information from the region of other people's eyes. Such impairment might show itself in two ways: (1) unlike those with typical development, people with autism might not be able to interpret how somebody is feeling or what that person is thinking based on clues from the eye region of the face; and (2) people with autism might have difficulty following the direction of another person's gaze, thus preventing joint attention. How these speculations could explain developmental delays in passing tests of belief remained unclear.

How well do people with autism interpret information from the eyes?

To address this question, Baron-Cohen and colleagues (Baron-Cohen, Jolliffe, Mortimore, & Robertson, 1997; Baron-Cohen, Wheelwright, Hill, Raste, & Plumb, 2001a; Baron-Cohen, Wheelwright, Scahill, Lawson, & Spong, 2001b) created a new test in which participants had to guess a target's mental state from a photograph of the person's facial expression. Under one condition the target's full face was visible while under another most of the face was masked and a rectangular window gave a view only on to the region of the target's eyes. High-functioning adults with autism were less successful than comparison participants in guessing the target's mental state and the difference between groups was greatest when only the target's eye region was visible. Baron-Cohen et al. interpreted this as a sign that people with autism are specifically impaired in processing psychological information from the region of a person's eyes. This research raises at least two questions. First, is it really true that participants with autism are specifically impaired in processing psychological information from a target's eyes? Second, is it more generally true that people with autism are less effective than typically developing individuals in processing clues in another person's behaviour to make psychological inferences?

The first question is answered by the results of a study conducted by Back, Ropar, and Mitchell (2007). Adults with and without autism who had intelligence measured in the normal range watched a video of an actress posing facial expressions associated with a variety of mental states. Participants had to make their judgement in a four-way forced-choice procedure, where chance responding was 25 per cent correct. Participants with autism were correct 55 per cent of the time and participants without autism were correct 65 per cent of the time. Several things can be said about this finding. First, participants without autism were only 10 per cent better on the task than those with autism, but this difference was nevertheless highly significant in statistical terms. Second, the task was unquestionably quite difficult in that participants, including those without autism, were well below ceiling. Third, notwithstanding, participants, including those with autism, were systematically correct in their judgements and performed well above chance in statistical terms.

How can we explain the finding that participants with autism had a lower rate of success compared with those who did not have autism? Perhaps Baron-Cohen would say that participants with autism were disadvantaged in being unable to interpret psychological information from the target's eyes. Indeed, in the light of Back et al.'s results (2007), he might even say that this disadvantage could be quantified as a 10 per cent decrement in performance. However, this explanation proved to be incorrect. Under another condition in the same experiment, part of the target's face was seamlessly frozen by digital editing, such that the eyes were the only part of the face that was animated (and therefore revealing of a mental state – non-animated parts were neutral and revealed nothing about mental states). Under this condition, performance in those with autism dropped from 55 per cent to 40 per cent – a level that was still systematically correct to a highly significant level, demonstrating that those with autism were definitely capable of processing psychological information exclusively from the target's eyes. Perhaps most importantly, though, the participants without autism also experienced a decrement to precisely the same extent, dropping from 65 per cent to 50 per cent. Hence, the decrement in performance was 15 per cent in both groups. If it had been the case, as Baron-Cohen suggests, that people with autism have specific difficulty interpreting information from the eyes, then they should have experienced a bigger decrement in performance compared with those who did not have autism when only the eye region conveyed psychological information.

Under a further condition in the same experiment, the eyes of the target were frozen such that only the mouth conveyed psychological information. Those with autism were correct approximately 45 per cent of the time, indicating a significant decrement in performance at the level of about 10 per cent compared with the condition in which all of the face was animated (and therefore psychologically informative). The result suggests that participants with autism were able to process information from the target's eyes when all of the face was animated. If they had effectively been blind to the target's eyes, as Baron-Cohen seemed to argue, then withholding information from the target's eyes should not have led to any further decrement in performance – but it did! Hence, where the face is fully animated and there is a 10 per cent difference in performance between those with and without autism, we cannot conclude that this is explained by people with autism being disadvantaged in processing information from the target's eyes. Instead, it seems that people with autism can make systematically correct judgements about mental states based on the target's facial expressions but for some unknown reason they are slightly less effective in doing this compared with typically developing people.

Why is it useful and adaptive to be able to guess mental states from clues in behaviour? If we can guess how another person is feeling, for example, when that person is upset, perhaps this will help us to show concern and offer comfort. Doing so no doubt will foster friendship, will encourage others to help us when we are in need and will enhance our esteem within the social group. A further benefit would ensue if we could actually penetrate beyond another person's mental states to the world as seen through that individual's eyes (or mind's eye). Mental states do not happen in a vacuum; rather, they are usually reactions to events that occur in the world. Presumably, the ability to see through a facial expression and to look beyond the underlying mental state to a precipitating event that happened in the world is of monumental adaptive value. Rather than knowledge having to be based entirely on first-hand experience, we would instead be able to see the world through the lens of another mind. A more highly developed form of the same faculty might allow us to learn from others through the medium of language and hence the accumulated wisdom of a culture can thus be transferred from one mind to another – in the modern world this would in many cases take place through formal education.

Psychological inferences from clues in behaviour

How effectively can people with and without autism guess what happened on observing a target's reaction? To find the answer, Pillai, Sheppard, and Mitchell (2012) began by testing the ability of typically developing adults. Participants viewed a short video (lasting around 7 seconds) of a target reacting to one of four scenarios. The targets had enrolled in a study and, before testing ostensibly began, the researcher paid a compliment, told a joke, described her difficult day or kept the target waiting while she rudely sent text messages and spoke to a friend on her mobile phone. From a 7-second video clip, would participants be able to guess which scenario the target experienced? The answer was yes! How did participants guess what happened – by scrutinising the eyes of the target? No! Participants viewed the target reactions on a screen that was equipped with sensors for record-ing eye movements and the data revealed that they spent about twice as much time looking at the target's mouth as they did looking at the eyes.

Using the same procedure, Pillai et al. (2014) tested adults with autism and comparison participants. Those with autism were systematically able to guess what happened to the target but performed less well than comparison participants. The eye movements of those with autism were indistinguishable from those of comparison participants, showing greater time spent looking at the mouth than the eyes of the target. A study by Cassidy, Ropar, Mitchell, and Chapman (2013) employed a similar procedure, except that targets were reacting to different kinds of events. In this case, targets had ostensibly completed the main part of the task whereupon the experimenter offered an additional reward for participating – some chocolate, a childish homemade gift or Monopoly money. Generally, those with autism performed less well in guessing which gift the target received than the comparison participants. This was evident in the case of the target receiving chocolate or a homemade gift, where those in the comparison group gave systematically correct judgements while those with autism did not. In this study there was evidence of participants in the two groups having different patterns of eye movements. Notably, there were signs in some conditions that participants with autism looked more to the target's mouth and less to the target's eyes compared with typically developing participants.

In summary, participants with autism are less proficient in processing facial expressions than typically developing participants. They are less effective in guessing the mental states of a target and they are less effective in guessing what caused a target's facial expression. Consequently, it seems they are disadvantaged in seeing things that happened in the world through the lens of another person's mind. What is the cause of this lack of proficiency in autism? Is it because they are specifically unable to interpret information from the target's eyes? While there is no compelling evidence to support such a suggestion, it remains a possibility that people with autism are not effective in following another person's direction of gaze. Even in circumstances when they spent as much time looking at the eyes of a target compared with typically developing participants, they still might not be able to follow gaze; and perhaps an inability to follow gaze could have cascading negative developmental consequences for broader mentalising abilities.

Can people with autism follow gaze?

One of the earliest studies designed to address this question was conducted by Baron-Cohen, Campbell, Karmiloff-Smith, Grant, and Walker (1995). Participants were shown a schematic face (Charlie) whose eye pupils were looking to one or other of the corners in the frame. In each corner was a type of candy and the observing participant was invited to guess which kind of candy Charlie wanted. Five-year-old children with typical development usually judged that Charlie wanted the candy that he was looking at while those with autism who had a mental age of 5 years judged unsystematically. The authors concluded that children with autism are unable to make psychological inferences (of desire) from direction of gaze. A subsequent study by Klin, Jones, Schultz, and Volkmar (2003) seemed to offer an explanation: while wearing an eye movement-recording device participants watched a movie and the evidence seemed to suggest that participants with autism spent far less time looking at the eyes of the principal actor than those with typical development; their attention seemed to be captured more by the mouth of the support actor. It would be difficult for participants with autism to follow gaze if they were not even looking at other people's eyes!

In order to investigate whether or not participants can follow gaze, Freeth, Ropar, Chapman, and Mitchell (2010) conducted the following task. Participants

FIGURE 9.1   (a and b). Participants with autism look at the face and follow gaze direction to the same degree as comparison participants, though they are slower to do these things. Reproduced from Freeth, M., Ropar, D., Chapman, P., & Mitchell, P. (2010). The eye-gaze direction of an observed person can bias perception, memory and attention in adolescents with and without autism spectrum disorders. *Journal of Experimental Child Psychology, 105*, 20–37. Copyright (2010) with permission from Elsevier.

were shown photos of targets in a context in which they were either looking directly out of the photo or looking sideways (even though they were directly facing the camera) at a conspicuous object in the scene (Figure 9.1). These photos were presented on a computer screen and participants were invited to slide the photo left and right using the arrow keys until they were satisfied that 'it looked best'. When the target was looking directly out of the photo, there was a strong tendency to adjust the photo until the target was in the middle of the screen, which was apparent to the same degree in those with and without autism. This is not surprising and perhaps is a sign that participants were sensitive to a convention that people are normally the central subject matter in photography.

Participants performed differently under the condition in which the target was looking sideways. In this case there are two areas of psychological interest: the target person remains a centre of psychological interest and in addition the object being looked at by the target now assumes psychological relevance because this object is invested with importance by virtue of being the subject of the target's gaze. If participants' adjustment of the photograph is based on what they perceive as the psychological centre of gravity, then how would they behave in this condition? It is reasonable to suppose that the psychological centre of gravity is located somewhere between the target person and the object the target is looking at. Accordingly, we should expect participants to adjust this point to be in the centre of the frame, and that is precisely what happened. Notably, participants adjusted the photos differently depending on whether the target was looking out of the photo or looking sideways, at least suggesting that they were heavily influenced by the gaze direction of the target. There was no difference in the strength of this effect between participants who did and did not have autism. Hence, those with autism were influenced by eye gaze to the same degree as comparison participants.

This is but one piece of evidence – is there any converging evidence to corroborate the suggestion that people with autism are effective in following gaze? To find the answer, Freeth, Ropar, et al. (2010) employed a change blindness procedure in which a photograph appears on the screen, alternating rapidly between versions in which a target object is present or absent – the participant's task is to detect the changing object as quickly as possible. Critically, under one condition a person in the photograph is looking at the point in the scene where the object is present or absent; under another condition the person is looking directly out of the photograph. Participants were significantly faster in detecting the changing object when it was the subject of the gaze of the person in the photo than when it was not. Most importantly, this effect was apparent to the same degree in participants with and without autism.

In summary, there is evidence that participants with autism followed the gaze direction of another person to the same degree as typically developing participants. However, this evidence, although compelling, is nevertheless circumstantial. We assume that if the behaviour of the participant was affected by the gaze direction of a target person in a photo, then the participant must have been following the gaze of the target. This is an inference made on the circumstantial evidence of an effect we observed on the participant's behaviour. But we do not actually know from this evidence that participants with autism appropriately shifted their gaze after looking at the eyes of a target. To find out for sure, eye movement-recording technology is needed.

Evidence from eye movement recordings

Participants were shown the same photographs of targets either looking directly out or looking sideways at an object within the scene for a period of 5 seconds (Freeth, Chapman, Ropar, & Mitchell, 2010). They did not have to make any response; they were asked only to look at the photo. These photos were displayed on a screen discreetly fitted with sensors capable of detecting where the participant was looking over the 5-second period of viewing. The results were multifaceted, often subtle but highly revealing.

Taking into consideration the scale of the photo and the size of the target's face therein, the resolution of the eye movement recording was sufficient to tell us whether the participant was looking at the top part of the face (including the eyes) or the lower part of the face (including the mouth). To begin, it is interesting to know whether the participants looked more at the top part of the face and whether or not there was any difference between groups in this respect. The results were absolutely clear: over the five seconds participants spent more than twice as much time looking at the top than the bottom part of the target's face and the data for those with autism were indistinguishable from those without autism.

Just because participants were looking at the region of the eyes, it does not necessarily follow that they would be influenced by that target's gaze direction. To clarify this matter, the researchers examined the probability that participants shifted their gaze to the salient object (the object being looked at by the target in some of the photos) immediately after looking at the target's eyes (the top part of the target's face). The results clearly showed that whether or not participants shifted their gaze in this way depended on the direction of gaze of the target. When the target was looking at the salient object, participants were more than twice as likely to shift their gaze to this same object than in photos where the target was not look-ing at the salient object. This large effect was indistinguishable between those with and without autism. Hence, the findings offer direct evidence of a circumstance in which people with autism strongly follow eye gaze to the same degree as people without autism.

More detailed examination of the results revealed subtle group differences in the *timing* of eye movements. While it was true that participants with and without autism equally spent a high proportion of time looking at the target's face, there was a significant group difference in how quickly participants started to look at the face. Those without autism started to look at the face after about a third of a second while those with autism started to look after about half a second. It is commonly known that sometimes people with autism are slow to respond to stimuli and we might wonder whether the relative delay in looking at the face is but a detail in a broader tendency to be slow in responding. To find out, Freeth, Chapman, et al. (2010) examined how quickly participants looked at other features in the photo, including physical objects as well as people. Interestingly, participants with autism were not slower but faster than comparison participants in looking at physical objects under some conditions. Hence, their slowness in looking at the face of the target apparently cannot be explained as a general tendency to respond slowly to any and all stimuli.

Finally, we consider perhaps the most important finding in Freeth, Chapman, et al.'s (2010) study: how long did it take participants to be cued by the gaze direction of the target? To find the answer, the researchers examined the probability of looking to the salient object after looking at the top part of the target's face to determine if this was greater when the target was looking at the object than when the target was not looking at the object. Such an effect was apparent in typically developing participants after viewing the photo for two seconds (but not after viewing it for one second). In other words, it took two seconds for typically developing participants to be cued by the target's direction of gaze. In contrast, it took participants with autism as long as three seconds to be cued by the target's eye gaze, and this amounted to a statistically significant difference between groups in the response time to a social cue.

In summary, eye movement data revealed subtle but potentially important differences between participants with and without autism. It was not the case that participants with autism looked at the eyes of a target less than comparison participants and neither were those with autism less likely to follow the gaze of a target. The vital differences between groups were related to timing. Those with autism were slower to look at faces but faster to look at physical objects than comparison participants. Moreover, those with autism were slower to be cued by a target's direction of gaze.

Developmental implications and consequences of responding slowly to social cues

In this section I will offer a highly speculative interpretation of these findings. Slow attention to the social world (e.g. a target's face) might be an indication that people with autism assign lower attentional priority to this subject matter compared with typically developing people. Perhaps a core feature of autism surrounds such differences in attentional priority. If a particular subject matter is assigned higher attentional priority than others, perhaps this will have developmentally cascading consequences in the way cognition is shaped. For example, a typically developing individual who prioritises looking at social stimuli like faces might eventually develop more expertise in analysing such stimuli compared with a person (for example, a person with autism) who assigns lower attentional priority to such stimuli.

Having attentional preference for certain kinds of stimuli will quite possibly mean that the individual becomes highly proficient in detecting subtle details that will help not only in distinguishing between one person and another but also in distinguishing between one expression and another in the same face. Being thus able to distinguish various expressions is undoubtedly a necessary skill for being able to recognise different emotions. In short, attentional priority for faces is probably the basis for developing expertise in processing faces along with an understanding of the psychological states that underlie facial expressions. Perhaps the lack of developing expertise in processing faces could explain why those with autism were 10 per cent less successful in interpreting facial expressions than comparison participants in the study reported by Back et al. (2007), summarised above.

Being slow to respond to facial cues not only gives an indication of lack of attentional priority to the social world; this feature might also impact on the very character of social development. While it is possible that being able to mentalise has an innate basis (Mitchell, 1994), such capacity could not reach its potential in a social vacuum. By analogy, although the human capacity for language might be innate, any child reared in social isolation will not acquire the ability to speak. Through conversation with others we learn of their likes, dislikes, what they are thinking, their hopes, ambitions and their moods. Further psychological enlightenment is afforded by observing the manner in which friends and family engage with third parties. They adapt their social style to suit the occasion, sometimes adopting charm, sometimes being blunt and sometimes being economical with the truth. In short, as an active or passive participant in social life we stand to gain tremendous insights into the minds of other people.

Is it possible that being slow in responding to social cues could be a barrier to participating in social life? Effectively, anyone who was slow in reacting to social cues would struggle to keep up with the pace of a social exchange. Moreover, talking to a person who is interpersonally slow might prove to be tedious and unrewarding. Perhaps not realising that your conversational partner has a developmental disorder, you would be forgiven for thinking that the person you are talking to is not paying full attention and is perhaps distracted by other matters. Presumably, people ordinarily have but limited patience in dealing with an unresponsive partner before moving on to talk to someone who seems more stimulating.

If this speculation has any merit then the implications for social development would be profound, for individuals with autism would find themselves feeling lonely and isolated from social life. In such a state there would be few opportunities to benefit from the informal interpersonal education that one normally gains from conversation. People with autism might thus be denied the kind of experiences that are vital for becoming socially adroit. Such lack of social expertise, coupled with basic slowness in responding to social cues, would put the individual at a further developmental disadvantage. Hence, the individual would developmentally lag further and further behind in this arena.

The speculation offered here is inspired by the transactional account of development, articulated by Sameroff (1975). He assigned a central role in the child's development to his or her caretaker. Specifically, he suggested that if, for example, the parent thought that the child was constitutionally abnormal and not developing well, then this would give rise to a sequence of negative transactions that cause the child's development to be hampered even further. Hence, the parent's interpretation of the child's behaviour will lead to a perception of his or her abilities that impacts on the way in which the parent relates to the child in future, thereby creating a self-fulfilling prophecy. Although Sameroff focused on the relationship between the parent and child, there is no reason to suppose that the transactional model should be confined to this specific relationship. Interactions between any individuals will inevitably lead to impressions being formed, which in turn will impact on behaviour which in turn will impact on the learning and development opportunities of the parties concerned. Accordingly, the suggestion here is that a basic attentional feature of autism could have cascading negative social-developmental consequences that create an obstacle to the acquisition of social competence.

Developmental implications and consequences of attending quickly to physical stimuli

Development seems to be driven by a potent force that almost seems unstoppable. Take language development as a case in point: the child learns a sophisticated code in a short period of time in the absence of formal or deliberate instruction. One might wonder if language is a special case, and perhaps it is; but children learn many things quite rapidly and often spontaneously. Granted, some children might have the potential to learn quicker than others and the capacity to learn more than others – no doubt there are individual differences in development. But the thirst for development might need to be quenched and an obstruction in one domain (the social domain) might present an opportunity in another domain (the non-social domain).

In most cases it is perhaps natural for children to develop expertise in the social world – doing so surely increases the chance that the individual will thrive. It is important for the child to bond with the caregiver, to communicate through language and to learn social customs. Suppose, though, that there was an obstacle to developing expertise in the social domain. In that circumstance, perhaps the drive to develop could be satisfied by acquiring expertise in the non-social domain. Specifically, perhaps prioritised attention to the physical world could allow heightened perceptual abilities to develop.

Various pieces of evidence support the suggestion that individuals with autism enjoy heightened perceptual abilities. They are better than matched controls in visual search (Plaisted, O'Riordan, & Baron-Cohen, 1998), in performing the embedded figures task (Shah & Frith, 1983) and in performing the block design test (Shah & Frith, 1993). People with autism might also experience less perceptual distortion than typically developing individuals and I offer two pieces of evidence in support of this suggestion. The first piece of evidence concerns the perception of a slanted circle. Thouless (1931) classically demonstrated that, when asked to draw a slanted circle, such as a dinner plate viewed obliquely from the head of the table, participants tend to exaggerate circularity: while a rather thin ellipse might be projected on to the retina, people reproduce a much fatter ellipse when asked to draw what they see. One might wonder if this is caused by an error in perception or an error in the process of drawing and it seems to be best explained as an error in perception (Taylor & Mitchell, 1997).

If people with autism experience less perceptual distortion than typically developing participants, then perhaps they will be able to reproduce a slanted circle more accurately in the kind of task devised by Thouless. To find out, Ropar and Mitchell (2002) presented a circular disc at a slant in a chamber and invited participants to look at the shape through a view hole. Typically developing participants exaggerated circularity as expected, and this occurred under normal conditions of illumination as well as under a condition in which the ambient visual context was not visible. In the latter, participants could only see the slanted circle; they could not see any of the surrounding context that provides information to indicate that the target is indeed a slanted circle (and not an ellipse presented squarely to the line of sight). But they knew nevertheless that the target was actually a circle because before testing began they were freely allowed to examine the properties of the target object.

Participants with autism showed a different pattern of performance. Although they exaggerated circularity to the same degree as comparison participants when the ambient context was visible, they made much more accurate judgements when the visual context was hidden. Hence, while knowledge (purely knowledge, not visual context) was sufficient to cause exaggeration of circularity in typically developing participants, this was not the case in participants with autism. At least in one sense, those with autism perceived more accurately.

It also seems that people with autism are less susceptible to certain kinds of visual illusion compared with typically developing individuals. Mitchell, Mottron, Soulieres, and Ropar (2010) demonstrated this with the Shepard Illusion (Figure 9.2), where the figure on the right looks squarer than the figure on the left but in fact the two are identical in size and shape (Shepard, 1990). Susceptibility was investigated with a custom-made program (Mitchell, Ropar, Ackroyd, & Rajendran, 2005) that presented the shapes shown in Figure 9.2 and participants were invited to adjust the shape on the right such that it was identical to the shape on the left (except that the shape on the left is standing up and the shape on the right is lying on its side). On experiencing perceptual distortion, participants tend to make the shape on the right too long and thin relative to the adjustment that would have been needed in order to make the two shapes physically identical. While participants with and

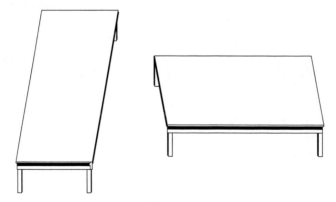

FIGURE 9.2 The Shepard Illusion – the figure on the right is exactly the same size and shape as the figure on the left (except it is rotated clockwise through 90 degrees). Participants with autism experienced lower illusion strength than comparison participants.

without autism made such errors, the degree of error was much more severe in the typically developing participants. Hence, by a matter of degree, it seems participants with autism were able to perceive the shapes more accurately than comparison participants.

Probably the Shepard Illusion owes its effect to the features that induce us to interpret the figure three-dimensionally. Indeed, it is quite possible that typically developing individuals automatically interpret the figure as a representation of a three-dimensional object. Perhaps those with autism are liberated from the compunction to interpret such a figure three-dimensionally and are free instead, at least to a degree, to interpret it as a two-dimensional pattern of lines. If so, then this would explain why the illusion is less potent for those with autism.

Some individuals with autism exhibit *savant* abilities, meaning that they develop expertise in specialised areas of activity despite being unable to perform well in other areas. Various topics can be the subject of a special interest and there are a few well-known cases of *savant* artists: people with autism who show remarkable ability in drawing, even though they have not received instruction and despite having extensive socio-cognitive disabilities. Granted, being good at art depends on dexterity in manipulating an instrument for drawing but it also depends on an aptitude for scrutinising and analysing what one sees. The latter is an aptitude that might be common in autism, as suggested above. Hence, a heightened ability in visual processing, which could be a compensating consequence of underdevelopment in the social sphere, might be an enabling factor in the development of artistic skills. Obviously this artistic potential would only be realised if the individual were also able to develop the relevant motor skills and therefore we would not expect all people with autism to be *savant* artists.

Conclusion: autism in a socio-developmental context

Autism should be understood in a socio-developmental context. This condition might be associated with a distinctive attentional profile that is sensed but misinterpreted by other people. Such basic interpersonal misunderstanding might create barriers to engaging in social life and in consequence might result in lost opportunities for learning how others think and feel (amongst other things). Because autism affects development, associated features will inevitably change over time. Unfortunately, though, development is likely to be tardy and aberrant. Looking to the future, if we had a better understanding of how autism impacts on development, then not only would we have deeper insights into this condition, but we would also have a better grasp of the processes that figure in typical development.

References

Back, E., Ropar, D., & Mitchell, P. (2007). Do the eyes have it? Inferring mental states from animated faces in autism. *Child Development, 78*, 397–411.

Baron-Cohen, S. (1989). The autistic child's theory of mind – a case of specific developmental delay. *Journal of Child Psychology and Psychiatry and Allied Disciplines, 30*, 285–297.

Pillai, D., Sheppard, E., Ropar, D., Marsh, L., Pearson, A., & Mitchell, P. (2014). Using other minds as a window onto the world: guessing what happened from clues in behavior. *Journal of Autism and Developmental Disorders, 44,* 2430–2439.

Plaisted, K., O'Riordan, M., & Baron-Cohen, S. (1998). Enhanced visual search for a conjunctive target in autism: a research note. *Journal of Child Psychology and Psychiatry and Allied Disciplines, 39,* 777–783.

Rajendran, G., & Mitchell, P. (2007). Cognitive theories of autism. *Developmental Review, 27,* 224–260.

Ropar, D., & Mitchell, P. (2002). Shape constancy in autism: the role of prior knowledge and perspective cues. *Journal of Child Psychology and Psychiatry, 43,* 647–653.

Sameroff, A. (1975). Transactional models in early social relations. *Human Development, 18,* 65–79.

Shah, A., & Frith, U. (1983). An islet of ability in autistic-children – a research note. *Journal of Child Psychology and Psychiatry and Allied Disciplines, 24,* 613–620.

Shah, A., & Frith, U. (1993). Why do autistic individuals show superior performance on the block design task? *Journal of Child Psychology and Psychiatry and Allied Disciplines, 34,* 1351–1364.

Shepard, R. N. (1990). *Mindsights: Original visual illusions, ambiguities, and other anomalies with a commentary on the play of mind in perception and art.* San Francisco: W. H. Freeman.

Taylor, L. M., & Mitchell, P. (1997). Judgments of apparent shape contaminated by knowledge of real shape. *British Journal of Psychology, 88,* 653–670.

Thouless, R. H. (1931). Phenomenal regression to the real object. I. *British Journal of Psychology 21,* 339–359.

Baron-Cohen, S. (1995). *Mindblindness*. Cambridge, MA: MIT Press.

Baron-Cohen, S., Campbell, R., Karmiloff-Smith, A., Grant, J., & Walker, J. (1 Are children with autism blind to the mental significance of the eyes? *British Jour Developmental Psychology, 13*, 379–398.

Baron-Cohen, S., Jolliffe, T., Mortimore, C., & Robertson, M. (1997). Another adva test of theory of mind: evidence from very high functioning adults with autis Asperger syndrome. *Journal of Child Psychology and Psychiatry and Allied Discipline* 813–822.

Baron-Cohen, S., Leslie, A. M., & Frith, U. (1985). Does the autistic-child have a tl of mind? *Cognition, 21*(1), 37–46.

Baron-Cohen, S., & Ring, H. (1994). A model of the mindreading system: neuropsy logical and neurobiological perspectives. In P. Mitchell & C. Lewis (Eds.), *Origins understanding of mind*. Hove, UK: Lawrence Erlbaum.

Baron-Cohen, S., Wheelwright, S., Hill, J., Raste, Y., & Plumb, I. (2001a). The "re the mind in the eyes" test revised version: a study with normal adults, and adults Asperger syndrome or high-functioning autism. *Journal of Child Psychology and Psy(and Allied Disciplines, 42*, 241–251.

Baron-Cohen, S., Wheelwright, S., Scahill, V., Lawson, J., & Spong, A. (2001b). Are tive physics and intuitive psychology independent? A test with children with Asp syndrome. *Journal of Developmental and Learning Disorders, 5*, 47–78.

Bowler, D. M. (1992). Theory of mind in Asperger's syndrome. *Journal of Child Psyc and Psychiatry and Allied Disciplines, 33*, 877–893.

Cassidy, S., Ropar, D., Mitchell, P., & Chapman, P. (2013). Can adults with autism spe disorders infer what happened to someone from their emotional response? *Autism Re 7*, 112–123.

Freeth, M., Chapman, P., Ropar, D., & Mitchell, P. (2010). Do gaze cues in coi scenes capture and direct the attention of high functioning adolescents with Evidence from eye-tracking. *Journal of Autism and Developmental Disorders, 40*, 537

Freeth, M., Ropar, D., Chapman, P., & Mitchell, P. (2010). The eye-gaze directi an observed person can bias perception, memory and attention in adolescents wit without autism spectrum disorders. *Journal of Experimental Child Psychology, 105*, 2(

Hadwin, J., Baron-Cohen, S., Howlin, P., & Hill, K. (1996). Can we teach childrer autism to understand emotions, belief, or pretence? *Development and Psychopatholo* 345–365.

Happé, F. G. E. (1995). The role of age and verbal-ability in the theory of mind performance of subjects with autism. *Child Development, 66*, 843–855.

Klin, A., Jones, W., Schultz, R., & Volkmar, F. (2003). The enactive mind, or from a to cognition: lessons from autism. *Philosophical Transactions of the Royal Society, Sei 358*, 345–360.

Mitchell, P. (1994). Realism and early conception of mind: phylogenetic and ontoge issues. In C. Lewis and P. Mitchell (Eds). *Children's early understanding of mind: Origi development*. Hove, UK: Erlbaum.

Mitchell, P., Mottron, L., Soulieres, I., & Ropar, D. (2010). Susceptibility to the Sh illusion in participants with autism: reduced top-down influences within percep *Autism Research, 3*, 113–119.

Mitchell, P., Ropar, D., Ackroyd, K., & Rajendran, G. (2005). How perception in on drawings. *Journal of Experimental Psychology: Human Perception and Performanc(996–1003.

Pillai, D., Sheppard, E., & Mitchell, P. (2012). Can people guess what happened to (from their reactions? *PLoS ONE* 7(11): e49859. doi:10.1371/journal.pone.004985'

APPENDIX

Standard theory of mind tasks

These versions of the tasks illustrate the structure and scoring principles for standard tests used with children. Specific details, such as the names and genders and objects of the story protagonists, the type of props used when presenting the tasks (e.g., dolls, cartoons), as well as inclusion of additional test and control questions, can be altered.

Changed location false belief (adapted from Wimmer & Perner, 1983)

Also known as the Sally-Anne task or the Maxi task. Suitable for children ages 2–6.

> Here is Sally. She puts her shoes in the shoebox and goes away. [Move shoes into box and hide Sally.] Now Anne comes. Anne takes the shoes out of the shoebox and puts them in the basket. Now Sally is coming back. She wants her shoes.

Test question: "Where will Sally look for the shoes?" or "Where does Sally think her shoes are now?" (correct answer = shoebox).

Control question: "Where are the shoes now?" (correct answer = basket) and/or "Where did Sally put her shoes before she left?" (correct answer = shoebox).

Score "pass" if both the test and control questions are answered correctly; score fail if any questions are incorrectly answered.

Unexpected contents false belief (adapted from Perner, Leekam & Wimmer, 1987)

Also known as Smarties task. Suitable for children ages 2–6.

> Here is a box. [Show candy box.] What do you think is inside it? Candy, that's a good idea. Let's open the box. [Open the box to reveal pebbles inside. Return pebbles and reclose box.]

Test question #1 (other's belief): "When your friend looks at this box, what will he/she think is inside it?" (correct answer = candy).

Test question #2 (self belief, also known as representational change question): "What did you think was inside this box when you first saw it, before we opened it up?" (correct answer = candy).

Control question for both test questions: "What is really inside the box?" (correct answer = pebbles).

Score "pass" for each test question if both the test and control questions are answered correctly; score fail if either the test or control question is incorrectly answered. Scores on the two test questions can be summed to create a 0–2 score.

Theory of Mind Scale (adapted from Wellman & Liu, 2004 and Peterson, Wellman, & Slaughter, 2012)

Suitable for children ages 2–12. Tasks should be given in the order listed below as they are scaled from easiest to hardest. For each task, score "pass" if test and control questions are answered correctly; score "fail" otherwise. Individual tasks can be dropped at the easy or hard end of the scale to suit the age group being tested. The proportion of tasks passed (out of the total administered) can be calculated to represent a total theory of mind score.

Task 1: Diverse desire

[Show cake and carrots.] Here are two foods. Which do you like to eat best? [Record child's answer.] Here is a lady. She doesn't like _____ [say the food that was the child's choice, e.g., cake]. She likes to eat _____ [say the opposite of the child's choice, e.g., carrots]. Now it is snack time. The lady is going to have something to eat.

Test question: "Which one does she want to eat?" (correct answer = food that matches lady's stated preference).

Task 2: Diverse beliefs

Here is a boy. He wants to find his cat. The cat is hiding. It could be in the garage. Or, it could be in the bushes. [Show garage and bushes.] Now, where do you think the cat is? [Record child's answer.] That's a good guess. But the boy thinks his cat is _____ [say the location that is opposite to what the child said.]

Test question: "Where will the boy look for the cat?" (correct answer = location that matches boy's stated belief).

Task 3: Knowledge access

[Display closed unmarked box] Here is a box. What do you think could be inside it? [Record child's answer.] That's a good guess. Lets open it. Oh, look! There is a book in it. [Close box.]

Control question: "What's really in the box?"(correct answer = book).

Here's a girl. This girl has never seen the box before. She has never opened it.

Control question: "So has she looked in the box?" (correct answer = no).
Test question: "Does the girl know what's in the box?" (correct answer = no).

Task 4: False belief

Here is a box. [Show Band-Aid box.] What do you think is inside it? Band-Aids, that's a good idea. Let's open the box. [Open the box to reveal paperclips inside. Return paperclips and reclose box.]

Test question: "When your friend looks at this box, what will he/she think is inside it?" (correct answer = Band-Aids).
Control question: "What is really inside the box?" (correct answer = paperclips).

Task 5: Hidden emotion

Here is a boy. [Show back of boy's head.] The boy and his friends were playing. A girl teased the boy and his friends all laughed. They thought it was funny. But not the boy. He did not think it was funny. But he did not want the others to see how he felt, or they would call him a baby.

Test question: "How did the boy really and truly feel when everyone laughed and teased him?" (correct answer: sad, embarrassed, unhappy, etc.)
Test question: "How did the boy try to look on his face when everyone laughed and teased him?" (correct answer: happy, OK, normal, etc.)
Test question: "Why did he try to look like that?" (correct answer: so the others wouldn't know how he felt, so they would stop teasing him, etc.)
Note: passing score requires that child chooses a more negative facial expression in response to "really and truly feel" compared to "try to look on his face" and response to final test question indicates that the boy was trying to hide his genuine emotion.

Task 6: Sarcasm

This girl and boy are going on a picnic. It is the boy's idea. He says it will be a lovely sunny day. But when they get the food out, big storm clouds come. [Show rainy picnic.] It rains and the food gets all wet. The girl says: "It's a lovely day for a picnic."

Control question: "Is it true, what the girl said?" (correct answer = no).

Test question: "Why did the girl say, 'It's a lovely day for a picnic'?" (correct answer = she was being sarcastic, she was joking, to be funny, she didn't mean it).

Control question: "Was the girl happy about the rain?" (correct answer = no).

References

Perner, J., Leekam, S. R., & Wimmer, H. (1987). Three-year-olds' difficulty with false belief: the case for a conceptual deficit. *British Journal of Developmental Psychology, 5*, 125–137.

Peterson, C. C., Wellman, H., & Slaughter, V. (2012). The mind behind the message: advancing theory of mind scales for typically developing children, and those with deafness, autism, or Asperger syndrome. *Child Development, 83*, 469–485.

Wellman, H. M., & Liu, D. (2004). Scaling of theory-of-mind tasks. *Child Development, 75*(2), 523–541.

Wimmer, H., & Perner, J. (1983). Beliefs about beliefs: representation and constraining function of wrong beliefs in young children's understanding of deception. *Cognition, 13*(1), 103–128.

INDEX

abuse 91, 93, 99; *see also* maltreatment
accommodation 8, 15
adolescence: autistic teenagers 114; deaf teenagers 111, 112; false belief mastery 28
affective empathy 110–111, 112, 114, 115, 116
Africa 26
aggression 114, 115
Amsterlaw, Jennifer 14
anticipatory looking x, 5, 123, 124
artistic ability 148
Asian cultures 9–10
assimilation 8, 15
Astington, J. W. 28
attachment security 46, 47
attention: attentional priority in autism 144–145; Cognitive Complexity Theory 96; institutionalized children 93; joint attention 74, 91, 108–109, 113, 116, 122, 128–129; Montessori education 66–67; shared visual attention xv; social xx
atypical populations xii–xiii, 91; *see also* autism; deaf and hard of hearing children
Australian children 29, 32, 33, 35
autism xii, xviii, 1, 99, 106, 135–150; deaf children compared with 41; developmental psychopathology 89, 90; empathic mind 112–115; eye gaze 137–139, 140–144; false-belief tasks 10; implicit and explicit skills xix, 126; mental-state talk 73; mentalizing

136–137; perceptual ability 146–148; psychological inferences 139–140; social attention deficits xx
Avis, J. 26

Back, E. 137, 144
Baillargeon, R. 124, 125
Banerjee, R. 42, 51, 91
Baron-Cohen, S. 136–138, 140
Bartsch, K. xi, 76
Baydar, N. 98
Bayesian learning 6–7, 14, 15
behaviour 71–72, 76–77
beliefs xi, 2–3, 72, 123; *see also* diverse beliefs
Bernier, A. 46
bilingualism 27, 30, 34–35, 37, 121
Bowler, D. M. 137
Bretherton, I. xiii
Brockmeier, J. 79
Brown, J. R. xiii, 41
Bruce, J. 93

Caldi, S. 81, 124
Callaghan, T. 26
Campbell, R. 140
Canada 26, 27
Cassidy, S. 63, 139–140
causality 48–49
changed location false-belief task 151
Chapman, P. 139–142, 143–144
Chinese children 9–10, 11–12, 26–27, 29, 31–32, 33–38, 51–52, 63

Chomsky, N. 7
Cognitive Complexity Theory 96
cognitive deficits 135
cognitive development 6, 8; attachment
    security 47; institutionalized children 93;
    parent-child interactions 43–44
cognitive empathy 111–112, 114
cognitive state talk xv, 50, 74
Colvert, E. 94
communication impairments 106–117
communicative environment xii, xiv, xv,
    xvii, xix, 91–92
compassion 65
concentration 66–67
conflict resolution xiii
connectedness xiv
constructivism 6, 8, 15, 16, 17
conversations xi, xiv, 49–50, 91; access to
    89, 91–92, 127; autism 145; bilingualism
    27; children's experience of language in
    122–123; connected turns 129; cultural
    differences 38; deaf children 122, 126;
    institutionalized children 93; mental-
    state talk 45, 48–49, 64–65, 74, 81–82;
    preschool children 6; specific language
    impairments 115
Corina, D. 127
Crowe, E. 49
culture xvii–xviii, 25–40; bilingual
    preschooler study 34–38; cross-
    cultural similarities 5; definition of
    25; developmental sequences xvi,
    9–10, 28–33; family influences 51–52;
    influence on language acquisition 121;
    Pacific cultures 81

DB see diverse beliefs
DD see diverse desires
de Rosnay, Marc x–xxi
de Villiers, P. 122
De Waal, Frans B. M. 110
deaf and hard of hearing (DHH) children
    xii, xv, xvi, 1–2, 10–11, 106, 121–134;
    communicative environment xix, 91–92;
    comparison with autistic children 41;
    conversational access 38, 89; empathic
    mind 107–112, 117; mental-state talk
    27, 73; parent-child interactions 43–44;
    predictability of development xviii; social
    experiences 99; ToM Scale 11–13, 16
Demers, I. 46
desires 2–3, 107–108; empathic mind 106;
    folk psychology xi; maternal talk xv,
    74–76, 78–80, 91; see also diverse desires

developmental delays: autism 10, 137,
    145; cross-cultural research 9–10; deaf
    children 1, 11, 27, 41, 91, 124, 126,
    128, 130, 131; institutionalized children
    93, 94, 97, 99
developmental psychopathology 89, 90
developmental sequences xvi, 8–13, 17;
    cross-cultural research xvii, 28–33,
    34–38
Devine, Rory T. xiii, xiv, 30, 41–56
DHH see deaf and hard of hearing children
Dirks, Evelien 106–120
diverse beliefs (DB) xvi, 9, 152; cross-
    cultural research xvii, 10, 28, 29, 31–33,
    35–37; microgenetic data 16–17;
    Montessori education 62; see also beliefs
diverse desires (DD) xvi, 8–9, 152; cross-
    cultural research 10, 28, 29, 31–33,
    36; microgenetic data 16–17; specific
    language impairments 116; see also desires
Dunn, J. xiii, 41, 44

Eastern cultures 9–10, 29
education: Montessori education xiii, xiv,
    57–70; socioeconomic status 49
Eisen, Sierra xiii, 57–70
elaborativeness xiv, 45
emotions: affective empathy 110–111,
    112, 114, 115, 116; communicative
    interactions xiv; cultural differences
    in emotion talk 51–52; empathic
    mind 106; facial emotion recognition
    109–110, 113, 116, 137–139, 140, 144;
    institutionalized children 93; maternal
    talk xv; see also hidden emotion
empathy 65, 68, 73; affective 110–111,
    112, 114, 115, 116; autistic children
    114–115; cognitive 111–112, 114–115;
    deaf children 110–112; empathic mind
    106, 107–116
Ensor, R. xv, 45, 50
everyday chores 66
evidence 7, 8, 14, 15, 17
executive function: institutionalized
    children 93, 94–95, 96, 97; Montessori
    education 66, 67; verbal responses 123
eye gaze 72, 116, 128, 136, 137–139,
    140–144

facial emotion recognition 109–110, 113,
    116, 137–139, 140, 144
false-belief (FB) mastery xvi, 3–5, 9, 122,
    153; autism 10, 114, 136; cross-cultural
    research 5, 10, 25–26, 28, 30–33,

34–37, 38; deaf children 13, 16, 107, 111, 124–125; executive function 67; family influences 41–52; implicit and explicit skills xix; infants 5, 28, 72; institutionalized children 93; maltreated children 91; mental-state talk 65; microgenetic data 14–17; milestones xvii; Montessori education 61, 62; preschool development 5–6; specific language impairments 116; training 16, 17
false-belief (FB) tasks x–xii, 3–5, 72, 151–152; autistic children 114; cross-cultural research 34–35, 81; deaf children 107, 111–112; explicit versions 123; family influences 41; institutionalized children 95; Montessori education 59–60; multi-aged classrooms 63; replicability xvii
family xiii, 41–56; age of siblings 63–64; communicative environment xv; cultural differences 51–52; future research directions 48–52; mental-state talk 43, 44–45, 46, 48–52, 64–65; methodological progress in studies 47–48; mind-mindedness 43, 45–47, 52; size of 43, 44; social-cognitive understanding 14; socioeconomic status 42–44, 49–50; support from extended 98; see also parents; siblings
Fang, F. X. 29, 31
fathers 51
Fernyhough, C. 46–47
Fivush, R. 51
folk psychology xi–xii, xvi, 5
France 92
Freeth, M. 140–142, 143–144
Frith, C. D. 81, 126

Garcia-Sierra, A. 121
gender 51
genetics 50, 126–127
Gopnik, Alison 6
Grant, J. 140
Grazzani, I. 79
Greece 94
Green, B. F. 35
Gunnar, M. R. 93

Harris, Paul L. 26, 65
Harris-Waller, J. 46–47
HE see hidden emotion
heritability 43
Heyes, C. M. 81, 125, 126

hidden emotion (HE) 9, 153; cross-cultural research 10, 28, 31–33, 36; Montessori education 61, 62; see also emotions
Hjelmquist, Erland 121–134
Hong Kong 26–27, 52
Hughes, Claire xiii, xiv, 30, 41–56, 127

India 26
Indonesia 30, 33
infancy: anticipatory looking x, 123; behaviour and mental states 71–72, 77, 81, 82; early interactions with parents 126–127; false belief 5, 28, 72; implicit and explicit skills xix, 125, 126; mental-state talk 74
institutionalized children xii–xiii, 89–90, 92–99
intentionality xix, 107–109, 116, 128
intersubjectivity xix
Iranian children 10, 29, 31–32, 33, 35, 37

Jacob, François 57
Japan 31, 33
Jenkins, J. 48
joint attention 74, 91, 108–109, 113, 116, 122, 128–129
Jones, W. 140

KA see knowledge access
Karmiloff-Smith, A. 140
Kegal, J. 13
Kessler-Shaw, L. 76
Ketelaar, L. 112
Klin, A. 140
knowledge access (KA) xvi, 9, 153; cross-cultural research xvii, 10, 28, 29, 31–33, 35–37; microgenetic data 16–17; Montessori education 61, 62
Korea 26
Kovács, Á. M. 124
Krentz, U. 127
Kuntoro, I. 30, 31

language 72–73, 82; acquisition of 121; bilingualism 27, 30, 34–35, 37, 121; capacity for 106; cognitive empathy 112; communicative environment xii; deaf children 130–131; development xvii, 146; early infant interactions 126; empathic mind development 117; institutionalized children 94–96, 97; learning from others through 139; linguistic input and stimulation 91; mental states and behaviour 76–78;

specific language impairments 106,
115–116, 117; spontaneous reference
to mental states xi; ToM enabled by
122–123; Vygotsky's ideas xvi; *see also*
conversations
learning xvii, 1–2, 6–8, 17, 81, 82; cultural
37; microgenetic data 14–15; scaffolding
74, 77; social 106, 107, 110, 113, 115,
117; statistical 71–72
Leekam, S. R. 44, 63
lexical development 122
Lillard, Angeline S. xiii, 57–70
Liu, D. 26, 28–29, 30, 31, 34, 97
Liu, G. 29, 31
Lohmann, H. 79
Luke, N. 42, 51, 91
lying 6

maltreatment 42, 51, 90, 91, 93, 99
Maxi task x, 151
Meadow-Orlans, K. 128
Meins, E. 46–47, 65, 126, 127
Meltzoff, A. N. 108
mental-state talk xiv, xv, 73, 78–82; age
of children 63, 64–65; children's use of
75, 76; cultural differences 51–52; deaf
children 27, 129–130; family influences
xiii, 43, 44–45, 46, 48–49, 50–51;
institutionalized children 97; maltreated
children 91; model from behaviour
to mental states 72; multiple contexts
76–78; scaffolding 74
mentalism 71, 81
mentalizing: autism 135, 136–137, 140,
145; deaf children 124, 125, 129;
implicit and explicit 126; maltreated
children 91
Meristo, Marek 81, 121–134
meta-representational capacity x
methodological issues 47–48
microgenetic data 13–17
Middleton, D. 74
milestones xvi, xvii, 13, 28
mind-mindedness xiii, xiv, 43, 45–47, 52
mindfulness 65–67, 68
minimalism 71–72
mirror self-recognition 73, 79–80
Mitchell, Peter xix–xx, 135–150
Montessori education xiii, xiv, 57–70
Montessori, Maria 58–59, 64
Morgan, Gary xix, 13, 121–134
mothers: cognitive state talk xv, 50; deaf
children 128; mental-state talk 48, 52,
64–65, 72, 75, 76–81, 129; perceptual

state talk 74; research focus on 51;
responsivity 91; shared visual attention
xv; talk about desires 74–76, 78–80; *see
also* parents
Mottron, L. 147
multi-aged classrooms 63–64

nativism 1, 7
Nelson, K. 44–45, 76
Netten, A. P. 112
neurocognitive mechanisms 125
Nielsen, M. 32
non-verbal responses 123, 124

Onishi, K. 124, 125
O'Reilly, K. 32
Ornaghi, V. 79

Pacific cultures 81
parents: abusive parenting 91;
communicative environment xiv;
conversational input from 38, 49–50;
cultural differences 29–30, 37, 52;
deaf children xii, xix, 11, 27, 43–44,
107, 121–122, 123–124, 126–131;
interactions with 43–44, 90–91, 92,
98, 126–127; interpretation of child's
behaviour 145; mental-state talk 45, 46,
48–52, 63, 64–65, 73, 80–81, 129–130;
mind-mindedness 45–47, 52; *see also*
family; fathers; mothers
Peabody Picture Vocabulary Test (PPVT)
35, 95, 97
perceptual ability 146–148
perceptual talk 74
Perez-Zapata, D. 26
Perner, J. 44, 63, 123, 125
Peru 26
Peterson, Candida C. xvi, xvii, 89; culture
and ToM development 25–40; deaf
children xii, 1–2, 16, 41, 91, 107;
influence of 99; siblings 44, 47, 63–64
Piaget, Jean 6, 8, 15
Pillai, D. 139
play: autistic children 112; deaf children
117; Montessori education 60; pretend
play 63, 64, 90; specific language
impairments 115
PPVT *see* Peabody Picture Vocabulary Test
pragmatics 27, 130
Premack, D. 89, 122
preschool development 5–6
pretend play 63, 64, 90
pretense 6

Prime, H. J. 48
prior knowledge 8, 17
probabilistic learning 6–8
Provost, M. A. 46
psychopathology 89, 90
Pyers, J. E. 13, 122

Qu, L. 30, 32

Raven, J. C. 95
representation x, 6
Rieffe, Carolien xii, 106–120
Rochat, P. 73
Romania 94, 97
Ropar, D. 137, 139–142, 146–147
Ruffman, Ted xv–xvi, xviii, 44, 49, 63,
    64–65, 71–86, 125, 129
Russia 92, 94

Sabbagh, M. A. 26
Sally-Anne task x, xi, xvi, 123, 151
Sameroff, A. 145
Samoa 26, 81
Saraswati, L. 30, 31
sarcasm 154
savant abilities 148
scaffolding 74, 77, 80, 81
scaling xvii–xviii, 9–13, 15–17, 28–29; *see
    also* Theory of Mind Scale
Schultz, R. 140
Schweder, R. 25, 38
Searle, J. R. 107–108
secret keeping 6
Selcuk, Bilge xii, 89–105
self-awareness 73, 80
Senghas, A. 13
Senju, A. 126
sensory engagement 66
sequences xvi, 8–13, 17; cross-cultural
    research xvii, 9–10, 28–33, 34–38
SES *see* socioeconomic status
Shahaeian, A. 29, 30, 31, 32, 33, 35
shared visual attention xv
Shen, P. 30, 32
Shepard Illusion 147–148
Sheppard, E. 139
siblings xiii–xiv, 72, 90; age of 63–64;
    conversational input from 38, 51, 73;
    cross-cultural research 26–27; influence
    on false-belief mastery 44, 47–48;
    interactions with 92, 98; mental-state
    talk 49; *see also* family
Siegal, Michael xii, 41
Siegler, R. S. 13

sign language 11, 27, 107, 123, 127, 129,
    130–131
Singapore 30, 32, 34–38
Slade, L. 49
Slaughter, Virginia xvi, xvii, 25–40, 63–64
SLI *see* specific language impairments
Slomkowski, C. L. xiii, 41
Smarties task 151–152
Smith, A. 114
social attention xx
social-cognitive understanding xi, xii, xvi,
    xix; environmental influences 91; family
    influence 14; institutionalized children
    93
social competence 6, 59–60, 145–146
social context xii, xiii, xvii
social cues 144–145
social interaction 2, 6, 63, 89, 90; autistic
    children 112–113; deaf children 11, 107,
    117, 131; facial emotion recognition
    110; specific language impairments 115;
    Vygotsky's ideas xvi
social learning 106, 107, 110, 113, 115,
    117
social motivation 112, 113, 115
social problem-solving 60, 61, 62
social sense 123, 124
socioeconomic status (SES) xiii, xiv, 49–50;
    cross-cultural research 30; false-belief
    mastery 42–44; low and middle-SES
    backgrounds 95–96, 98
Soulieres, I. 147
specific language impairments (SLI) 106,
    115–116, 117
Spencer, P. 128
Sperber, D. 81, 124
Su, Y. 32
Surian, L. 81, 124
syntax 122

Tarabulsy, G. M. 46
Tardif, T. 26
Tarullo, A. R. 93–94, 97
Taumoepeau, Mele xv–xvi, xviii, 71–86,
    129
Tesla, C. xiii, 41
Thailand 26
theory of mind (ToM) x–xix; atypical
    populations xii–xiii, 91; autism 114–115,
    135, 137; belief-desire reasoning 2–3;
    conceptual sequences 8–13; culture
    and ToM development 25–40, 81;
    deaf children 1–2, 111–112, 121–131;
    environmental factors 127; family

influences 41–56, 90–91; implicit and
explicit skills xii, xviii–xix, 81–82, 123,
125–126; infancy 71; institutionalized
children 89–90, 93–99; interventions
78–81; language understanding 72–73;
learning 1–2, 17; maternal talk about
desires 75; mental-state conversations
81–82; microgenetic data 13–17;
Montessori education 57, 59–68;
social influences 41; specific language
impairments 116; *see also* false-belief
mastery
theory-of-mind mental module (ToMM) 1
Theory of Mind Scale (ToM Scale) 12,
15–17, 152–154; cultural differences
28–33, 34–38; deaf children 11;
institutionalized children 97; Montessori
education 61, 62
theory theory 6–8
thought bubbles 16
Thouless, R. H. 146
ToM *see* theory of mind
ToM Scale *see* Theory of Mind Scale
Tomasello, M. 79
ToMM *see* theory-of-mind mental module
Toyama, K. 31
training xiv, 14–15, 16, 17, 64, 99, 130
transactional model xix, 145
Trevarthen, C. xix
Turkey 92, 95–99
twins 63, 64, 65, 129

Ukraine 94
unexpected contents false-belief task 3–4,
151–152
United Kingdom: cross-cultural research
26, 30; deaf children 129, 130; foster

care and adoption 92; institutionalized
children 94; parental mind-mindedness
46, 52; socioeconomic status 43
United States: cross-cultural research 26,
27, 29; foster care and adoption 92;
institutionalized children 93, 94; ToM
Scale 11–12
universality 25, 26, 38

values 29–30, 37
van Vlerken, Wendy 106–120
Veiga, Guida 106–120
verbal skills 123, 126, 131
visual attention, shared xv
visual perception 146–148
Volkmar, F. 140
Vygotsky, L. xvi, 74

Walker, J. 140
Wang, Q. 51
Wellman, Henry M. xi, xvi, xvii, xviii,
1–21, 97; cross-cultural research 26,
28–30, 31, 33, 34–35; mental-state talk
65, 76
Western cultures 9–10, 29, 37, 38
Wimmer, H. 123
Woll, B. 129
Wood, D. 74
Woodruff, G. 89, 122
Wu, Z. 32

Yağmurlu, B. 95–98, 100n
Youngblade, L. xiii, 41
Yucel, N. Meltem xii, 89–105

Zhu, L. 29, 31
zone of proximal development 74